Android Best Practices

Godfrey Nolan

Onur Cinar

David Truxall

Apress·

Android Best Practices

ISBN-13 (pbk): 978-1-4302-5857-5

ISBN-13 (electronic): 978-1-4302-5858-2

President and Publisher: Paul Manning
Lead Editor: Steve Anglin
Douglas Pundick: Douglas Pundick
Technical Reviewers: Nitin Khanna and Grant Allen
Editorial Board: Steve Anglin, Mark Beckner, Ewan Buckingham, Gary Cornell, Louise Corrigan, Jim DeWolf, Jonathan Gennick, Jonathan Hassell, Robert Hutchinson, Michelle Lowman, James Markham, Matthew Moodie, Jeff Olson, Jeffrey Pepper, Douglas Pundick, Ben Renow-Clarke, Dominic Shakeshaft, Gwenan Spearing, Matt Wade, Steve Weiss
Coordinating Editor: Christine Ricketts
Copy Editor: James Compton
Compositor: SPi Global
Indexer: SPi Global
Artist: SPi Global
Cover Designer: Anna Ishchenko

Distributed to the book trade worldwide by Springer Science+Business Media New York, 233 Spring Street, 6th Floor, New York, NY 10013. Phone 1-800-SPRINGER, fax (201) 348-4505, e-mail orders-ny@springer-sbm.com, or visit www.springeronline.com. Apress Media, LLC is a California LLC and the sole member (owner) is Springer Science + Business Media Finance Inc (SSBM Finance Inc). SSBM Finance Inc is a Delaware corporation.

For information on translations, please e-mail rights@apress.com, or visit www.apress.com.

Apress and friends of ED books may be purchased in bulk for academic, corporate, or promotional use. eBook versions and licenses are also available for most titles. For more information, reference our Special Bulk Sales–eBook Licensing web page at www.apress.com/bulk-sales.

Any source code or other supplementary material referenced by the author in this text is available to readers at www.apress.com. For detailed information about how to locate your book's source code, go to www.apress.com/source-code/.

Contents at a Glance

Contents

About the Authors

Godfrey Nolan is president of RIIS LLC, where he specializes in web site optimization. He has written numerous articles for magazines and newspapers in the United States, the United Kingdom, and Ireland. Nolan has had a healthy obsession with reverse-engineering bytecode since he wrote "Decompile Once, Run Anywhere," which first appeared in *Web Techniques* in September 1997.

Onur Cinar is the author of *Android Apps with Eclipse and Pro Android C++ with the NDK*, both from Apress. He has over 17 years of experience in design, development, and management of large-scale complex software projects, primarily in mobile and telecommunication space. His expertise spans VoIP, video communication, mobile applications, grid computing, and networking technologies on diverse platforms. He has been actively working with the Android platform since its beginning. He has a B.S. degree in Computer Science from Drexel University in Philadelphia, PA. He is currently working at the Skype division of Microsoft as the Principal Development Manager for the Skype and Lync clients on the Android platform.

David Truxall A long-time resident of metro Detroit, Dr. Truxall has programmed for a living since 1995, working with enterprise web technologies, modeling business processes, and building public web sites for some of the largest companies in Michigan. Always an enthusiast for troubleshooting systems, David has rescued numerous troubled applications and improved their performance. He speaks at local conferences and user groups. Currently David is working as a mobile architect, bringing mobile apps and their supporting systems to the enterprise.

About the Technical Reviewers

Nitin Khanna is a technology enthusiast and an evangelist with over 10 years of experience in various Computing technologies ranging from IP based telecom networks to mobile applications and infrastructure. Over the years Nitin has created and contributed to a number of Open Source projects; key being Sipdroid and Karura (hybrid application development framework) for Android.

Nitin works for Skype PLC, a Microsoft owned, world renowned communications application. He is currently responsible for Skype and Lync applications on Android with combined support over 100m users.

In his spare time, Nitin likes to contribute to Open Source projects, experimenting with new technologies and Arduino based automation systems.

Grant Allen has worked in the IT field for over 20 years, as a CTO, entrepreneur, enterprise architect, mobile computing and data management expert. Grant's roles have taken him around the world, specializing in global-scale systems design, development, and performance. He is a frequent speaker at industry and academic conferences, on topics such as data-mining, database systems, content management, collaboration, disruptive innovation, and mobile ecosystems like Android. His first Android application was a task list to remind him to finish all his other unfinished Android projects. Grant works for Google, and in his spare time is completing a PhD on building innovative high-technology environments. Grant is the author of six books, on topics including mobile development with Android and data management.

## Chapter 1

Before You Start

In late 2011 as I got more into Android development, I tried to look for a book that I hoped would take my development to the next level. I'd already completed a couple of apps and wanted to know what everyone else was doing that I might have missed. Sure, there was a wealth of Android documentation from Google, but the Android docs had some odd recommendations; they suggest using jUnit3 for my unit testing, which felt like going backwards. I already knew there were existing jUnit4 testing frameworks for Android, such as Roboelectric, so maybe there were other cool things out there that I'd missed that I simply didn't know about that could really help me write better code.

This book is an attempt to pull together the research on the best practices that developers have created for the Android platform in the hope that you can find all the information you need in one place.

Once you've written an app or are part of an Android team of developers, it quickly becomes clear that Android development, just like any other language or environment, can get messy and inefficient if you don't think about how you're going to get organized. This book will help you take those steps to become a well oiled, productive team.

You may want to consider reading this book if you want to do one or more of the following:

- Get better at Android Development by looking at best practices sample code.

- Write apps that are easier to extend and maintain.

- Write more secure apps.

- Learn how to write not only the client side of the app but also its often ignored server side.

Introduction to Android

Android is a Linux-based open source operating system for smartphones. The company started back in October 2003 and was acquired by Google in August 2005. The HTC Dream, released in October 2008, was the first phone to run Android.

From a developer's perspective typically Android apps are written in Java. Google provides an Android SDK which provides the necessary libraries and applications to convert the Java code into a format that can run on Android phones. Most people use Eclipse or the command line to create Android apps. The Android Studio has recently emerged as an alternative to Eclipse and is likely to become the IDE of choice over the next year or two.

Android is the premier operating system for mobile devices, with over 75% of the world's devices and 52% of the US market running on it.

In my own personal experience there was a time when Android development was the redheaded stepchild. All development was first done on iOS and then developed in Android once the app became successful. This has changed now that Android phones have such a large market share.

Who Should Read This Book?

This book is designed to be approachable by developers who have any level of familiarity with Android. However, your degree of experience will dictate which parts you find most useful. If you're entirely new to Android development, or have only tinkered here and there, this book should help you develop great habits and practices for your future Android work. This is especially true if you find yourself doing more and more work with Android. The approaches and tools for testing, performance profiling, and so forth are great for instilling productive habits and avoiding some classic pitfalls and anti-patterns of good development. If you end up never saying "I'll write the tests later," then this book has served you well.

For the intermediate or advanced Android developer, this book will walk you through details of the current state of the art in Android tool chains; you'll see how best to refactor and improve existing code and applications, and it will push you to embrace some of the advanced topics you might have put off until now. If you've never thought of NDK-based development, you'll learn how to do it right the first time. If you've never had the wherewithal to do multiplatform, multihandset testing and modeling, you'll take the plunge and see what you've been missing all this time.

What You Need Before You Begin

To get the most out of this book, having a few of the housekeeping items sorted out up front will remove distractions later, and it will let you get straight to implementing the tools and techniques you'll learn in each chapter.

An Actual Android Application

To get the best return from this book it will help if you have already written one or two Android apps. They don't even need to have made it all the way to Google Play; but ideally it helps if you've gone through the process and have real-world users who have kicked the tires on your Android app, and you've made revisions based on their feedback or reviews.

A Working Development Environment

You need to have the Android SDK installed with the IDE of your choice: either Eclipse with the ADT toolset; Android Developer Studio; or for the more adventurous, one of the exotic third-party development environments like Intel's Beacon Mountain. You'll need an actual device to follow along with some of our examples, but the emulator will do for most of the code in the book.

All the Bells and Whistles

In addition to the stock Android Developer Studio, Eclipse with ADT, or other IDE, you should also ensure that you have the optional libraries available for the Android SDK. These include the SDK Build-tools, the Google APIs associated with your SDK release level, Android Support Library, and Web Driver and USB driver if available for your operating system.

As each chapter unfolds, you will also be introduced to specific additional tools for unit testing, handset diversity testing, performance profiling and so on. We'll discuss those tools one by one in the relevant chapters.

Source Code for the Sample Application

The Android app we're using in each of the chapters is a simple to-do list and task reminder application. You should download the code from www.apress.com/9781430258575/ so you can follow along. We'll be using the to do list app to show best practices for Android walking you through design patterns, performance issues, security problems and more in each chapter.

What's in This Book

Here's a chapter-by-chapter summary of what you can expect over the course of this book:

Chapter 2: We begin in Chapter 2 with Patterns. You may already have some familiarity with Android's user interface (UI) patterns, which help create a consistent user experience (UX) across multiple devices. You'll also learn about how you can use other libraries such as ActionBarSherlock and NineOldAndroids to help your users on older devices get a more up-to-date Android experience.

Chapter 3: Following on from UI and UX patterns, Chapter 3 looks at implementing the MVC and MVVM developer design patterns as an alternative to the standard Android design before we dive deeply into Android Annotations and how that can help you create clean understandable Android code.

Chapter 4: Chapter 4 takes a close look at the basic Agile elements of test-driven Development (TDD), behavior-driven design (BDD), and continuous integration (CI) that you can use during development. We look at the unit testing available in the Android SDK and the benefits of looking further afield at tools such as Roboelectric, Calabash, and Jenkins and how you can use them to create a more efficient Agile development environment.

Chapter 5: Android allows you to incorporate C++ code directly using the Android NDK, but there can be a significant performance hit because of the context switch between Java and C++. There are still times, however, when it makes more sense to use new or existing C++ code in Android without porting it to Java. Chapter 5 looks at the reasons when C++ is the right answer and the best way to approach using it for Android.

Chapter 6: Chapter 6 is an up-to-date look at several industry-standard Top 10 security lists that have emerged to give you a much better idea on the do's and don'ts of Android security. The chapter ends with a new list that combines the best elements of Google and OWASP's top 10 lists.

Chapter 7: Device testing can be the bane of Android development. Whether you want to create your own testing platform or using one of the many online services Chapter 8 looks at practical approaches to tame device fragmentation.

Chapter 8: For most Android applications in the business world, the Android part of the application acts as a client to a back-end server. Information is usually but not always sent as JSON via a REST API. Chapter 8 explores in depth how to talk to both REST and SOAP APIs. You'll learn how to create a REST API and why the Richardson Maturity model is important for the longevity of your API. You'll also create your own web services using Google App Engine.

## Chapter 2

Android Patterns

We begin in Chapter 2 by looking at Android *design patterns*. In my mind this can mean two things, *user Interface design* and *architecture*; and we'll look at both here. In the "UI Design Patterns" section we'll take a look at Android UI guidelines that Google released around the time Ice Cream Sandwich was released.

You don't have to follow the out-of-the-box programming structure when you're coding Android applications; there are MVC, MVVM, and DI alternatives. And in the second half of this chapter, "Architectural Design Patterns," we're going to look at some of the alternatives to classic Android programming design.

UI Design Patterns

Before Ice Cream Sandwich, Android design was not very well defined. Many early apps looked very similar to the example shown in Figure 2-1. This app has built-in Back button functionality and iOS-like tabs because more than likely it was a port of an existing iOS app; the app even has a name, iFarmers, that belongs in the iTunes app store.

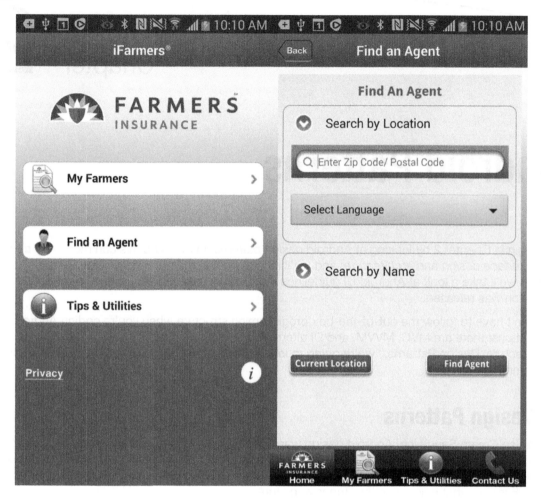

Figure 2-1. iFarmers is a typical early Android app

I don't want to single out the iFarmers app, as there are many examples of similar apps on Google Play. I'm sure the app developers pushed for more of an Android design, and no doubt at the time they were not able to point to a design resource and say it was the industry standard way of designing an Android app; they were probably told to just get on with it.

These days, the Android platform is less about iOS conversions and more about leveraging the massive Android user base. Google has also produced a design guide, available at `http://developer.android.com/design/get-started/principles.html`, and those principles are what this section is going to explain.

To help demonstrate different best practices we're going to be using a simple To Do List app throughout this book. So to begin with, let's look at the code for the sample app; at the moment it has a splash screen, shown in Figure 2-2, and a to-do list screen to add items, shown in Figure 2-3.

Figure 2-2. *The TodDoList app splash screen*

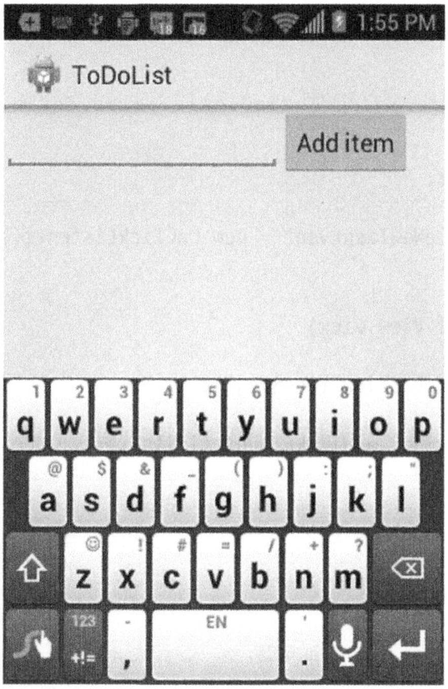

Figure 2-3. *The app's main To Do List screen*

The complete code for this app is provided with the book's downloadable source code, but for our purposes here there are two Java files we will work with, TodoActivity.java, shown in Listing 2-1, and TodoProvider.java, which you'll see in Listing 2-2.

Listing 2-1. TodoActivity.java

```java
package com.logicdrop.todos;

import java.util.ArrayList;
import java.util.List;

import android.app.Activity;
import android.os.Bundle;
import android.util.Log;
import android.view.View;
import android.view.View.OnClickListener;
import android.widget.AdapterView;
import android.widget.AdapterView.OnItemClickListener;
import android.widget.ArrayAdapter;
import android.widget.Button;
import android.widget.EditText;
import android.widget.ListView;
import android.widget.TextView;
import android.os.StrictMode;

public class TodoActivity extends Activity
{
    public static final String APP_TAG = "com.logicdrop.todos";

    private ListView taskView;
    private Button btNewTask;
    private EditText etNewTask;
    private TodoProvider provider;

    private OnClickListener handleNewTaskEvent = new OnClickListener()
    {
        @Override
        public void onClick(final View view)
        {
            Log.d(APP_TAG, "add task click received");

            TodoActivity.this.provider.addTask(TodoActivity.this
                    .getEditText()
                    .getText()
                    .toString());

            TodoActivity.this.renderTodos();
        }
    };
```

```java
@Override
protected void onStart()
{
    super.onStart();
}

private void createPlaceholders()
{
    this.getProvider().deleteAll();

    if (this.getProvider().findAll().isEmpty())
    {
        List<String> beans = new ArrayList<String>();
        for (int i = 0; i < 10; i++)
        {
            String title = "Placeholder " + i;
            this.getProvider().addTask(title);
            beans.add(title);
        }
    }
}

EditText getEditText()
{
    return this.etNewTask;
}

private TodoProvider getProvider()
{
    return this.provider;
}

private ListView getTaskView()
{
    return this.taskView;
}

public void onCreate(final Bundle bundle)
{
    super.onCreate(bundle);

    this.setContentView(R.layout.main);

    this.provider = new TodoProvider(this);
    this.taskView = (ListView) this.findViewById(R.id.tasklist);
    this.btNewTask = (Button) this.findViewById(R.id.btNewTask);
    this.etNewTask = (EditText) this.findViewById(R.id.etNewTask);
    this.btNewTask.setOnClickListener(this.handleNewTaskEvent);

    this.showFloatVsIntegerDifference();
```

```
        this.createPlaceholders();

        this.renderTodos();
}

        private void renderTodos()
        {
        List<String> beans = this.getProvider().findAll();

        Log.d(APP_TAG, String.format("%d beans found", beans.size()));

        this.getTaskView().setAdapter(
                new ArrayAdapter<String>(this,
                        android.R.layout.simple_list_item_1, beans
                                .toArray(new String[]
                                {})));

        this.getTaskView().setOnItemClickListener(new OnItemClickListener()
        {
            @Override
            public void onItemClick(final AdapterView<?> parent,
                    final View view, final int position, final long id)
            {
                Log.d(APP_TAG, String.format(
                        "item with id: %d and position: %d", id, position));

                TextView v = (TextView) view;
                TodoActivity.this.getProvider().deleteTask(
                        v.getText().toString());
                TodoActivity.this.renderTodos();
            }
        });
    }

}
```

TodoActivity.java controls the layout of the app, and TodoProvider.java, shown in Listing 2-2, manages the data for the items you add to your list. In the app we've populated it with a list of initial placeholder items.

Listing 2-2. TodoProvider.java

```
package com.logicdrop.todos;

import java.util.ArrayList;
import java.util.List;

import android.content.ContentValues;
import android.content.Context;
import android.database.Cursor;
import android.database.sqlite.SQLiteDatabase;
import android.database.sqlite.SQLiteOpenHelper;
import android.util.Log;
```

```java
import com.logicdrop.todos.TodoActivity;

public class TodoProvider
{
    private static final String DB_NAME = "tasks";
    private static final String TABLE_NAME = "tasks";
    private static final int DB_VERSION = 1;
    private static final String DB_CREATE_QUERY = "CREATE TABLE " + TABLE_NAME + " (id integer
primary key autoincrement, title text not null);";

    private SQLiteDatabase storage;
    private SQLiteOpenHelper helper;

    public TodoProvider(final Context ctx)
    {
        this.helper = new SQLiteOpenHelper(ctx, DB_NAME, null, DB_VERSION)
        {
            @Override
            public void onCreate(final SQLiteDatabase db)
            {
                db.execSQL(DB_CREATE_QUERY);
            }

            @Override
            public void onUpgrade(final SQLiteDatabase db, final int oldVersion,
                    final int newVersion)
            {
                db.execSQL("DROP TABLE IF EXISTS " + TABLE_NAME);
                this.onCreate(db);
            }
        };

        this.storage = this.helper.getWritableDatabase();
    }

    public synchronized void addTask(final String title)
    {
        ContentValues data = new ContentValues();
        data.put("title", title);

        this.storage.insert(TABLE_NAME, null, data);
    }

    public synchronized void deleteAll()
    {
        this.storage.delete(TABLE_NAME, null, null);
    }

    public synchronized void deleteTask(final long id)
    {
        this.storage.delete(TABLE_NAME, "id=" + id, null);
    }
```

```
public synchronized void deleteTask(final String title)
{
    this.storage.delete(TABLE_NAME, "title='" + title + "'", null);
}

public synchronized List<String> findAll()
{
    Log.d(TodoActivity.APP_TAG, "findAll triggered");

    List<String> tasks = new ArrayList<String>();

    Cursor c = this.storage.query(TABLE_NAME, new String[] { "title" }, null, null, null, null, null);

    if (c != null)
    {
        c.moveToFirst();

        while (c.isAfterLast() == false)
        {
            tasks.add(c.getString(0));
            c.moveToNext();
        }

        c.close();
    }

    return tasks;
    }
}
```

This is a very basic app, and the design and functionality are reminiscent of an early Android 2.x app, or what we can call classic Android.

The layout for the To Do List screen is defined in the Layout.xml file, which is available in the book's resources folder and is also shown in Listing 2-3.

Listing 2-3. Layout.xml

```
<?xml version="1.0" encoding="utf-8"?> (change to LinearLayout)
<RelativeLayout xmlns:android="http://schemas.android.com/apk/res/android"
    android:id="@+id/widget31"
    android:layout_width="fill_parent"
    android:layout_height="fill_parent" >
    <TableRow
        android:id="@+id/row"
        android:layout_width="fill_parent"
        android:layout_height="wrap_content"
        android:layout_alignParentLeft="true"
        android:layout_below="@+id/tasklist"
        android:orientation="horizontal" >
```

```
    <EditText
        android:id="@+id/etNewTask"
        android:layout_width="200px"
        android:layout_height="wrap_content"
        android:text=""
        android:textSize="18sp" >
    </EditText>

    <Button
        android:id="@+id/btNewTask"
        android:layout_width="wrap_content"
        android:layout_height="wrap_content"
        android:text="@+string/add_button_name" >
    </Button>
</TableRow>
<ListView
    android:id="@+id/tasklist"
    android:layout_width="fill_parent"
    android:layout_height="wrap_content"
    android:layout_alignParentLeft="true"
    android:layout_alignParentTop="true" >
</ListView>
</RelativeLayout>
```

Holo

Sometimes it's hard to think in terms of a contrast between the classic (2.x) design style we've just seen and the modern Holo Android design (4.x), as the technology itself is so young. However, the changes in the phone's UI have been significant over the last couple years, so we really do need to differentiate between the two.

And before we look at the newer approach, remember that our apps still need to account for the relatively large proportion of users who are still on the classic phones, currently around a quarter of your users (but that number is shrinking all the time; see http://developer.android.com/about/dashboards/index.html). There is also an argument that we should further separate out Android 3.x from Android 4.x phones, but based on the numbers you'll see later in Figure 7-2 in Chapter 7, Honeycomb or Android 3.x is dead.

So what exactly does Holo Android design mean?

The following is a list of the most basic Android elements:

- Action Bar
- Navigation Drawers
- Mult Pane

We'll focus on the Action Bar in this chapter as its changes are all-pervasive and relevant to every application you build. There has been a move away from the hardware action bars in Android 4.x to the software Action Bar, which is shown in Figure 2-4. This design pattern is becoming more and more common in Android and is a difference between Android and iOS. The less-used app settings, however, should still be found via the hardware buttons.

Figure 2-4. Action Bar

Figure 2-5 shows the Action Bar used in conjunction with *tabs*, which can be useful for more complex menu structures.

Figure 2-5. Action Bar with tabs

Figure 2-6 shows *navigation drawers* or *swipe menus*, which can be used as an alternative pattern to action bars.

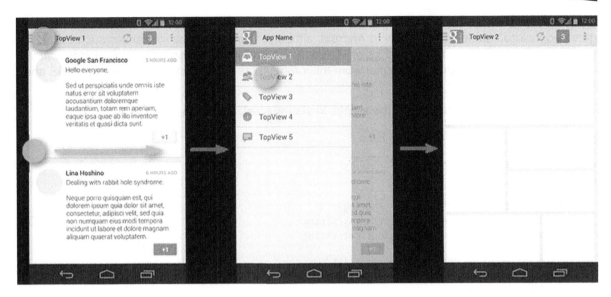

Figure 2-6. *Navigation drawers*

Figure 2-7 shows our TodoList app with an added Action Bar.

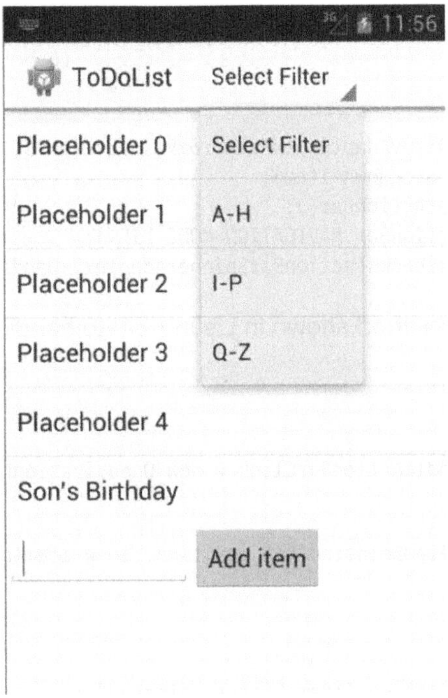

Figure 2-7. *TodoList with Action Bar*

The UI design patterns for Android are significantly different from those for the iOS, which often gets people into trouble who are new to Android, although there are some similarities such as the navigation drawers. There is no need for on-screen Back button or putting tabs in the bottom bar. Cross-platform HTML5 apps often suffer from this problem, as they often have a mixture of iOS and Android design patterns.

To implement the Action bar, create the strings in `strings.xml`, shown in Listing 2-4.

Listing 2-4. Strings.xml

```xml
<?xml version="1.0" encoding="utf-8"?>
<resources>

    <string name="app_name">ToDoList</string>
    <string name="action_settings">Settings</string>
    <string name="add_button_name">Add item</string>

    <string-array name="action_bar_action_list">
        <item>Select Filter</item>
        <item>A-H</item>
        <item>I-P</item>
        <item>Q-Z</item>
    </string-array>

</resources>
```

In Listing 2-5 we set up the adapter code for the Action Bar, which in this case is an Action Bar Spinner.

Listing 2-5. actionBarSpinnerAdapter

```java
this.actionBarSpinnerAdapter = ArrayAdapter.createFromResource(this, R.array.action_bar_action_list,
android.R.layout.simple_spinner_dropdown_item);
final ActionBar myActionBar = getActionBar();
myActionBar.setNavigationMode(ActionBar.NAVIGATION_MODE_LIST);
myActionBar.setListNavigationCallbacks(actionBarSpinnerAdapter, handleActionBarClick);
```

Add the OnNavigationListener method shown in Listing 2-6 to handle when the menu items are selected in the spinner list.

Listing 2-6. Action Bar Listener

```java
private OnNavigationListener handleActionBarClick = new OnNavigationListener()    {

    @Override
    public boolean onNavigationItemSelected(int position, long itemId) {

        switch (position) {

            case 0:
                Log.d(APP_TAG, "Action Clear Filter selected");
                TodoActivity.this.provider.clearFilter();
                TodoActivity.this.renderTodos();
                break;
```

```
            case 1:
                Log.d(APP_TAG, "Action A-H selected");
                    TodoActivity.this.provider.setFilter('A', 'H');
                    TodoActivity.this.renderTodos();
                break;
            case 2:
                    Log.d(APP_TAG, "Action I-P selected");
                    TodoActivity.this.provider.setFilter('I', 'P');
                    TodoActivity.this.renderTodos();
                break;
            case 3:
                        Log.d(APP_TAG, "Action Q-Z selected");
                        TodoActivity.this.provider.setFilter('Q', 'Z');
                        TodoActivity.this.renderTodos();
                        break;
            default:
                    break;
        }
        return true;
    }
};
```

There are no changes needed to the renderTodos method, as it's already being filtered.

ActionBarSherlock Navigation

Now that the Action Bar has become the design pattern of choice for Android 4.0 and above, where does that leave earlier versions of Android and more specifically the folks still running 2.x? If you're releasing a consumer app, chances are you or your business stakeholders don't want to ignore those customers.

One option is to use the hardware buttons in earlier phones that were largely replaced by the Action Bar pattern and code around the different functionality based on the Android version or API level.

A better option is to use a library called Action Bar Sherlock, from Jake Wharton, which is available at http://actionbarsherlock.com/.

In Jake's words, ActionBar Sherlock is a "Library for implementing the action bar design pattern using the native action bar on Android 4.0+ and a custom implementation on pre-4.0 through a single API and theme." It allows you to code once for all versions of Android and the hardware buttons can be largely ignored. Figure 2-8 shows the ToDoList app using ActionBarSherlock.

Download and install the library in Eclipse and add the items to the resources file shown Listing 2-7.

Listing 2-7. main.xml

```xml
<?xml version="1.0" encoding="utf-8"?>
<menu xmlns:android="http://schemas.android.com/apk/res/android" >
    <item
        android:id="@+id/action_A_H"
        android:title="A-H"
        android:showAsAction="always"
        android:orderInCategory="100">
    </item>
    <item
        android:id="@+id/action_I_P"
        android:title="I-P"
        android:showAsAction="always">
    </item>
    <item
        android:id="@+id/action_Q_Z"
        android:title="Q-Z"
        android:showAsAction="always">
    </item>
</menu>
```

Add the onCreateOptionsMenu and onOptionsItemSelected code to ToDoActivity as shown in Listing 2-8.

Listing 2-8. OnCreateOptionsMenu and onOptionsItemSelected

```java
public boolean onCreateOptionsMenu(Menu menu) {
    MenuInflater inflater = getSupportMenuInflater();
    inflater.inflate(R.menu.activity_itemlist, menu);
    return true;
}

@Override
public boolean onOptionsItemSelected(MenuItem item) {
    // Handle item selection
    switch (item.getItemId()) {
        case R.id.action_A_H:
            // filter & render
            return true;
        case R.id.action_I_P:
            // filter & render
            return true;
        case R.id.action_Q_Z:
            // filter & render
            return true;
        default:
            return super.onOptionsItemSelected(item);
    }
}
```

The Action Bar is now implemented, regardless of the Android OS version; Figure 2-8 shows it running on Android 2.1.

Figure 2-8. *Action Bar implemented using ActionBarSherlock on Android 2.1*

Designing for Different Devices

Android allows you to offer images and layouts for different generic screen sizes and screen pixel densities. There are a couple of key variables that you need to understand to create a good user experience across multiple devices. The most common screen sizes are small, normal, large, and xlarge (for tablets). As of September 4, 2013, almost 80 percent of all devices on the market were normal size; see Table 2-1.

Table 2-1. *Screen Pixel Density and Screen Sizes*

	ldpi	mdpi	tvdpi	hdpi	xhdpi	xxhdpi	Total
Small	9.5%						9.5%
Normal	0.1%	15.7%		33.6%	23.1%	7.1%	79.6%
Large	0.6%	3.4%	1.2%	0.4%	0.5%		6.1%
Xlarge		4.4%		0.3%	0.1%		4.8%
Total	10.2%	23.5%	1.2%	34.3%	23.7%	7.1%	

Also shown in Table 2-1 is our second variable, the number of pixels per square inch of the display or screen pixel density. The most common screen pixel densities are mdpi (medium), hdpi (high), xhdpi (extra high) and xxhdpi (extra extra high) density. An image or layout will have a different size based on the screen density or number of pixels in a device screen.

An up to date version of this table can always be found at `http://developer.android.com/about/dashboards/index.html`.

Figure 2-9 shows just the layouts in the resources directory for the open source Wordpress app. It contains all the default normal layouts in the `layout` folder as well as small, large, and xlarge. There are also further resources defined for portrait and landscape for some but not all screen sizes.

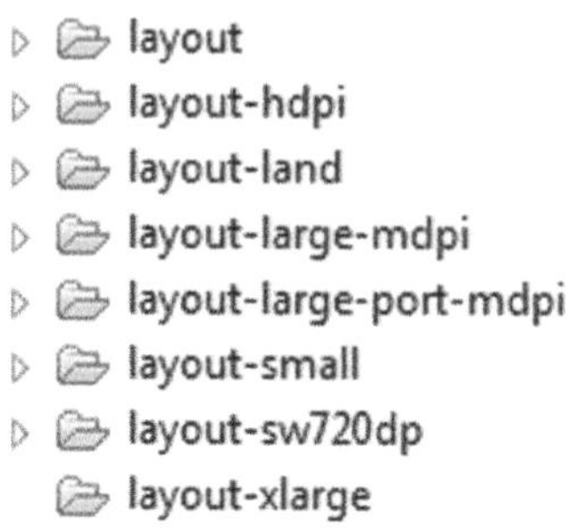

▷ 📂 layout
▷ 📂 layout-hdpi
▷ 📂 layout-land
▷ 📂 layout-large-mdpi
▷ 📂 layout-large-port-mdpi
▷ 📂 layout-small
▷ 📂 layout-sw720dp
   📂 layout-xlarge

Figure 2-9. Wordpress layouts

But what is layout-sw720dp? In Android 3.2, new layout definitions were included to handle tablets; in this example the *sw* stands for smallest width and the layout targets tablets that have a minimum width of 720 density pixels for a 10" tablet. These new qualifiers also allow you to target specific widths (w) and heights (h).

Fragments

Google introduced *fragments* in Android 3.0 as a way to create a more modular user interface design so that the same fragments could be used in a modular fashion on Android phones and Android tablets.

An activity is now split into multiple fragments, allowing for much more complex layouts based on the device. Figure 2-10 shows a task item with the corresponding task detail on a phone.

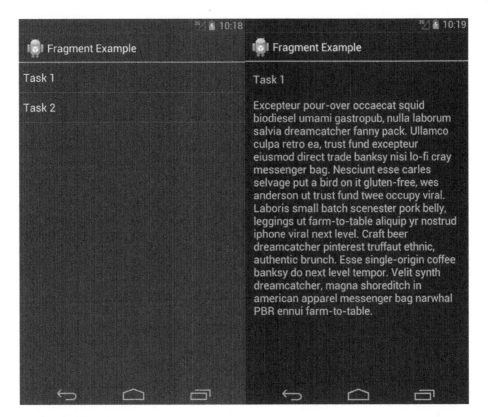

Figure 2-10. Task Item and Task Detail on a phone

Figure 2-11 shows how this look on a tablet, where there is more real estate and the task item and detail can be viewed on a single screen.

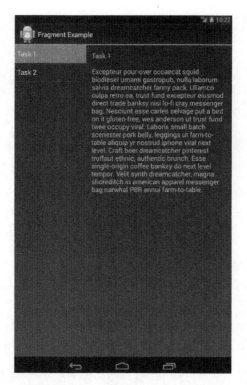

Figure 2-11. Task Item and Task Detail on a tablet

Listing 2-8 shows the updated and commented ToDoActivity.java code for the new fragment layout. ToDoActivity now extends FragmentActivity, and we create a TaskFragment and NoteFragment, which are swapped in and out depending on the device layout. The code shown in Listing 2-9 checks to see if the note fragment exists in the layout and displays it. The note fragment is only found in the layout-large/main.xml resource and not the layout/main.xml file.

Listing 2-8. ToDoActivity.java Fragment Source

```
public class TodoActivity extends FragmentActivity implements TaskFragment.OnTaskSelectedListener
{
    @Override
    public void onCreate(final Bundle savedInstanceState)
    {
        super.onCreate(savedInstanceState);

        this.setContentView(R.layout.main);

        // Check whether the activity is using the layout version with
        // the fragment_container FrameLayout. If so, we must add the first
        // fragment
        if (this.findViewById(R.id.fragment_container) != null)
```

```java
        {
            // However, if we're being restored from a previous state,
            // then we don't need to do anything and should return or else
            // we could end up with overlapping fragments.
            if (savedInstanceState != null)
            {
                return;
            }

            final TaskFragment taskFrag = new TaskFragment();

            // In case this activity was started with special instructions
            // from an Intent,
            // pass the Intent's extras to the fragment as arguments
            taskFrag.setArguments(this.getIntent().getExtras());

            // Add the fragment to the 'fragment_container' FrameLayout
            this.getSupportFragmentManager().beginTransaction().add(R.id.fragment_container,
taskFrag).commit();
        }
    }

    /**
     * User selected a task
     */
    @Override
    public void onTaskSelected(final int position)
    {
        // Capture the title fragment from the activity layout
        final NoteFragment noteFrag = (NoteFragment) this.getSupportFragmentManager()
                .findFragmentById(R.id.note_fragment);

        if (noteFrag != null)
        {
            // If note frag is available, we're in two-pane layout…
            noteFrag.updateNoteView(position);
        }
        else
        {
            // If the frag is not available, we're in the one-pane layout
            // Create fragment and give it an argument for the selected task
            final NoteFragment swapFrag = new NoteFragment();
            final Bundle args = new Bundle();
            args.putInt(NoteFragment.ARG_POSITION, position);
            swapFrag.setArguments(args);
            final FragmentTransaction fragTx = this.getSupportFragmentManager().beginTransaction();

            // Replace whatever is in the fragment_container view
            // and add the transaction to the back stack so the user can
            // navigate back
            fragTx.replace(R.id.fragment_container, swapFrag);
            fragTx.addToBackStack(null);
```

```
            // Commit the transaction
            fragTx.commit();
        }
    }
}
```

Listing 2-9. layout-large/main.xml

```xml
<?xml version="1.0" encoding="utf-8"?>

<LinearLayout xmlns:android="http://schemas.android.com/apk/res/android"
    android:orientation="horizontal"
    android:layout_width="match_parent"
    android:layout_height="match_parent">

    <fragment
        android:id="@+id/tasks_fragment"
        android:name="com.example.TaskFragment"
        android:layout_width="0dp"
        android:layout_height="match_parent"
        android:layout_weight="1" />

    <fragment
        android:id="@+id/note_fragment"
        android:name="com.example.NoteFragment"
        android:layout_width="0dp"
        android:layout_height="match_parent"
        android:layout_weight="2" />

</LinearLayout>
```

Architectural Design Patterns

One of the fundamental problems with all types of software can be summed up in the concept of *entropy*, which suggests that ordered code naturally becomes disordered over time. Or in other words, no matter how hard you try, your code will gradually go from an organized state to a disorganized state in what is also known as highly coupled, or perhaps more frankly, spaghetti code.

For smaller Android applications with one or two careful developers, this at first doesn't seem to be an issue. But as new versions are released and new people join, as Bob Martin would say the code starts to smell and if you want to keep the code clean it needs to be regularly reorganized or refactored.

For larger enterprise Android applications, the way you organize your code is going to be an issue from the very beginning. And unfortunately, classic Android design doesn't lend itself to long-term cleanliness.

In this section we'll look at some of the frameworks or software design patterns that you might want to consider when you're thinking about your app's architecture.

If you want to have less coupling and greater separation in your Android app, you need to move your logic to classes other than the main `Activity` class. We begin with classic Android design, then look at MVC and MVVM and finish off with Dependency Injection to help you see how you can use these frameworks to better organize your code.

Classic Android

In classic Android design, the user interface is defined in XML layout files. Activities then use these XML files to draw the screens and load images, size information and strings for multiple screen resolutions and hardware. Any other user interface code is written in other classes outside of the main UI thread.

The code for the TodoList app, shown in Listings 2-1 and 2-2 earlier, is for a classic Android design. We'll be using a number of different versions of this application throughout the book.

MVC

MVC (Model-View-Controller) is a software design pattern that separates the user interface (view) from the business rules and data (model) using a mediator (controller) to connect the model to the view.

The main benefit of MVC for us is separation of concerns. Each part of MVC takes care of its own job and no more: the View takes care of the user interface, the Model takes care of the data, and the Controller sends messages between the two.

The Controller provides data from the Model for the View to bind to the UI. Any changes to the Controller are transparent to the View, and UI changes won't affect the business logic and vice-versa.

Design patterns help to enforce a structure on the developers so that the code becomes more controlled and less likely to fall into disrepair. MVC's separation of concerns makes it much easier to add unit testing if we want to at a later stage.

There is an argument that Android already uses an MVC pattern, with the XML files acting as the View. However this does not provide us any real possibilities for separation of concerns.

In the following example the Classic Android code has been refactored into an MVC framework as follows.

The Model

The MVC Model component, shown in Listing 2-10, largely replaces the ToDoProvider.java code from before.

Listing 2-10. MVC Model code

```
final class TodoModel
{
    private static final String DB_NAME = "tasks";
    private static final String TABLE_NAME = "tasks";
    private static final int DB_VERSION = 1;
    private static final String DB_CREATE_QUERY = "CREATE TABLE " + TodoModel.TABLE_NAME +
" (id integer primary key autoincrement, title text not null);";

    private final SQLiteDatabase storage;
    private final SQLiteOpenHelper helper;
```

```java
    public TodoModel(final Context ctx)
    {
        this.helper = new SQLiteOpenHelper(ctx, TodoModel.DB_NAME, null, TodoModel.DB_VERSION)
        {
            @Override
            public void onCreate(final SQLiteDatabase db)
            {
                db.execSQL(TodoModel.DB_CREATE_QUERY);
            }

            @Override
            public void onUpgrade(final SQLiteDatabase db, final int oldVersion,
                                  final int newVersion)
            {
                db.execSQL("DROP TABLE IF EXISTS " + TodoModel.TABLE_NAME);
                this.onCreate(db);
            }
        };

        this.storage = this.helper.getWritableDatabase();
    }

    public void addEntry(ContentValues data)
    {
        this.storage.insert(TodoModel.TABLE_NAME, null, data);
    }

    public void deleteEntry(final String field_params)
    {
        this.storage.delete(TodoModel.TABLE_NAME, field_params, null);
    }

    public Cursor findAll()
    {
        Log.d(TodoActivity.APP_TAG, "findAll triggered");

        final Cursor c = this.storage.query(TodoModel.TABLE_NAME, new String[]
                { "title" }, null, null, null, null, null);

        return c;
    }
}
```

The View

The View code in MVC, shown in Listing 2-11, is a modified version of the ToDoActivity.java code from before. Any UI changes now happen here, and the control code is now moved to the ToDoController.java file.

Listing 2-11. MVC View code

```java
public class TodoActivity extends Activity
{
    public static final String APP_TAG = "com.example.mvc";

    private ListView taskView;
    private Button btNewTask;
    private EditText etNewTask;

    /*Controller changes are transparent to the View. UI changes won't
     *affect logic, and vice-versa. See below: the TodoModel has
     * been replaced with the TodoController, and the View persists
     * without knowledge that the implementation has changed.
     */
    private TodoController provider;

    private final OnClickListener handleNewTaskEvent = new OnClickListener()
    {
        @Override
        public void onClick(final View view)
        {
            Log.d(APP_TAG, "add task click received");

            TodoActivity.this.provider.addTask(TodoActivity.this
                    .etNewTask
                    .getText()
                    .toString());

            TodoActivity.this.renderTodos();
        }
    };

    @Override
    protected void onStop()
    {
        super.onStop();
    }

    @Override
    protected void onStart()
    {
        super.onStart();
    }

    @Override
    public void onCreate(final Bundle bundle)
    {
        super.onCreate(bundle);

        this.setContentView(R.layout.main);
```

```
        this.provider = new TodoController(this);
        this.taskView = (ListView) this.findViewById(R.id.tasklist);
        this.btNewTask = (Button) this.findViewById(R.id.btNewTask);
        this.etNewTask = (EditText) this.findViewById(R.id.etNewTask);
        this.btNewTask.setOnClickListener(this.handleNewTaskEvent);

        this.renderTodos();
    }

    private void renderTodos()
    {
        final List<String> beans = this.provider.getTasks();

        Log.d(TodoActivity.APP_TAG, String.format("%d beans found", beans.size()));

        this.taskView.setAdapter(new ArrayAdapter<String>(this,
                android.R.layout.simple_list_item_1,
                beans.toArray(new String[]
                        {})));

        this.taskView.setOnItemClickListener(new OnItemClickListener()
        {
            @Override
            public void onItemClick(final AdapterView<?> parent, final View view, final int
position, final long id)
            {
                Log.d(TodoActivity.APP_TAG, String.format("item with id: %d and position: %d", id,
position));

                final TextView v = (TextView) view;
                TodoActivity.this.provider.deleteTask(v.getText().toString());
                TodoActivity.this.renderTodos();
            }
        });
    }
}
```

The Controller

Shown in Listing 2-12, the controller binds the UI to the data but also creates a layer of separation between the model and view code above. This interface between the two layers provides a framework for the code to expand and for new developers to follow the MVC pattern to know what new code belongs where.

Listing 2-12. MVC Controller code

```
public class TodoController {
    /*The Controller provides data from the Model for the View
     *to bind to the UI.
     */
```

```java
private TodoModel db_model;
private List<String> tasks;

public TodoController(Context app_context)
{
    tasks = new ArrayList<String>();
    db_model = new TodoModel(app_context);
}

public void addTask(final String title)
{
    final ContentValues data = new ContentValues();
    data.put("title", title);
    db_model.addEntry(data);
}

//Overrides to handle View specifics and keep Model straightforward.
public void deleteTask(final String title)
{
    db_model.deleteEntry("title='" + title + "'");
}

public void deleteTask(final long id)
{
    db_model.deleteEntry("id='" + id + "'");
}

public void deleteAll()
{
    db_model.deleteEntry(null);
}

public List<String> getTasks()
{
    Cursor c = db_model.findAll();
    tasks.clear();

    if (c != null)
    {
        c.moveToFirst();

        while (c.isAfterLast() == false)
        {
            tasks.add(c.getString(0));
            c.moveToNext();
        }

        c.close();
    }

    return tasks;
}
}
```

MVVM

The MVVM (Model-View-ViewModel) pattern comes from the Microsoft world. It's a specialized case of MVC that deals with UI development platforms like Silverlight, and although its origins are in .Net, it might also be applicable to Android. The difference between MVC and MVVM is that the Model should contain no logic specific to the view—only logic necessary to provide a minimal API to the ViewModel.

The Model only needs to add/delete, and the ViewModel handles the specific needs of the View. All event logic and delegation is handled by the ViewModel, and the View handles UI setup only.

In our example the Model component largely stays the same, as you can see in Listing 2-13. The ViewModel, shown in Listing 2-15 acts as a delegate between the ToDoActivity (View) and the ToDoProvider (Model). The ViewModel receives references from the View and uses them to update the UI. The ViewModel handles rendering and changes to the view's data and the View, shown in Listing 2-14, simply provides a reference to its elements.

The Model

Shown in Listing 2-13, the Model largely stays the same in MVVM as it was in the MVC version.

Listing 2-13. MVVM Model Code

```
package com.example.mvvm;

import java.util.ArrayList;
import java.util.List;

import android.content.ContentValues;
import android.content.Context;
import android.database.Cursor;
import android.database.sqlite.SQLiteDatabase;
import android.database.sqlite.SQLiteOpenHelper;
import android.util.Log;

final class TodoModel

{

    //The Model should contain no logic specific to the view - only
    //logic necessary to provide a minimal API to the ViewModel.
  private static final String DB_NAME = "tasks";
  private static final String TABLE_NAME = "tasks";
  private static final int DB_VERSION = 1;
  private static final String DB_CREATE_QUERY = "CREATE TABLE " + TodoModel.TABLE_NAME + " (id
integer primary key autoincrement, title text not null);";

  private final SQLiteDatabase storage;
  private final SQLiteOpenHelper helper;
  public TodoModel(final Context ctx)
```

```
{
  this.helper = new SQLiteOpenHelper(ctx, TodoModel.DB_NAME, null, TodoModel.DB_VERSION)
  {
    @Override
    public void onCreate(final SQLiteDatabase db)
    {
      db.execSQL(TodoModel.DB_CREATE_QUERY);
    }

    @Override
    public void onUpgrade(final SQLiteDatabase db, final int oldVersion,
        final int newVersion)
    {
      db.execSQL("DROP TABLE IF EXISTS " + TodoModel.TABLE_NAME);
      this.onCreate(db);
    }
  };

  this.storage = this.helper.getWritableDatabase();
}

  /*Overrides are now done in the ViewModel. The Model only needs
   *to add/delete, and the ViewModel can handle the specific needs of the View.
   */
public void addEntry(ContentValues data)
{
  this.storage.insert(TodoModel.TABLE_NAME, null, data);
}

public void deleteEntry(final String field_params)
{
  this.storage.delete(TodoModel.TABLE_NAME, field_params, null);
}

public Cursor findAll()
{
      //Model only needs to return an accessor. The ViewModel will handle
      //any logic accordingly.
      return this.storage.query(TodoModel.TABLE_NAME, new String[]
  { "title" }, null, null, null, null, null);
  }
}
```

The View

The View, shown in Listing 2-14, in MVVM simply provides a reference to its elements.

Listing 2-14. MVVM View Code

```
package com.example.mvvm;
import android.app.Activity;
import android.os.Bundle;
import android.view.View;
```

```
import android.widget.Button;
import android.widget.EditText;
import android.widget.ListView;

public class TodoActivity extends Activity
{
  public static final String APP_TAG = "com.logicdrop.todos";

  private ListView taskView;
  private Button btNewTask;
  private EditText etNewTask;
    private TaskListManager delegate;

    /*The View handles UI setup only. All event logic and delegation
     *is handled by the ViewModel.
     */

    public static interface TaskListManager
    {
        //Through this interface the event logic is
        //passed off to the ViewModel.
        void registerTaskList(ListView list);
        void registerTaskAdder(View button, EditText input);
    }

  @Override
  protected void onStop()
  {
    super.onStop();
  }

  @Override
  protected void onStart()
  {
    super.onStart();
  }

  @Override
  public void onCreate(final Bundle bundle)
  {
    super.onCreate(bundle);

    this.setContentView(R.layout.main);

        this.delegate = new TodoViewModel(this);
        this.taskView = (ListView) this.findViewById(R.id.tasklist);
        this.btNewTask = (Button) this.findViewById(R.id.btNewTask);
        this.etNewTask = (EditText) this.findViewById(R.id.etNewTask);
        this.delegate.registerTaskList(taskView);
        this.delegate.registerTaskAdder(btNewTask, etNewTask);
  }
}
```

The ViewModel

The ViewModel component, shown in Listing 2-15, acts as a delegate between the ToDoActivity (View) and the ToDoProvider (Model). The ViewModel handles rendering and changes to the View's data; it receives references from the View and uses them to update the UI.

Listing 2-15. MVVM View-Model Code

```
package com.example.mvvm;

import android.content.ContentValues;
import android.content.Context;
import android.database.Cursor;
import android.view.View;
import android.widget.AdapterView;
import android.widget.ArrayAdapter;
import android.widget.EditText;
import android.widget.ListView;
import android.widget.TextView;

import java.util.ArrayList;
import java.util.List;

public class TodoViewModel implements TodoActivity.TaskListManager
{
    /*The ViewModel acts as a delegate between the ToDoActivity (View)
     *and the ToDoProvider (Model).
     * The ViewModel receives references from the View and uses them
     * to update the UI.
     */

    private TodoModel db_model;
    private List<String> tasks;
    private Context main_activity;
    private ListView taskView;
    private EditText newTask;

    public TodoViewModel(Context app_context)
    {
        tasks = new ArrayList<String>();
        main_activity = app_context;
        db_model = new TodoModel(app_context);
    }

    //Overrides to handle View specifics and keep Model straightforward.

    private void deleteTask(View view)
    {
        db_model.deleteEntry("title='" + ((TextView)view).getText().toString() + "'");
    }
```

```
private void addTask(View view)
{
    final ContentValues data = new ContentValues();

    data.put("title", ((TextView)view).getText().toString());
    db_model.addEntry(data);
}

private void deleteAll()
{
    db_model.deleteEntry(null);
}

private List<String> getTasks()
{
    final Cursor c = db_model.findAll();
    tasks.clear();

    if (c != null)
    {
        c.moveToFirst();

        while (c.isAfterLast() == false)
        {
            tasks.add(c.getString(0));
            c.moveToNext();
        }

        c.close();
    }

    return tasks;
}

private void renderTodos()
{
    //The ViewModel handles rendering and changes to the view's
    //data. The View simply provides a reference to its
    //elements.
    taskView.setAdapter(new ArrayAdapter<String>(main_activity,
            android.R.layout.simple_list_item_1,
            getTasks().toArray(new String[]
                    {})));
}

public void registerTaskList(ListView list)
{
    this.taskView = list; //Keep reference for rendering later
    if (list.getAdapter() == null) //Show items at startup
    {
        renderTodos();
    }
```

```
        list.setOnItemClickListener(new AdapterView.OnItemClickListener()
        {
            @Override
            public void onItemClick(final AdapterView<?> parent, final View view, final int
position, final long id)
            { //Tapping on any item in the list will delete that item from the database and
re-render the list
                deleteTask(view);
                renderTodos();
            }
        });
    }

    public void registerTaskAdder(View button, EditText input)
    {
        this.newTask = input;
        button.setOnClickListener(new View.OnClickListener()
        {
            @Override
            public void onClick(final View view)
            { //Add task to database, re-render list, and clear the input
                addTask(newTask);
                renderTodos();
                newTask.setText("");
            }
        });
    }
}
```

Dependency Injection

If our aim is to move away from highly coupled code, then the Dependency Injection pattern probably allows a greater degree of separation across the application than MVC or MVVM. It removes any hard-coded dependencies between classes and allows you to plug in different classes at compile-time. This is very useful for multiple developers working in teams because it can enforce a much stricter framework to follow.

Just as important is that dependency injection also facilitates the writing of testable code, which we'll see more of in Chapter 4, on Agile Android.

Dependency Injection or DI has been around for many years in Java development. It usually comes in two flavors, compile-time DI (such as Guice) or run-time DI (such as Spring). In compile-time DI, the injections are known at compile time and are controlled by a mapping file. Run-time DI takes more of an aspect oriented programming approach, where classes are injected while the app is running.

There are a number of DI frameworks available in Android such as Roboelectric and Dagger, all of them are compile time DI.

In the following example we're going to look at using Dagger to mock out a database connection. Often you want to test the app and not the database.

There are four pieces in this example that we need to wire together. The ToDoModule.java contains the injection map that tells the app whether to use the ToDoProvider stub file or the ToDoProvider2 file that connects to the database. ToDoProvider.java contains the stub file that returns a fake task list, ToDoProvider2.java contains the real database connection, and ToDoApplication.java contains a currentChoice Boolean flag that tells the app whether to use the stub or the real connection.

The ToDoModule

Listing 2-16 shows how the ToDoModule wires in the two database providers; the first is the real database and the second is a stub function.

Listing 2-16. Dagger ToDoModule.java

```java
import dagger.Module;
import dagger.Provides;
import android.content.Context;
import android.database.sqlite.SQLiteDatabase;
import android.database.sqlite.SQLiteOpenHelper;
import android.util.Log;

@Module(complete = true, injects = { TodoActivity.class })
public class TodoModule {

    static final String DB_NAME = "tasks";
    static final String TABLE_NAME = "tasks";
    static final int DB_VERSION = 1;
    static final String DB_CREATE_QUERY = "CREATE TABLE "
            + TodoModule.TABLE_NAME
            + " (id integer primary key autoincrement, title text not null);";

    private final Context appContext;
    public static boolean sourceToggle = false;
    private TodoApplication parent;

    /** Constructs this module with the application context. */
    public TodoModule(TodoApplication app) {
        this.parent = app;
        this.appContext = app.getApplicationContext();

    }

    @Provides
    public Context provideContext() {
        return appContext;
    }

    /**
     * Needed because we need to provide an implementation to an interface, not a
     * class.
     *
     * @return
```

```
    */
    @Provides
    IDataProvider provideDataProvider(final SQLiteDatabase db) {
        //Here we obtain the boolean value for which provider to use
        boolean currentChoice = parent.getCurrentSource();
        if(currentChoice == true){
            //Here is a log message to know which provider has been chosen
            Log.d(TodoActivity.APP_TAG, "Provider2");
            return new TodoProvider2(db);
        }else{
            Log.d(TodoActivity.APP_TAG, "Provider");
            return new TodoProvider(db);
        }
    }

    /**
     * Needed because we need to configure the helper before injecting it.
     *
     * @return
     */
    @Provides
    SQLiteOpenHelper provideSqlHelper() {
        final SQLiteOpenHelper helper = new SQLiteOpenHelper(this.appContext,
                TodoModule.DB_NAME, null, TodoModule.DB_VERSION) {
            @Override
            public void onCreate(final SQLiteDatabase db) {
                db.execSQL(TodoModule.DB_CREATE_QUERY);
            }

            @Override
            public void onUpgrade(final SQLiteDatabase db,
                    final int oldVersion, final int newVersion) {
                db.execSQL("DROP TABLE IF EXISTS " + TodoModule.TABLE_NAME);
                this.onCreate(db);
            }
        };

        return helper;
    }

    @Provides
    SQLiteDatabase provideDatabase(SQLiteOpenHelper helper) {
        return helper.getWritableDatabase();
    }
}
```

The Database Provider

The Boolean currentChoice tells the code which database provider to use; we can connect either to the real database, ToDoProvider2, as shown in Listing 2-17, or the stub, ToDoProvider, as shown in Listing 2-18.

Listing 2-17. Dagger ToDoProvider2.java

```java
package com.example.dagger;

import java.util.ArrayList;
import java.util.List;

import javax.inject.Inject;

import android.content.ContentValues;
import android.database.Cursor;
import android.database.sqlite.SQLiteDatabase;
import android.util.Log;

class TodoProvider2 implements IDataProvider {

    private final SQLiteDatabase storage;

    @Inject
    public TodoProvider2(SQLiteDatabase db)
    {
        this.storage = db;
    }

    @Override
    public void addTask(final String title) {
        final ContentValues data = new ContentValues();
        data.put("title", title);

        this.storage.insert(TodoModule.TABLE_NAME, null, data);
    }

    @Override
    public void deleteAll() {
        this.storage.delete(TodoModule.TABLE_NAME, null, null);
    }

    @Override
    public void deleteTask(final long id) {
        this.storage.delete(TodoModule.TABLE_NAME, "id=" + id, null);
    }

    @Override
    public void deleteTask(final String title) {
        this.storage.delete(TodoModule.TABLE_NAME, "title='" + title + "'",
                null);
    }

    @Override
    public List<String> findAll() {
        Log.d(TodoActivity.APP_TAG, "findAll triggered");

        final List<String> tasks = new ArrayList<String>();
```

```
    final Cursor c = this.storage.query(TodoModule.TABLE_NAME,
            new String[] { "title" }, null, null, null, null, null);

    if (c != null) {
        c.moveToFirst();

        while (c.isAfterLast() == false) {
            tasks.add(c.getString(0));
            c.moveToNext();
        }

        c.close();
    }

    return tasks;
    }

}
```

The Stub Provider

Listing 2-18 shows the fake or stubbed out database; we include this to make sure we're only testing our code and not the database connections.

Listing 2-18. ToDoProvider.java

```java
package com.example.dagger;

import java.util.ArrayList;
import java.util.List;

import javax.inject.Inject;

import android.content.ContentValues;
import android.database.Cursor;
import android.database.sqlite.SQLiteDatabase;
import android.util.Log;

class TodoProvider implements IDataProvider {

    private final SQLiteDatabase storage;

    @Inject
    public TodoProvider(SQLiteDatabase db)
    {
        this.storage = db;
    }

    @Override
    public void addTask(final String title) {
        final ContentValues data = new ContentValues();
        data.put("title", title);
```

```
        this.storage.insert(TodoModule.TABLE_NAME, null, data);
    }

    @Override
    public void deleteAll() {
        this.storage.delete(TodoModule.TABLE_NAME, null, null);
    }

    @Override
    public void deleteTask(final long id) {
        this.storage.delete(TodoModule.TABLE_NAME, "id=" + id, null);
    }

    @Override
    public void deleteTask(final String title) {
        this.storage.delete(TodoModule.TABLE_NAME, "title='" + title + "'",
                null);
    }

    @Override
    public List<String> findAll() {
        Log.d(TodoActivity.APP_TAG, "findAll triggered");

        final List<String> tasks = new ArrayList<String>();

        final Cursor c = this.storage.query(TodoModule.TABLE_NAME,
                new String[] { "title" }, null, null, null, null, null);

        if (c != null) {
            c.moveToFirst();

            while (c.isAfterLast() == false) {
                tasks.add(c.getString(0));
                c.moveToNext();
            }

            c.close();
        }

        return tasks;
    }

}
```

ToDoApplication

Finally we need to tell the code what code to inject. We do this in the getCurrentSource method of
ToDoApplcation.java, shown in Listing 2-19. Ideally, we'd like to set this in a config file somewhere,
but here it is hard-coded in a file.

Listing 2-19. ToDoApplication.java

```java
package com.example.dagger;

import android.app.Application;
import android.content.SharedPreferences;
import android.content.SharedPreferences.Editor;
import dagger.ObjectGraph;

public class TodoApplication extends Application {

    private ObjectGraph objectGraph;
    SharedPreferences settings;

    @Override
    public void onCreate()
    {
        super.onCreate();

        //Initializes the settings variable
        this.settings = getSharedPreferences("Settings", MODE_PRIVATE);
        Object[] modules = new Object[] {
                new TodoModule(this)
        };

        objectGraph = ObjectGraph.create(modules);
    }

    public ObjectGraph getObjectGraph() {
        return this.objectGraph;
    }

    //Method to update the settings
    public void updateSetting(boolean newChoice){
        Editor editor = this.settings.edit();
        editor.putBoolean("CurrentChoice", TodoModule.sourceToggle);
        editor.commit();
    }

    //Method to obtain the value of the provider setting
    public boolean getCurrentSource(){
        return this.settings.getBoolean("CurrentChoice", false);
    }
}
```

Summary

In this chapter we looked at the Holo GUI design pattern to see best practices for GUIs as well as the MVC, MVVM and DI architectural design patterns using Dagger to see how to best organize or separate your code so that it's got some room for growth. We'll return to Dagger in Chapter 4, on Agile Android, to show how we can use DI for mock testing. All the code for the examples in this chapter and the book is available on the Apress website if you want to investigate it further.

Chapter **3**

Performance

Michael A. Jackson famously coined the first and second rules of program optimization:

> Rule 1. *Don't do it.*
>
> Rule 2. (For experts only!): *Don't do it yet.*

This can be interpreted in a number of ways. To me, it really means "keep your code clean and don't worry about optimizing its flow." Avoid making the code too complicated. It also points to the fact that as computers and JIT compilers get more advanced, you probably won't have to worry about it in six months, as the hardware will have overtaken any minimal optimizations that you can apply.

What it doesn't mean is to do nothing if your mobile app takes 10 or more seconds to load an activity and is a terrible user experience. Remember that whatever you thought was an acceptable time on the Web is most definitely not acceptable on a phone, whether that's on Android or iOS.

And it gets worse, because if your app takes too long, then Android will display the dreaded Android Not Responding image (see Figure 3-1), and your user will probably leave the app. This is more likely to happen on older devices with less memory and less power; and contrary to the second law of program optimization there are many of older Android devices from the Gingerbread era that continue to hang around in the field and are not expected to go away any time soon.

Figure 3-1. Android "not responding" popup

For comparison's sake we're going to talk a little about how performance tuning works on the Web. Optimizing Android apps is still a bit of a black art; while there's a general consensus on how you should go about optimizing your web server, it's nowhere as neat and tidy on the Android platform. After all, the variety of Android devices on the market makes optimizing your app a moving target.

We'll also spend some time on Android performance tips that can really make a difference to your code. Finally, we'll look at the some of the tools that come with the Android SDK, such as Dalvik Debug Monitor Server (DDMS) and Traceview, that can help identify bottlenecks and hopefully point the way to creating a better app.

History

Back in the 2000s, performance optimization was all about how to optimize web applications typically sitting on IIS or Apache web servers, and many of the same points apply to what we are trying to do in this chapter. Unfortunately, it's not as easy to measure Android performance as it is on a web server.

The Web server metric that is often aimed for is that 95% of pages should be returned in a second or less. The raw stats, such as the number of page hits and page timings (using the time-taken token, as shown in Figure 3-2), are all there to see in the log files. The trick is to optimize the slowest, most visited pages, which give the perception of a faster web server; perception is reality when it comes to performance. The same is true on mobile devices.

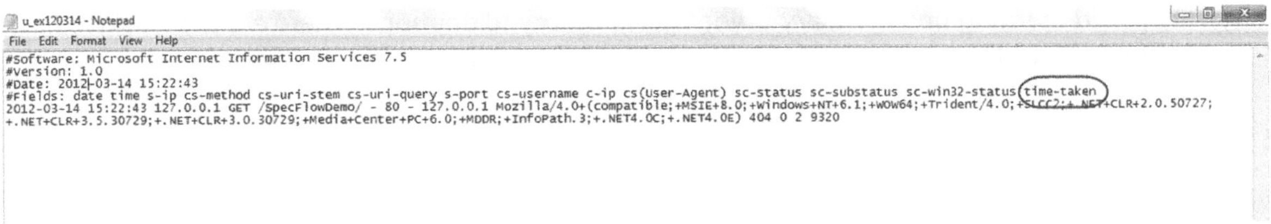

Figure 3-2. Web Server log files with time-taken token

Dramatic increases in page speed are commonly achieved on the worst-performing pages by adding indexes on the database, fixing SELECT statements to limit the amount of data returned, or fixing problems with programming control flow logic. Iteratively fixing the most-visited, worst-performing pages over an extended time can transform a web server's speed using this "wash, rinse, repeat" approach.

Android, on the other hand, is not as simple. In Android there is no metric like "95% of pages should be returned in a second or less." There really isn't any consensus on how responsive an app needs to be. And the metric would probably also vary from one device to the next. It's also a lot harder to measure how long each activity takes, as there are no log files with a handy time-taken token that you can easily use.

It's not all bad news, however, as the Android SDK does come with a number of tools, such as DDMS and Traceview, that really help debug performance problems, but they measure different aspects of an Android app's performance.

Ideally, you want a good load testing tool with some sort of reliable time measurement. If possible, it should run as part of a build on a continuous integration server so you could see regression test reports; by seeing how long the same actions are taking as the app progresses, you'll be able to identify if something is suddenly taking dramatically longer than it was in the past.

We will need to look at Web server statistics when we're trying to optimize Web services, which we'll return to later in the book.

Performance Tips

Let's take a look at some Android, Java, Web services, and SQL tips that you might want to try if your app is not responding correctly.

Android Performance

Google publishes an excellent list of performance tips (see `http://developer.android.com/training/articles/perf-tips.html`), which the following are largely taken from and expanded upon. Some of these optimizations take a very macro approach, and some take a very micro approach to optimization and will only remove a line or two of bytecode from the generated `classes.dex` in the APK. These micro-optimizations will probably be handled by future just-in-time DVM optimizations or ahead of time by the new ART or Android Runtime virtual machine, which is a replacement for the DVM. However as ART is at the time of writing available only on Android KitKat, it may be a while before these automated optimizations become commonplace.

Avoid creating unnecessary objects or memory allocations. There are two basic rules for writing efficient code:

- Don't do work that you don't need to do.

- Don't allocate memory if you can avoid it.

Mobile development is relatively simple right now; we don't have the layers and layers of complexity that always appear as a technology matures, such EJBs.

But it is inevitable that this is going to happen sooner or later on Android. People are already putting ORMs into their Android apps, so try to move to more of a TDD (test-driven development) model, and think about what you're introducing. Do you really need to reinvent some caching mechanism to satisfy the feature you're implementing, or not? If you are still worried, then apply the YAGNI concept— You Aren't Going to Need It, because you really don't need it.

Avoid internal getters/setters. Virtual method calls are expensive, more so than instance field lookups. It's reasonable to follow common object-oriented programming practices and have getters and setters in the public interface, but within a class you should always access fields directly. This is an example of a micro-optimization that removes a line or two of bytecode from the generated classes.dex in the APK.

Use static/final where appropriate. Because of the way the code is compiled into Davlik bytecode, any code that refers to intVal will use the integer value 42 directly if you use a static final, and accesses to strVal will use a relatively inexpensive "string constant" instruction instead of a field lookup.

Use floats judiciously. Floating-point calculation is expensive, usually taking twice as long as integer calculations on Android devices.

Make fewer, more productive, NDK calls. Context switching between Java and C++ using the JNI or NDK can be expensive. There are also no JIT optimizations.

But if the app uses some core algorithm or functionality that doesn't need to be tied to the UI in any significant way, it should probably be run natively. Running things natively is almost always going to be faster than Java even with the JIT compiler. The NDK also comes with some major security benefits, as it's much harder to reverse-engineer C++ code.

Inflate Views only when needed. Basically, the idea here is that you only inflate the views a minimum number of times or better still delay displaying the view, because inflating views is pretty expensive.

Use standard libraries and enhancements. Use libraries rather than rolling your own code. Android also sometimes replaces library methods with optimized hand-coded assembler. For example, using `String.indexOf()` and the `System.arraycopy()` method is about nine times faster than a hand-coded loop.

Use StrictMode. To limit the chance of an Android Not Responsive (ANR) error, it helps to not include any slow network or disk access in the applications main thread. Android provides a utility called StrictMode, which is typically used to detect if there are any unwanted disk or network accesses introduced into your application during the development process. Add StrictMode to your onCreate() method as shown in Listing 3-1. StrictMode calls are also pretty expensive, so make sure the code isn't shipped as production code.

Listing 3-1. Using the Strictmode utility

```
public void onCreate()
{
        // remove from production code
        if (BuildConfig.DEBUG){
                StrictMode.setThreadPolicy(new StrictMode.ThreadPolicy.Builder(),
                .detectDiskReads()
                .detectDiskWrites()
                .detectNetwork()
                .penaltyLog()
                .build());
    {
        super.onCreate();

}
```

Optimize the onSomething() classes. Earlier we talked about perception being reality for web applications; in the Android world, if your onStart(), onCreate(), and onResume() classes are lightning fast, then the application is going to be perceived to be a faster Android app. So if there is any code that you can put elsewhere or optimizations that you might want to apply, then spending time in these classes will bring rewards. Wait as long as you can to inflate any views. Using android.view. ViewStub will allow objects to be created when needed, a technique known as lazily inflating a view.

Use Relativelayouts instead of Linearlayouts. New Android developers tend to create a UI over-using LinearLayouts. As the application becomes more complex, these linear layouts can often become quite nested. Replacing these LinearLayouts with a single RelativeLayout will improve your UI loading speed. Lint and the Hierarchy Viewer will help you identify deeply nested LinearLayouts.

Java Performance

There are books and books written about Java performance, and Android can also benefit from some well-written Java code. The Java Performance Tuning page (http://www.javaperformancetuning.com/tips/rawtips.shtml) is a page of links to articles about Java optimization with summaries and reviews of each of these pages of optimization tips.

The most common optimizations are as follows:

1. Use + for concatenating two Strings; use `Stringbuffer` for concatenating more Strings.

   - Don't synchronize code unless synchronization is required.

   - Close all resources, such as connections and session objects, when finished.

   - Classes and methods that aren't going to be redefined should be declared as final.

   - Accessing arrays is much faster than accessing vectors, Strings, and StringBuffers.

SQLite Performance

Website inefficiencies could often be summed up as "It's the database, Stupid." And while it's less of an issue on Android, where SQLite is used more for client-side caching of information, there is no reason why EXPLAIN PLAN cannot still be very useful in your performance tuning. And don't forget you can create indexes on SQLite, too, if you need them (see Figure 3-3).

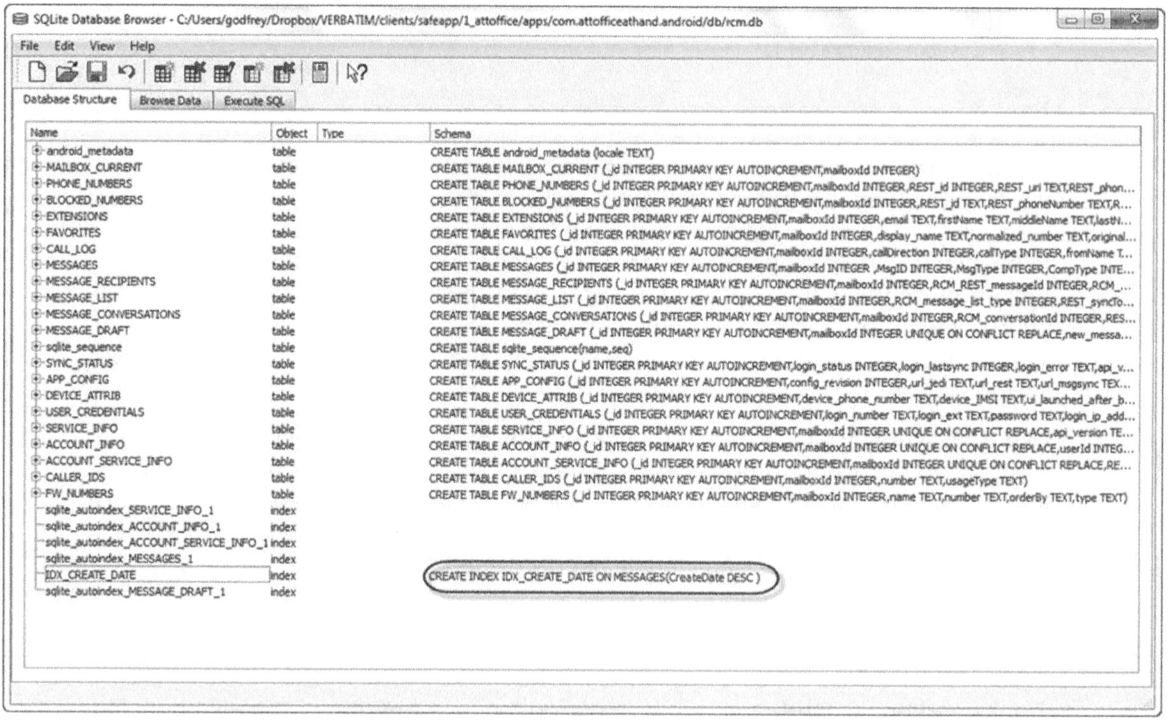

Figure 3-3. SQLite indexes

Learn the SQLite Android libraries and use the `DatabaseUtils.InsertHelper` command for inserting large amounts of data or use `compileStatement` where appropriate. Don't store the database on the SD Card. Finally, don't return the entire table of data in a SELECT statement; always return the minimum of rows using carefully crafted SQL statements.

Web Services Performance

For Web services it's a case of "everything old is new again." We're right back to the web site optimization techniques I mentioned earlier. Use the server logs, as shown in Figure 3-2 earlier, to see how long each call is taking and optimize the slowest, most-used Web services. Some common optimizations for Web services are as follows:

- Minimize the size of the Web service envelopes; choose REST over SOAP and JSON over XML where possible.

- Reduce the number of round trips, steer clear of chatty Web service calls, and keep the number of Web service transactions to a minimum.

- Remove any duplicate calls, which are not as uncommon as they might seem.

- Similar to database SELECT * FROM TABLE statements, careful choice of query parameters can dramatically limit the amount of data returned via the Web service.

- Avoid maintaining state across calls; the most scalable of Web services maintain no state.

- Gzip the data.

Web proxy tools such as Charles Proxy (http://www.charlesproxy.com/) are an excellent way to see how your app is interacting with Web services.

The topic of Web services is covered in more detail in Chapter 8.

Optimized Code

In the next few pages you're going to see how some of these optimizations are used in the ToDo List application. To begin, Listing 3-2 shows Splash.java, which has a bare-bones onCreate() method.

Listing 3-2. The ToDo List Application's Splash.java page

```java
package com.logicdrop.todos;

import android.app.Activity;
import android.os.Bundle;
import android.content.Intent;

public class Splash extends Activity {
    public void onCreate(Bundle savedInstanceState) {
        // TIP: Optimized the onSomething() classes, especially onCreate()
        super.onCreate(savedInstanceState);

        // TIP: View - inflate the views a minimum number of times
        // inflating views are expensive
        /*for (int i=0; i<10000; i++)
            setContentView(R.layout.splash);*/
```

```
        // TIP: Splashscreen optional  (DONE)
        setContentView(R.layout.splash);
        Thread timer = new Thread() {
            public void run() {
                try {
                    sleep(1000);
                } catch (InterruptedException e) {
                    e.printStackTrace();
                } finally {
                    Intent openStartingPoint = new Intent("com.logicdrop.todos.TodoActivity");
                    startActivity(openStartingPoint);
                }
            }
        };
        timer.start();
    }
}
```

ToDoActivity.java, shown in Listing 3-3, has many of the Android and Java optimizations mentioned in this chapter; see comments in the code for more information. It also shows how to stop and start profiling using the Traceview API.

Listing 3-3. The ToDo List Application's ToDoActivity.java page

```
package com.logicdrop.todos;

import java.util.List;
import java.util.ArrayList;

import android.app.Activity;
import android.os.Bundle;
import android.util.Log;
import android.view.View;
import android.view.View.OnClickListener;
import android.widget.AdapterView;
import android.widget.AdapterView.OnItemClickListener;
import android.widget.ArrayAdapter;
import android.widget.Button;
import android.widget.EditText;
import android.widget.ListView;
import android.widget.TextView;
import android.os.StrictMode;

import com.logicdrop.todos.R;

public class TodoActivity extends Activity
{
    public static final String APP_TAG = "com.logicdrop.todos";

    private ListView taskView;
    private Button btNewTask;
    private EditText etNewTask;
    private TodoProvider provider;
```

```
// TIP: Use static/final where appropriate
private final OnClickListener handleNewTaskEvent = new OnClickListener()
{
    @Override
    public void onClick(final View view)
    {
        Log.d(APP_TAG, "add task click received");

        TodoActivity.this.provider.addTask(TodoActivity.this
                .etNewTask
                        .getText()
                        .toString());

        TodoActivity.this.renderTodos();
    }
};

// TIP: Traceview
@Override
protected void onStop()
{
    super.onStop();

    // Debug.stopMethodTracing();
}

@Override
protected void onStart()
{
    // Debug.startMethodTracing("ToDo");

    super.onStart();
}

// TIP: Use floats judiciously
@SuppressWarnings("unused")
private void showFloatVsIntegerDifference()
{
    int max = 1000;
    float f = 0;
    int i = 0;
    long startTime, elapsedTime;

    // Compute time for floats
    startTime = System.nanoTime();
    for (float x = 0; x < max; x++)
    {
        f += x;
    }
    elapsedTime = System.nanoTime() - startTime;
    Log.v(APP_TAG, "Floating Point Loop: " + elapsedTime);
```

```
        // Compute time for ints
        startTime = System.nanoTime();
        for (int x = 0; x < max; x++)
        {
            i += x;
        }
        elapsedTime = System.nanoTime() - startTime;
        Log.v(APP_TAG, "Integer Point Loop: " + elapsedTime);
    }

    // TIP: Avoid creating unnecessary objects or memory allocation
    private void createPlaceholders()
    {
        // TIP: Avoid internal getters/setters
        provider.deleteAll();

        if (provider.findAll().isEmpty())
        {
          // TIP: Arrays are faster than vectors
            List<String> beans = new ArrayList<String>();

            // TIP: Use enhanced for loop (DONE)
            // This is example of the enhanced loop but don't allocate objects if not necessary
              /*for (String task : beans) {
                  String title = "Placeholder ";
                this.provider.addTask(title);
                beans.add(title);
              }*/

            /*for (int i = 0; i < 10; i++)
            {
                String title = "Placeholder " + i;
                this.getProvider().addTask(title);
                beans.add(title);
            }*/
        }
    }

        // TIP: Avoid private getters/setters - consider using package (DONE)
    /*EditText getEditText()
    {
        return this.etNewTask;
    }*/

    /*private TodoProvider getProvider()
    {
        return this.provider;
    }*/

    /*private ListView getTaskView()
    {
        return this.taskView;
    }*/
```

```
    @Override
    public void onCreate(final Bundle bundle)
    {
        // TIP: Use Strictmode to detect unwanted disk or network access
        // Remove from production code (DONE)
        //StrictMode.setThreadPolicy(new StrictMode.ThreadPolicy.Builder()
        //        .detectDiskReads()
        //        .detectDiskWrites()
        //        .detectNetwork()
        //        .penaltyLog()
        //        .build());
        super.onCreate(bundle);

            // TIP: Do not overuse Linearlayouts, as they become more complex (DONE)
            // Replace them with Relativelayouts, increasing UI loading speed
        this.setContentView(R.layout.main);

        this.provider = new TodoProvider(this);
        this.taskView = (ListView) this.findViewById(R.id.tasklist);
        this.btNewTask = (Button) this.findViewById(R.id.btNewTask);
        this.etNewTask = (EditText) this.findViewById(R.id.etNewTask);
        this.btNewTask.setOnClickListener(this.handleNewTaskEvent);

        this.renderTodos();

            // TIP: Again, don't allocate unnecessary objects that expand the heap size to
significant proportions (DONE)
        // Once GC occurs, a large amount of the heap memory is dumped, especially with
        // local data structures, which renders a large portion of the heap unused.
        // SEE: optimizedHeap.png, deoptimizedHeap.png, heap-before.tiff, heap-after.tiff
        /*ArrayList<uselessClass> uselessObject = new ArrayList<uselessClass>();
        for (int i=0; i<180000; i++)
            uselessObject.add(new uselessClass());*/
    }

    private void renderTodos()
    {
        final List<String> beans = this.provider.findAll();

        Log.d(TodoActivity.APP_TAG, String.format("%d beans found", beans.size()));

        this.taskView.setAdapter(new ArrayAdapter<String>(this,
                android.R.layout.simple_list_item_1,
                beans.toArray(new String[]
                {})));

        this.taskView.setOnItemClickListener(new OnItemClickListener()
        {
            @Override
            public void onItemClick(final AdapterView<?> parent, final View view, final int
position, final long id)
```

```
                {
                        Log.d(TodoActivity.APP_TAG, String.format("item with id: %d and position: %d",
id, position));

                        final TextView v = (TextView) view;
                        TodoActivity.this.provider.deleteTask(v.getText().toString());
                        TodoActivity.this.renderTodos();
                }
            });
        }

    // Class with 26 double data members used to expand heap size in example
    /*private class uselessClass {
        double a,b,c,d,e,f,g,h,i,j,k,l,m,n,o,p,q,r,s,t,u,v,w,x,y,z;
    }*/
}
```

Finally, ToDoProvider.java, shown in Listing 3-4, has examples of some of the remaining optimizations, such as always closing resources and only using SELECT statements to return a minimum of data.

Listing 3-4. The ToDo List Application's ToDoProvider.java Page

```
package com.logicdrop.todos;

import java.util.ArrayList;
import java.util.List;

import android.content.ContentValues;
import android.content.Context;
import android.database.Cursor;
import android.database.sqlite.SQLiteDatabase;
import android.database.sqlite.SQLiteOpenHelper;
import android.util.Log;

final class TodoProvider
{
    private static final String DB_NAME = "tasks";
    private static final String TABLE_NAME = "tasks";
    private static final int DB_VERSION = 1;
    private static final String DB_CREATE_QUERY = "CREATE TABLE " + TodoProvider.TABLE_NAME +
" (id integer primary key autoincrement, title text not null);";

    // TIP: Use final wherever possible (DONE)
    private final SQLiteDatabase storage;
    private final SQLiteOpenHelper helper;

    public TodoProvider(final Context ctx)
    {
        this.helper = new SQLiteOpenHelper(ctx, TodoProvider.DB_NAME, null, TodoProvider.DB_VERSION)
        {
```

```java
        @Override
        public void onCreate(final SQLiteDatabase db)
        {
            db.execSQL(TodoProvider.DB_CREATE_QUERY);
        }

        @Override
        public void onUpgrade(final SQLiteDatabase db, final int oldVersion,
                final int newVersion)
        {
            db.execSQL("DROP TABLE IF EXISTS " + TodoProvider.TABLE_NAME);
            this.onCreate(db);
        }
    };

    this.storage = this.helper.getWritableDatabase();
}

// TIP: Avoid synchronization (DONE)
public void addTask(final String title)
{
    final ContentValues data = new ContentValues();
    data.put("title", title);

    this.storage.insert(TodoProvider.TABLE_NAME, null, data);
}

public void deleteAll()
{
    this.storage.delete(TodoProvider.TABLE_NAME, null, null);
}

public void deleteTask(final long id)
{
    this.storage.delete(TodoProvider.TABLE_NAME, "id=" + id, null);
}

public void deleteTask(final String title)
{
    this.storage.delete(TodoProvider.TABLE_NAME, "title='" + title + "'", null);
}

// TIP: Don't return the entire table of data. (DONE)
// Unused
public List<String> findAll()
{
    Log.d(TodoActivity.APP_TAG, "findAll triggered");

    final List<String> tasks = new ArrayList<String>();

    final Cursor c = this.storage.query(TodoProvider.TABLE_NAME, new String[]
    { "title" }, null, null, null, null, null);
```

```
        if (c != null)
        {
            c.moveToFirst();

            while (c.isAfterLast() == false)
            {
                tasks.add(c.getString(0));
                c.moveToNext();
            }

            // TIP: Close resources (DONE)
            c.close();
        }

        return tasks;
    }
}
```

Tools

In this section we'll look at two types of tools useful in finding performance bottlenecks—tools that come with the Android SDK, and Unix command-line tools.

The Android SDK ships with the following tools to help us identify any performance issues:

- DDMS
- Traceview
- Lint
- Hierarchy Viewer
- Viewer

The Dalvik Debug Monitor Server (DDMS) is an Android SDK application that works as either a standalone tool or an Eclipse plugin. DDMS does lots of things, including device screen capture and providing a place to find logging output. But it also provides heap analysis, method allocation, and thread monitoring information. The Android SDK also has the Traceview tool for method profiling, `layoutopt` for optimizing your XML layouts, and Hierarchy Viewer for optimizing your UI.

And because Android is basically a Linux shell, we can leverage many of the following command-line Unix tools for performance testing:

- `Top`
- `Dumpsys`
- `Vmstat`
- `Procstats`

In this section we're going to look at how to use those tools to get a quick idea of where your application is spending most of its time.

DDMS

In this section we'll be covering the System Performance, Heap Usage, Threads, and Traceview tools, all of which come as part of DDMS. We'll also look at the Memory Analyzer Tool (MAT), which can be downloaded as part of the Eclipse tool and used to report on how memory is being managed in the Heap.

System Performance

The most basic tool in the DDMS suite is System Performance, which gives a quick snapshot overview of the current CPU load, memory usage, and frame render time, as shown in Figure 3-4. The first sign that you have an underperforming app is when your application is consuming too much CPU or memory.

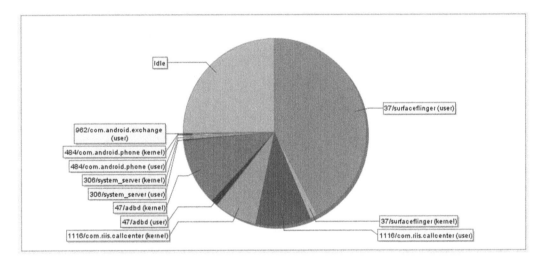

Figure 3-4. The System Performance tool displaying CPU load for CallCenterApp

Heap Usage

DDMS also offers a Heap Usage tool. Take the following steps to view the memory heap, where you can see what objects are being created and if they're being destroyed correctly by the garbage collection. (See Figure 3-5.)

1. In the Devices tab, select the process for which you want to view the heap.

2. Click the Update Heap button to enable heap information for the process.

3. Click Cause GC in the Heap tab to invoke garbage collection, which enables the collection of heap data.

4. When garbage collection completes, you will see a group of object types and the memory that has been allocated for each type.

5. Click an object type in the list to see a bar graph that shows the number of objects allocated for a particular memory size in bytes.

6. Click Cause GC again to refresh the data. Details of the heap are given along with a graph of allocation sizes for a particular allocation type. Watch the overall trend in Heap Size to make sure it doesn't keep growing during the application run.

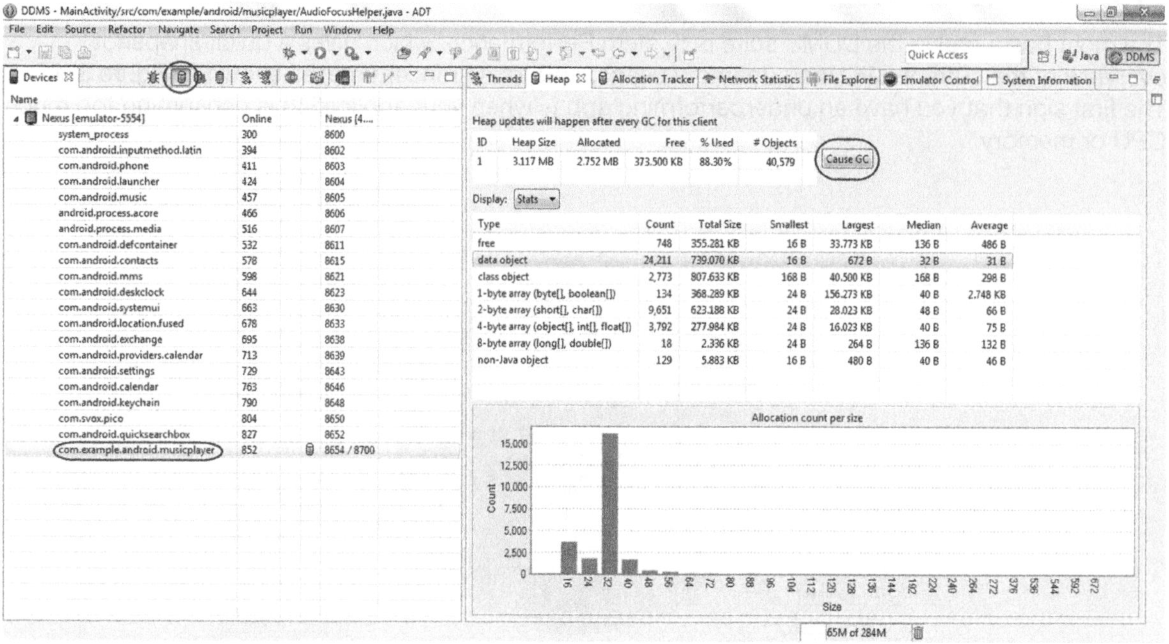

Figure 3-5. Viewing the DDMS heap

Eclipse Memory Analyzer

Eclipse has an integrated Memory Analyzer Tool (MAT) plugin, which you can download and install from http://www.eclipse.org/mat/downloads.php. MAT can help you make sense of the heap output. Now when you dump the heap profile or hprof file (see Figure 3-6), it will be automatically analyzed so you can make some sense of the heap file.

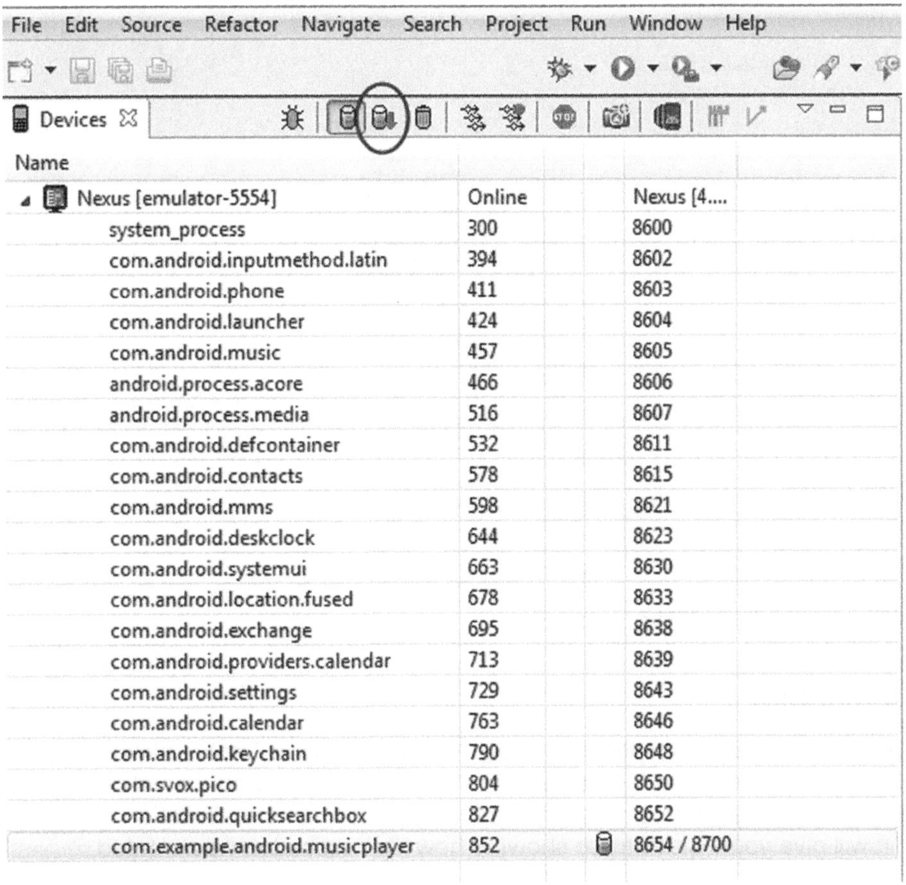

Figure 3-6. *Dumping the hprof file*

MAT provides a number of reports, including a Dominator Tree for the biggest class, a Top Consumers report, and a Leak Suspects report. Figure 3-7 shows Biggest Objects by Retained Size.

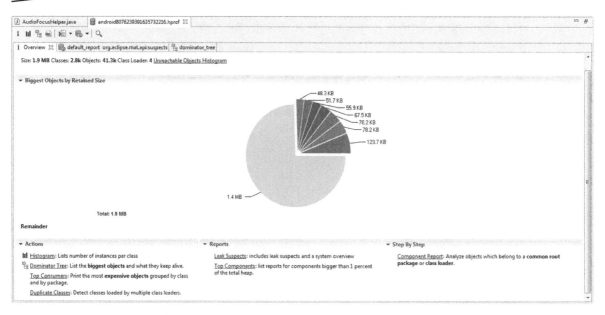

Figure 3-7. Memory Analyzer Tool overview

Memory Allocation

The next level of detail about allocations is shown in the Allocation Tracker view (Figure 3-8). To display it, click Start Tracking, perform an action in the application, and then click Get Allocations. The list presented is in allocation order, with the most recent memory allocation displayed first. Highlighting it will give you a stack trace showing how that allocation was created.

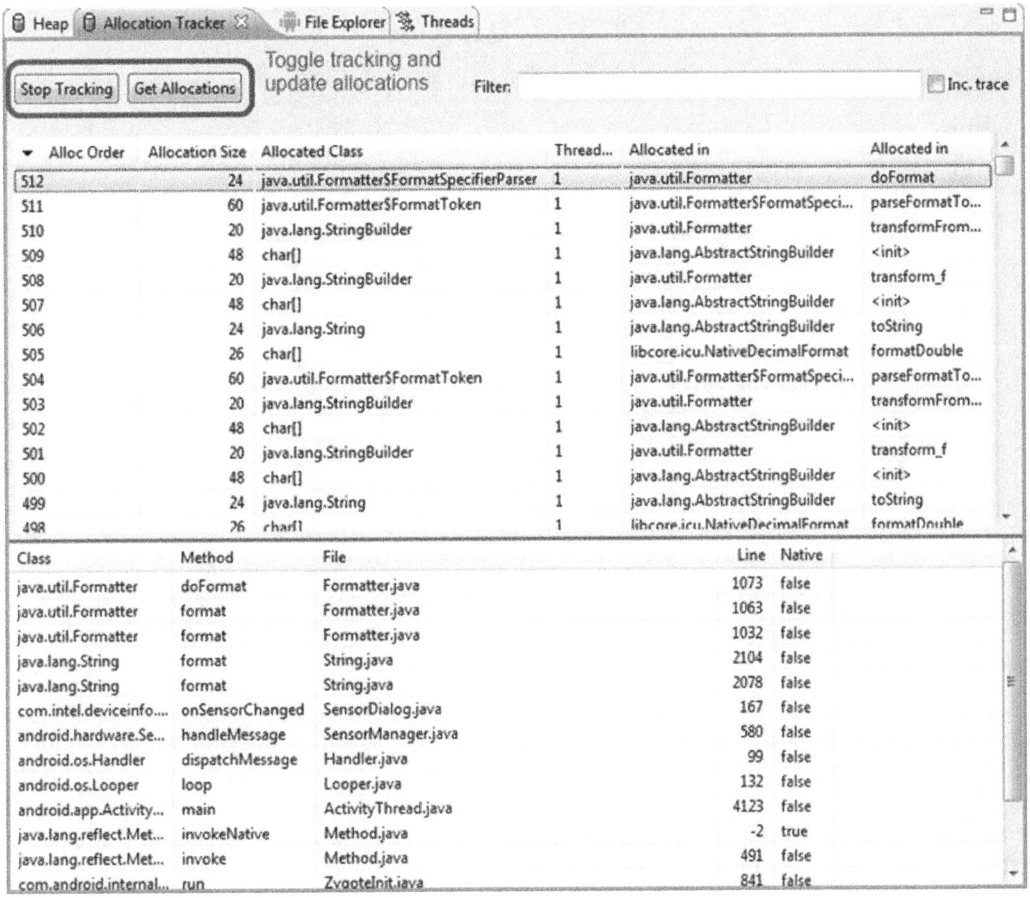

Figure 3-8. Allocation Tracker

Threads

The thread monitor and profiling view in DDMS is useful for applications that manage a lot of threads. To enable it, click the Update Threads icon, shown in Figure 3-9.

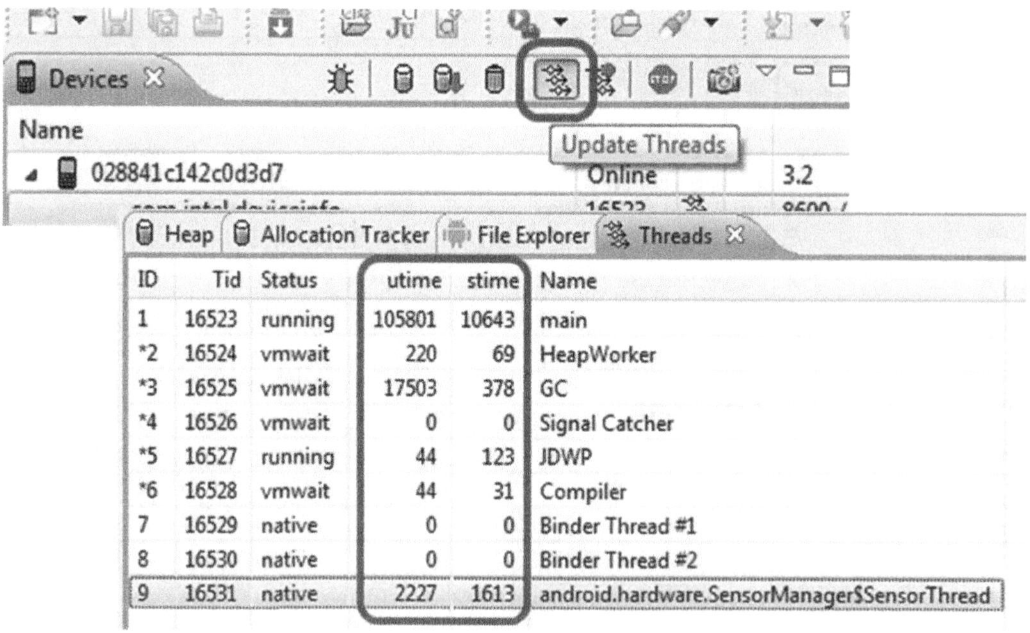

Figure 3-9. *DDMS threads*

The total time spent in a thread running user code (utime) and system code (stime) is measured in what are known as jiffies. A jiffy was originally the time it takes light to travel 1cm, but for Android devices it is the duration of one tick of the system timer interrupt. It varies from device to device but is generally accepted to be about 10ms. The asterisk indicates a daemon thread, and the status Native means the thread is executing native code.

Looking at the sample data in Figure 3-9, it is clear that an unusual amount of time is spent doing GC. A closer look at how the application is handling object creation might be a good idea for improving performance.

Method Profiling

Method Profiling is the tool of choice within DDMS for getting a quick overview of where time is really spent in your application and is the first step in homing in on methods that are taking too much time. With your application running and ideally performing some interesting task that you would like to get more performance data about, take the following steps to use Method Profiling:

1. Click on Start Method Profiling.

2. Click the icon again to stop collection after a couple of seconds.

3. The IDE will automatically launch the Traceview window and allow you to analyze the results from right within the IDE.

4. Click a method call in the bottom pane to create a hierarchy, showing you the current method, the parent(s) that call this method, and then the children methods called from within the selected method (Figure 3-10).

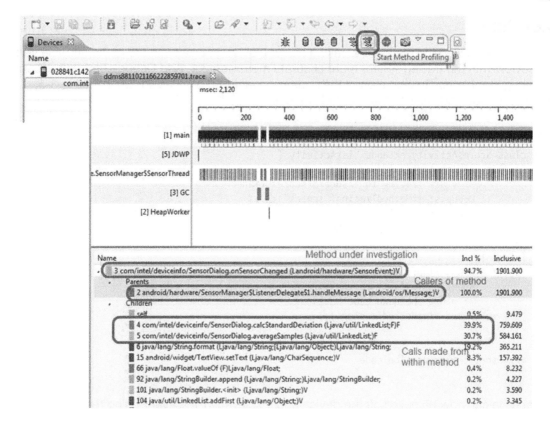

Figure 3-10. Method Profiling in DDMS using Traceview

5. Identify the methods that are taking the most time so you can look at them closer by creating Traceview files, which we'll explore later in this section.

Each method has its parents and children, and the columns are as follows:

Inc % The percentage of the total time spent in the method plus any called methods

Inclusive The amount of time spent in the method plus the time spent in any called methods

Excl % The percentage of the total time spent in the method

Exclusive The amount of time spent in the method

Calls + Recursive The number of calls to this method plus any recursive calls

Time/Call The average amount of time per call

Traceview

Once you've identified the methods to take a closer look at, you can use the command-line version of Traceview with the tracing API for more accurate measurement. Add Debug.startMethodTracing, and Debug.stopMethodTracing around the code you want to profile, as shown in Listing 3-5. Compile your code again and push the APK to your device.

Listing 3-5. startMethodTracing and stopMethodTracing

```
public class ScoresActivity extends ListActivity {
        public void onStart() {
                // start tracing to "/sdcard/scores.trace"
                Debug.startMethodTracing("scores");
                super.onStart();
                // other start up code here
        }

        public void onStop() {
                super.onStop();
                // other shutdown code here
                Debug.stopMethodTracing();
        }

        // Other implementation code
}
```

The trace file can now be pulled off the device and displayed in Traceview using the following commands:

```
adb pull /sdcard/scores.trace scores.before.trace
```

Figure 3-11 shows the results before code optimization.

Name	Incl %
▶ ▮ 0 (toplevel)	100.0%
▶ ▮ 1 android/os/Handler.dispatchMessage (Landroid/os/Message;)V	96.0%
▶ ▮ 2 android/view/ViewRoot.handleMessage (Landroid/os/Message;)V	71.7%
▶ ▮ 3 android/widget/ListView.makeAndAddView (IIZIZ)Landroid/view/View;	70.5%
▶ ▮ 4 android/widget/AbsListView.trackMotionScroll (II)V	52.5%
▶ ▮ 5 android/widget/ListView.fillGap (Z)V	52.2%
▶ ▮ 6 android/widget/AbsListView.obtainView (I)Landroid/view/View;	52.2%
▶ ▮ 7 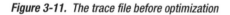Adapter.getView (ILa	52.1%

Figure 3-11. The trace file before optimization

Optimize the code using some of the suggestions earlier in the chapter and measure again, this time using the following command:

```
adb pull /sdcard/scores.trace scores.after.trace
```

Figure 3-12 shows the results after optimization; the difference is clear.

```
▷  12 android/widget/ListView.dispatchDraw (Landroid/graphics/Canvas;)V                      32.0%
▷  13 android/widget/AbsListView.dispatchDraw (Landroid/graphics/Canvas;)V                   32.0%
▷  14 android/graphics/Canvas.native_drawBitmap (IILandroid/graphics/Rect;Landroid/          31.9%
▷  15 android/widget/ListView.makeAndAddView (IIZIZ)Landroid/view/View;                      15.9%
▷  16 android/graphics/Canvas.drawBitmap (Landroid/graphics/Bitmap;FFLandroid/gra            15.4%
▷  17 android/graphics/Canvas.native_drawBitmap (IIFFI)V                                      15.1%
▷  18 android/widget/AbsListView.trackMotionScroll (II)V                                      11.2%
▷  19 android/widget/AbsListView.obtainView (I)Landroid/view/View;                            11.1%
▷  20                                                          Adapter.getView (ILa           10.8%
```

Figure 3-12. The trace file after optimization

Lint

Lint is, like its original Unix namesake, a static code-analysis tool. It replaces the layoutopt tool, which was used to analyze your layout files and point out potential performance issues to get quick performance gains by reorganizing your UI layout. It now does so much more, including the following error-checking categories:

- Correctness
- Correctness:Messages
- Security
- Performance
- Usability:Typography
- Usability:Icons
- Usability
- Accessibility
- Internationalization

If you run the command `lint --list Performance` it will tell you that Lint does the following performance checks, many of which we've already seen in the Android Tips section:

FloatMath: Suggests replacing `android.util.FloatMath` calls with `java.lang.Math`.

FieldGetter: Suggests replacing use of getters with direct field access within a class.

InefficientWeight: Looks for inefficient weight declarations in `LinearLayouts`.

NestedWeights: Looks for nested layout weights, which are costly.

DisableBaselineAlignment: Looks for LinearLayouts, which should set android:baselineAligned=false.

ObsoleteLayoutParam: Looks for layout params that are not valid for the given parent layout.

MergeRootFrame: Checks whether a root `<FrameLayout>` can be replaced with a `<merge>` tag.

UseCompoundDrawables: Checks whether the current node can be replaced by a TextView using compound drawables.

UselessParent: Checks whether a parent layout can be removed.

UselessLeaf: Checks whether a leaf layout can be removed.

TooManyViews: Checks whether a layout has too many views.

TooDeepLayout: Checks whether a layout hierarchy is too deep.

ViewTag: Finds potential leaks when using View.setTag.

HandlerLeak: Ensures that Handler classes do not hold on to a reference to an outer class.

UnusedResources: Looks for unused resources.

UnusedIds: Looks for unused IDs.

SecureRandom: Looks for suspicious usage of the SecureRandom class.

Overdraw: Looks for overdraw issues (where a view is painted only to be fully painted over).

UnusedNamespace: Finds unused namespaces in XML documents.

DrawAllocation: Looks for memory allocations within drawing code.

UseValueOf: Looks for instances of "new" for wrapper classes, which should use valueOf instead.

UseSparseArrays: Looks for opportunities to replace HashMaps with the more efficient SparseArray.

Wakelock: Looks for problems with wakelock usage.

Recycle: Looks for missing recycle() calls on resources.

Lint can be run from within Eclipse or on the command line. If you just want to run the performance checks on your project, type lint --check Performance `<ProjectName>` on the command line. Listing 3-6 displays the output of this command for the sample application, showing that there are some layouts that need to be better organized.

Listing 3-6. Lint Performance output for the CallCenterApp project

```
Scanning CallCenterV3: ....................................................
Scanning CallCenterV3 (Phase 2): .....................
res\layout\custom_titlebar.xml:6: Warning: Possible overdraw: Root element paints background #004A82
with a theme that also paints a background (inferred theme is @style/CustomTheme) [Overdraw]
    android:background="#004A82"
    ~~~~~~~~~~~~~~~~~~~~~~~~~~~~~

res\layout\custom_titlebar_with_logout.xml:6: Warning: Possible overdraw: Root element paints
background #004A82 with a theme that also paints a background (inferred theme is @style/CustomTheme)
[Overdraw]
    android:background="#004A82"
    ~~~~~~~~~~~~~~~~~~~~~~~~~~~~~

res\layout\custom_titlebar_with_settings.xml:6: Warning: Possible overdraw: Root element paints
background #004A82 with a theme that also paints a background (inferred theme is @style/CustomTheme)
[Overdraw]
    android:background="#004A82"
    ~~~~~~~~~~~~~~~~~~~~~~~~~~~~~

res\layout\login_screen.xml:5: Warning: Possible overdraw: Root element paints background
@drawable/bg_app with a theme that also paints a background (inferred theme is @style/CustomTheme)
[Overdraw]
    android:background="@drawable/bg_app"
    ~~~~~~~~~~~~~~~~~~~~~~~~~~~~~~~~~~~~~~~

res\layout\queues_screen.xml:5: Warning: Possible overdraw: Root element paints background
@drawable/bg_app with a theme that also paints a background (inferred theme is @style/CustomTheme)
[Overdraw]
    android:background="@drawable/bg_app"
    ~~~~~~~~~~~~~~~~~~~~~~~~~~~~~~~~~~~~~~~

res\layout\settings_screen.xml:5: Warning: Possible overdraw: Root element paints background #1D1D1D
with a theme that also paints a background (inferred theme is @style/CustomTheme) [Overdraw]
    android:background="#1D1D1D"
    ~~~~~~~~~~~~~~~~~~~~~~~~~~~~~

res\drawable-hdpi\bg_login.9.png: Warning: The resource R.drawable.bg_login appears to be unused
[UnusedResources]
res\drawable-hdpi\btn_ok_xlarge.png: Warning: The resource R.drawable.btn_ok_xlarge appears to be
unused [UnusedResources]
res\drawable-hdpi\no_xlarge.png: Warning: The resource R.drawable.no_xlarge appears to be unused
[UnusedResources]
res\menu\settings_menu.xml: Warning: The resource R.menu.settings_menu appears to be unused
[UnusedResources]
res\values\strings.xml:7: Warning: The resource R.string.loginMessage appears to be unused
[UnusedResources]
    <string name="loginMessage">Enter Your Login Credentials</string>
            ~~~~~~~~~~~~~~~~~~~~

res\values\strings.xml:8: Warning: The resource R.string.CSQ_default appears to be unused
[UnusedResources]
    <string name="CSQ_default">Log In</string>
            ~~~~~~~~~~~~~~~~~~~

res\values\strings.xml:11: Warning: The resource R.string.default_time appears to be unused
[UnusedResources]
    <string name="default_time">00:00:00</string>
```

```
                ~~~~~~~~~~~~~~~~~~~~~
res\values\strings.xml:12: Warning: The resource R.string.oldest_in_queue appears to be unused
[UnusedResources]
    <string name="oldest_in_queue">Oldest Call In Queue: </string>
                ~~~~~~~~~~~~~~~~~~~~~~~
res\values\strings.xml:16: Warning: The resource R.string.add_to_queue appears to be unused
[UnusedResources]
    <string name="add_to_queue">Add To Queue</string>
                ~~~~~~~~~~~~~~~~~~~
res\layout\login_screen.xml:9: Warning: This LinearLayout view is useless (no children, no
background, no id, no style) [UselessLeaf]
    <LinearLayout
     ^
res\layout\custom_titlebar.xml:10: Warning: This RelativeLayout layout or its LinearLayout parent is
useless; transfer the background attribute to the other view [UselessParent]
    <RelativeLayout
     ^
res\layout\custom_titlebar_with_logout.xml:10: Warning: This RelativeLayout layout or its
LinearLayout parent is useless; transfer the background attribute to the other view [UselessParent]
    <RelativeLayout
     ^
res\layout\custom_titlebar_with_settings.xml:10: Warning: This RelativeLayout layout or its
LinearLayout parent is useless; transfer the background attribute to the other view [UselessParent]
    <RelativeLayout
     ^
res\layout\queue_list_item.xml:13: Warning: This TableRow layout or its TableLayout parent is
possibly useless [UselessParent]
        <TableRow
         ^
res\layout\queue_list_item.xml:45: Warning: This TableRow layout or its TableLayout parent is
possibly useless [UselessParent]
        <TableRow
         ^
res\layout\custom_titlebar.xml:3: Warning: The resource R.id.photo_titlebar appears to be unused
[UnusedIds]·
    android:id="@+id/photo_titlebar"
                ~~~~~~~~~~~~~~~~~~~~~~~~~~~~~~~~~
res\layout\queue_list_item.xml:7: Warning: The resource R.id.nameTable appears to be unused
[UnusedIds]
        android:id="@+id/nameTable"
                    ~~~~~~~~~~~~~~~~~~~~~~
res\layout\queue_list_item.xml:14: Warning: The resource R.id.tableRow1 appears to be unused
[UnusedIds]
            android:id="@+id/tableRow1"
                        ~~~~~~~~~~~~~~~~~~~~~~~
res\layout\queue_list_item.xml:19: Warning: The resource R.id.activeIndicatorDummy appears to be
unused [UnusedIds]
                android:id="@+id/activeIndicatorDummy"
                            ~~~~~~~~~~~~~~~~~~~~~~~~~~~~~~~~~~~~
res\layout\queue_list_item.xml:46: Warning: The resource R.id.tableRow2 appears to be unused
[UnusedIds]
            android:id="@+id/tableRow2"
```

```
                ~~~~~~~~~~~~~~~~~~~~~~~~~~~~~~~
res\layout\queue_list_item.xml:62: Warning: The resource R.id.callsInQueueLabel appears to be unused
[UnusedIds]
                android:id="@+id/callsInQueueLabel"
                    ~~~~~~~~~~~~~~~~~~~~~~~~~~~~~~~~~~~~~~~~
```

0 errors, 27 warnings

```
res\layout\queue_list_item.xml:7: Warning: The resource R.id.nameTable appears to be unused [UnusedIds]
          android:id="@+id/nameTable"
              ~~~~~~~~~~~~~~~~~~~~~~~~~~~~
res\layout\queue_list_item.xml:14: Warning: The resource R.id.tableRow1 appears to be unused
[UnusedIds]
                android:id="@+id/tableRow1"
                    ~~~~~~~~~~~~~~~~~~~~~~~~~~~~
res\layout\queue_list_item.xml:19: Warning: The resource R.id.activeIndicatorDummy appears to be
unused [UnusedIds]
                android:id="@+id/activeIndicatorDummy"
                    ~~~~~~~~~~~~~~~~~~~~~~~~~~~~~~~~~~~~~~~~~~
res\layout\queue_list_item.xml:46: Warning: The resource R.id.tableRow2 appears to be unused
[UnusedIds]
                android:id="@+id/tableRow2"
                    ~~~~~~~~~~~~~~~~~~~~~~~~~~~~
res\layout\queue_list_item.xml:62: Warning: The resource R.id.callsInQueueLabel appears to be unused
[UnusedIds]
                android:id="@+id/callsInQueueLabel"
                    ~~~~~~~~~~~~~~~~~~~~~~~~~~~~~~~~~~~~~~~~
```

0 errors, 27 warnings

Hierarchy Viewer

Another useful tool in debugging performance issues, specifically for layouts, is the Hierarchy Viewer. At its most basic it will show you how long it takes to inflate the layouts. You start Hierarchy Viewer from within Eclipse by adding the perspective; this is similar to the way you would add back DDMS if it ever disappeared.

Hierarchy Viewer first displays a list of devices and emulators; click the name of your app from the list and then click Load View Hierarchy. The Tree View, the Tree Overview, and the Tree Layout will then open, as shown in Figure 3-13. The Tree View shows all the layouts that you defined in your XML files. We talked earlier in this chapter about how nested layouts can be bad for performance, and Tree Overview is a great way to see just how nested your layouts have become and figure out if it's time to merge them into a RelativeLayout. Tree View shows how long each layout took to display, so you can identify which views you need to debug and optimize to speed up your UI.

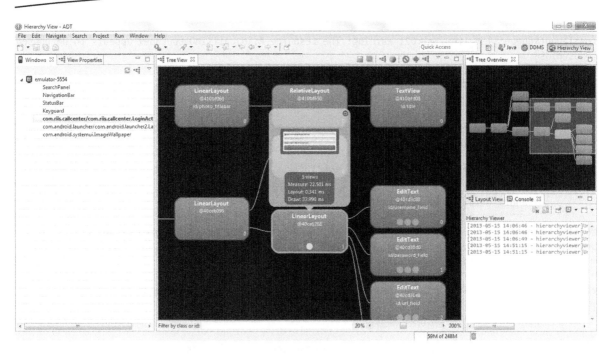

Figure 3-13. *Hierarchy Viewer for CallCenterApp login screen*

In Figure 3-13 we can see that our login view took almost 33ms to display. It also shows what layouts are part of the login view, and by hovering over specific views you can see just how long each took to display.

Hierarchy Viewer also includes a Pixel Perfect tool for designers. We won't be covering that in this book.

Unix Tools

Because Android is built on Linux, we can leverage many of the same shell command tools as Linux for performance testing. The main tools focus on total process load, individual process details, and memory utilization.

Top

The top command will give you an idea of where your app is in relation to all other processes on the device. The higher up the list, the more resources it is consuming. You can log onto the phone using the adb shell command, or you can run the command remotely using adb shell top from your command line. Figure 3-14 shows the results.

```
User 28%, System 12%, IOW 3%, IRQ 0%
User 69 + Nice 22 + Sys 40 + Idle 173 + IOW 12 + IRQ 0 + SIRQ 0 = 316

  PID PR CPU% S   #THR     VSS      RSS PCY UID      Name
  270  0   6% S     96 416256K   62584K fg  system   system_server
 1599  0   6% S      9 293056K   37488K fg  app_110  com.riis.callcenter
  129  0   5% S      9  57644K   10552K fg  system   /system/bin/surfaceflinger
 1586  0   3% R      1   1104K     472K fg  shell    top
31563  0   1% S      1      0K       0K fg  root     kworker/u:0
```

Figure 3-14. Output from the top command

Dumpsys

Top also gets you the process ID or PID of your application, which you can then use for the dumpsys command, as follows:

```
adb shell dumpsys meminfo 1599
```

Dumpsys will give you information about the memory and heap being used by your application; see Figure 3-15.

```
Applications Memory Usage (kB):
Uptime: 126416263 Realtime: 126416238

** MEMINFO in pid 1599 [com.riis.callcenter] **
                        Shared  Private    Heap    Heap    Heap
                  Pss    Dirty    Dirty    Size   Alloc    Free
                ------  ------   ------   ------  ------  ------
     Native      1113    1540     1076     4232    4168      63
     Dalvik      5794   13084     5544    16035   14912    1123
     Cursor         0       0        0
     Ashmem         0       0        0
  Other dev        4      40        0
   .so mmap      413    2176      280
  .jar mmap        4       0        0
  .apk mmap       55       0        0
  .ttf mmap        3       0        0
  .dex mmap      276       0        0
 Other mmap      543      16       28
    Unknown      640     348      636
      TOTAL     8845   17204     7564    20267   19080    1186

  Objects
             Views:      62        ViewRootImpl:       3
        AppContexts:      2          Activities:       1
            Assets:       3       AssetManagers:       3
      Local Binders:      7       Proxy Binders:      13
    Death Recipients:      1
    OpenSSL Sockets:       0

  SQL
              heap:       0         MEMORY_USED:       0
  PAGECACHE_OVERFLOW:      0         MALLOC_SIZE:       0
```

Figure 3-15. Dumpsys Meminfo

All of the Unix tools mentioned in this section are taking measurements at a point in time. Procstats was introduced in Android 4.4 or KitKat to show how much memory and CPU the apps running in the background will consume. Use the command to see the `procstats` output:

```
adb shell dumpsys procstats
```

with the results shown in Figure 3-16.

```
            Home: 0.00%
        (Cached): 67% (54MB–56MB–67MB/44MB–47MB–62MB over 32)
* com.google.android.gms / u0a7:
          TOTAL: 28% (10MB–11MB–11MB/8.0MB–8.1MB–8.2MB over 16)
            Top: 27% (10MB–11MB–11MB/8.0MB–8.1MB–8.2MB over 16)
         Imp Fg: 1.2%
        Service: 0.14%
       Receiver: 0.01%
           Home: 0.00%
      (Last Act): 0.09%
        (Cached): 70% (10MB–11MB–11MB/8.0MB–8.1MB–8.2MB over 15)
* com.google.android.apps.books / u0a26:
          TOTAL: 22% (50MB–80MB–113MB/43MB–63MB–82MB over 12)
            Top: 22% (50MB–80MB–113MB/43MB–63MB–82MB over 12)
        Service: 0.00%
      (Last Act): 4.6% (85MB–85MB–85MB/77MB–77MB–77MB over 2)
        (Cached): 58% (78MB–81MB–82MB/70MB–73MB–74MB over 4)
* com.android.settings / 1000:
          TOTAL: 2.8% (14MB–15MB–16MB/11MB–12MB–13MB over 3)
            Top: 2.8% (14MB–15MB–16MB/11MB–12MB–13MB over 3)
```

Figure 3-16. *Dumpsys Procstats*

Vmstat

Vmstat allows you to view virtual memory levels on the device; see Figure 3-17. It is a simple Linux command that reports about processes, memory, paging, block IO, traps, and CPU activity. The "b" column shows which processes are blocked. Use the command as follows: adb shell vmstat.

```
C:\adt\sdk\tools>adb shell vmstat
procs  memory                                system           cpu
 r  b    free  mapped    anon   slab         in    cs  flt    us ni sy id wa ir
 1  0   95308  296784  976812   67336       552  1259    0     4  0 12 79  0  0
 0  0   95324  296792  976816   67336       497  1250    0     6  0  6 79  0  0
 0  0   95324  296792  976820   67336       496  1231    0     6  0  6 80  0  0
 0  0   95280  296792  976828   67336       523  1415    1    19  0 14 99  0  0
 0  0   95280  296792  976892   67336       238   824    7     3  0 13 77  0  0
 1  0   95304  296792  976888   67336       178   772    0     9  0  5 87  0  0
 0  0   95312  296792  976884   67336       274   883    0     7  0 13 83  0  0
 1  0   95312  296792  976884   67336       222   832    0     8  0  6 86  0  0
 0  0   95312  296792  976888   67336       192   784    1     6  0  6 83  0  0
 0  0   95172  296792  976928   67336       368  1106    4    15  0 10 71  1  0
 4  0   95172  296792  976932   67336       490  1247    0     8  0  7 78  0  0
 0  0   95180  296792  976932   67336       510  1296    1     9  0  7 76  0  0
 0  0   95172  296792  976936   67336       575  1318    0     6  0  9 75  0  0
 0  0   94808  296792  976940   67336       444  1361    1    18  0  8 65  0  0
 0  0   94684  296792  976944   67336       243   931    0     8  1 10 75  0  0
```

Figure 3-17. Dumpsys Meminfo

Summary

In this chapter we've looked at the tools to first find out if you have a performance problem and then identify the call that needs to be fixed; we also saw some techniques you can use to optimize your application. The Android SDK, and the Android platform, because of their close Unix relationship, come with a wealth of tools that can help you identify issues.

Chapter 4

Agile Android

As a developer, you want to get better at Android development, have fewer bugs, make a better product, or simply make the customer happy. Whether you're developing for the web, mobile, or even the desktop, it pays to adopt an Agile approach to your development and testing.

Benefits

I'm going to talk about the real benefits of the Agile approach for Android and indeed mobile development in general. By the end of this chapter, it should be clear just how much of a sweet spot Agile really is for Android developers.

Let's begin with the most obvious benefits of Agile development:

- You'll have fewer errors.
- You'll get faster feedback.
- It's repeatable and reliable.
- You'll need less manual testing.
- It's cheaper.
- It offers built in regression testing.

Using test-driven development (TDD) will result in fewer defects and remove the need for lots of people doing manual testing, which makes the development of an app much cheaper. Continuous integration (CI) will provide faster feedback to the customer and by its nature make the APKs creation process repeatable and reliable as well as providing built-in regression testing for any new features that you introduce into your app.

Benefits to the Business

What is the goal behind adding Agile practices to your Android projects? If we're using continuous integration we're going to get faster feedback from the business, with repeatable and reliable

75

development and all the time making sure that you're producing something useful for what people are trying to do to perform their basic needs. In a nutshell, if you're using Agile in mobile development, it makes the business happy, as there are fewer defects and team members get to see how the app is progressing day to day.

For me, Agile is about lessons learned and how to integrate best practices to make sure we raise the bar for everyone, not just a single app. It's about trying to make sure that people are using Agile the right way and the customers are happy, whoever they may be.

Benefits to the Developer

When I first started working on mobile apps, it came as a surprise that when people started mobile development they got so excited they just started coding and seemed to forget everything we've learned in the last 10 years.

One of the main reasons I favor adopting Agile practices is to make sure everyone is following the same standard so we can have repeatable quality over many different apps. I see when people don't use Agile and when they do in mobile, and there is no reason we would go back to not using TDD and behavior-driven development (BDD) in our development. Without them the quality goes out the window. Using Agile is also about trying to make sure that as new developers come in, they're all doing their work the way they should be.

We'll look at the elements of Agile in the next section. I'm sure your list may be different, but for me at its most basic Agile development includes TDD, BDD, and CI. BDD isn't ever really an issue for developers to adopt. That's probably because it's mainly the job of the Business Analyst and QA folks to get BDD up and running. CI also tends to be readily adopted, as it allows any and all code deployment and integration issues to be fixed much earlier in the process. CI takes away those last-minute deployment snafus or issues that have plagued software development for decades now.

TDD, on the other hand, can be difficult for many developers to grasp and properly adopt. As its name suggests, TDD means writing a unit test first and then writing the simplest piece of code to make the test pass. Once it passes the test, the code is cleaned up or refactored. Then rinse and repeat to add any new requested features. TDD does not mean adding unit tests after the code is complete. This is a huge reversal of the coding practices for many developers; and for many it is the software world's equivalent of quantum mechanics, as it just does not make intuitive sense.

However, there are two great benefits that TDD provides to developers. First, it tilts development into a YAGNI—You Aren't Going to Need It—mindset. There is often a temptation to develop a truly wonderful new framework or architecture for your new app, but trust me, You Aren't Going to Need It. TDD takes away that temptation and makes sure that you're *only* writing code for functionality that is necessary and nothing more. Second, TDD also provides developer insurance against defects. For any new feature, you write a new test and then the corresponding code to make the test pass; then, if the unit tests all pass, you can be relatively sure that the new code did not introduce any unwanted side effects.

The Sweet Spot

Agile lends itself very well to mobile development for a number of reasons. I've mentioned some of its benefits in the previous sections, but Agile processes and mobile development make a particularly good partnership, as it is so much easier to do mobile Agile than it is to do mainframe Agile or even web Agile.

The first reason for this is that mobile projects have smaller teams and also have shorter development lifecycles than other development work. According to Kinvey, which runs cloud back-end services for mobile developers, the average time to create a mobile application is 18 weeks (see `http://www.kinvey.com/blog/2086/how-long-does-it-take-to-build-a-mobile-app`).

The reason for this is that mobile apps tend not to be as complex as web sites, and have fewer features developed from start to finish. Often the work can be completed in a handful of sprints, where s *sprint* is an Agile term that means a regular period of time (2 weeks is common) in which some work is completed and made ready for review.

The Kinvey report further notes that the work takes approximately 8 weeks for the front-end and 10 weeks for the back-end work.

Because mobile apps and teams tend to be smaller, adopting Agile practices for mobile application development does not require a huge company reorganization. All that is required is the team's interest in trying an Agile approach, and the benefits listed in previous section can be quickly realized.

Second, although we'll see later that the Google TDD and BDD aren't the best place to start, there are open source alternatives that make it very easy to adopt Agile Android development practices.

So even if you start off in small steps using just TDD or even something as simple as recording your scripts using Monkey Runner, Agile will help you in the long run keeping your customer happy, whoever that might be.

Elements of Agile

Let's take a look at what are we going to need to have in our Agile Android project in its basic form. There was a time when you could get away with just doing unit testing and claim you were doing Agile development. But what we're ultimately trying to do is make sure the customer is happy, and unit testing alone probably won't get us that. Ideally we're looking for more, at the very least for a continuous integration process with unit testing and functional tests.

The elements of Agile Android are as follows:

- Continuous integration server
- Unit testing
- BDD or functional testing
- Deployment; that is, emailing out an APK

The rest of this chapter will show how you can create Android projects using those elements.

Goals

Before we look at in the details of setting up an Agile Android project, let's talk a little about our goals.

Tests should be automated; we don't want to be running them manually over and over again, as that's not efficient. We also want to build early and build often so we don't have any deployment issues. And we want to run the unit and functional tests before sending out the APK to anyone. How often you run the whole process is up to you. Some people run it every evening, others choose to run tests every time any new code is checked in.

So ideally we want an automated build process that starts when the code is checked into our source code repository, such as GitHub. Then the CI server checks it out and builds the code, and the unit tests are automatically run, followed by the functional tests (in the form of executable requirements). If nothing fails—that is, if everything is green—then the APK is emailed to the customer so it can be installed on a device.

I'd be lying if I said we were completely finished. Code coverage is an issue, but the goal here is to pass on information so you can get started, too. I'll try to point out the main elements you're going to need and what you can and currently cannot do.

Following the Agile approach we can start small with the basic elements and build from there. You may want to add more elements later, such as load testing, performance testing, or security testing, but for now if we do TDD, BDD and CI, then we are including the primary elements of Agile Android.

Roll Call

Now I'd like to introduce you to the names behind these elements of Agile Android, as the rest of this chapter is going to be practical rather than theoretical. Table 4-1 shows the Android development tools we'll use for each element of the Agile model.

Table 4-1. Agile Android Element Names

Agile Element	Android Tool Name
TDD	Robolectric
BDD	Calabash
CI	Jenkins
Source Code Management	GitHub

From Table 4-1 we can see that our elements now become the following:

- Robolectric (robolectric.org): Although jUnit is the out-of-the-box unit-testing system with Android, it has some drawbacks and I do not recommend it as a good place to start. You should be able to run unit tests quickly and efficiently, but jUnit on Android device emulators does not lend itself to efficient unit testing. Instead we're going to use Robolectric, which has none of the jUnit drawbacks and is also jUnit4 and not jUnit3.

- Calabash (calaba.sh): We're going to use Calabash for our BDD or executable requirements. Calabash allows us to impose executable requirements in a given-when-then format. Calabash is the easiest system to get BDD up and running for your Android projects.

- Jenkins (jenkins-ci.org): The de facto industry standard continuous integration server, formerly known as Hudson.

- GitHub (github.org): Rapidly becoming the de facto industry standard source version control or source code repository. Although people often treat them as the same thing, I should point out that Git is the version control system and GitHub is a website where you can post your Git projects.

TDD

Test-driven development (TDD) has been around for some time now; it comes from XP's test-first programming in the late 1990s. The concept is simple: write a test for each new feature, run the test so that it fails, write code to satisfy the test, and finally tidy or refactor the code; Figure 4-1 illustrates the process. Each test is typically called a *unit test*.

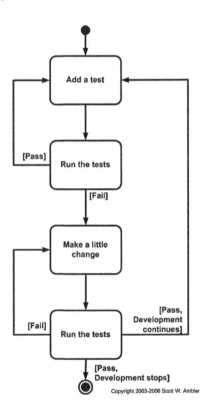

Figure 4-1. Test-driven development

And although the idea isn't exactly new, it hasn't been massively adopted by the programming community, as it seems counterintuitive to many developers. However, in smaller applications such as mobile development projects, TDD can show dramatic improvements. It can reduce the number of defects as well as increase the speed of development.

A huge benefit of TDD is the built-in regression testing. If the TDD tests all pass after you make a small change during the refactoring phase or when adding a new feature, then you can be sure your app is behaving correctly. Unit tests are the best insurance against problems that can be introduced by refactoring or adding new functionality.

The other major benefit of TDD is the focus it brings to the development process. Gone are the great architectural additions to the code or inventing new frameworks that no one will ever use again. The developer's job becomes writing a unit test or tests to satisfy the next feature and then writing the simplest code to make the unit test pass. This is also called YAGNI or You Aren't Going to Need It, another XP principle. So a decision about whether to use an ORM instead of just using SQLite, for example, becomes much simpler; the question becomes "do I need an ORM to make the unit test pass?" And the answer is inevitably no or YAGNI.

As noted earlier, we'll use Roboelectric to write our unit tests, because the built-in solution from Android uses an older version of jUnit and requires us to use the incredibly slow Android emulator to run tests, which makes TDD a very painful exercise. And while Roboelectric simplifies the process, code coverage reporting (how much of your code is covered by unit tests) can still be an issue.

BDD

Behavior-driven development (BDD), in this case in the form of executable requirements, extends TDD by adding another layer, as shown in Figure 4-2. What it means is that we're adding executable requirements as one of our elements. These are use case or user story–type requirements, which are written in the *gherkin* format, also known as given/when/then to you and me.

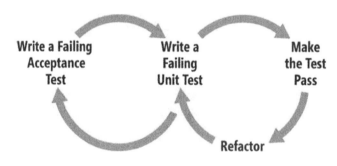

Figure 4-2. Behavior-driven development

Figure 4-3 shows a simple example of an executable requirement. It doesn't matter if this is for an Android game or something on the web; the description of the requirement is still the same. It's not a huge stretch to see how you would convert your old-style user stories into this gherkin format.

```
ScoreCalculation.feature
    Feature: Score Calculation
      In order to know my performance
      As a player
      I want the system to calculate my total score

    Scenario: Gutter Game
      Given a new bowling game
      When all of my balls are landing in the gutter
      Then my total score should be 0

    Scenario: All Strikes
      Given a new bowling game
      When all of my rolls are strikes
      Then my total score should be 300
```

Figure 4-3. A sample feature file

Executable requirements are written in feature files, which are made up of one or more scenarios, often with a small table of data to drive the scenarios. Feature files always go hand-in-hand with step definition files, which usually include some Ruby code to drive the web or mobile application. Simple regex expressions in the step definition files glue the two together and make your requirements executable.

It can sometimes take a few minutes for the whole given/when/then idea (as used by the Cucumber approach we discuss later in the chapter) to sink in. I hope Figure 4-4 will make the penny drop for you, too. Given a set of preconditions, when you do *X*, then you expect the following testable outcome.

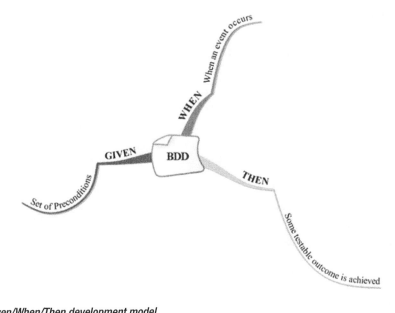

Figure 4-4. The Given/When/Then development model

When I started trying to adopt Agile practices to Android work, BDD tools simply weren't available, but now there is plenty of scope to allow you to use given/when/then development.

We're going to use Calabash for our BDD tool because it's so easy to use. One of the main reasons Calabash is so easy is its library of step definition functions that allow you to test Android apps, often without needing to write any of your own step definitions.

So how do you decide how much unit testing vs. functional testing to do? The Agile pyramid shown in Figure 4-5 gives us a good idea. How does this diagram apply to Android? The GUI Tests and Acceptance Tests layers are implemented using BDD, and the Unit Tests/Component Tests layer is obviously done using unit tests.

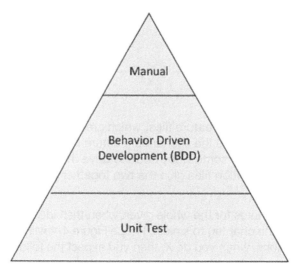

Figure 4-5. The Agile testing triangle

What is the difference between a unit test and a GUI test? Unit tests act on a method, typically a public method; by contrast, GUI tests or BDD functional tests are tests that typically run against the emulator.

Android apps are usually client-server apps; they're front-ends with corresponding back-end databases. So they typically have APIs that we'll test using BDD. We'll also be testing for exceptions and wrong paths as well as the "ideal path."

Continuous Integration

Continuous Integration (CI) takes the form of a build server where each developer's code is merged together on a regular basis, usually daily or whenever any code is checked into the project's source code repository. Originally CI was created to stop the integration hell that arose when multiple developers' code was merged just before an application is released; all sorts of new defects, unforeseen dependencies, and performance issues could conspire to delay a project's launch. CI makes the code merging happen much more often, so theoretically the integration should be less painful, as it's only at most a day's code that you're merging.

CI servers automate the build process, simplifying deployment and making it much easier to spot any dependencies earlier in the project. CI servers also allow us to do other things, such as run our unit tests (TDD) and executable requirements (BDD) along with performance testing, device testing and all sorts of reporting. They will even stop the deployment if any of tests fail, preventing the app from getting the business user when it's not ready for prime time.

We'll be using Jenkins as the CI server in this chapter. Jenkins and CI in general work very well for mobile projects. If you can run a command manually from the command line, then you can automate it in Jenkins. There are also lots of plugins available that make the build, test, and deployment stages easy to set up and maintain.

We'll also look at using CI for automated testing on multiple phones and tablets, which for me has long been the holy grail of Android development.

Putting It All Together

We start off adopting Agile in our mobile development processes by using Jenkins as our CI server. Download Jenkins from `http://jenkins-ci.org/`. You can also download and install a windows or Mac OS native binary, but it's just as easy to download the war file and run `java -jar jenkins.war` from the command line. Next, point your browser at `http://localhost:8080` to load Jenkins; you should see something like the dashboard page in Figure 4-6.

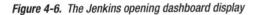

Figure 4-6. *The Jenkins opening dashboard display*

> **Tip**   There are also web sites such as Cloudbees (`cloudbees.com`) that will host Jenkins for you. With Cloudbees you can have it simply compile your apps or set up slave clients to compile the code and just get Cloudbees to orchestrate everything.

There are two areas where we typically go when we're working with Jenkins, as shown in the Manage Jenkins screen in Figure 4-7. The first is Manage Plugins, where we can pull in the Ant, GitHub, and Android emulator plugins. We also need to go to Configure System to add the default project settings for the JDK, Ant location, and so on.

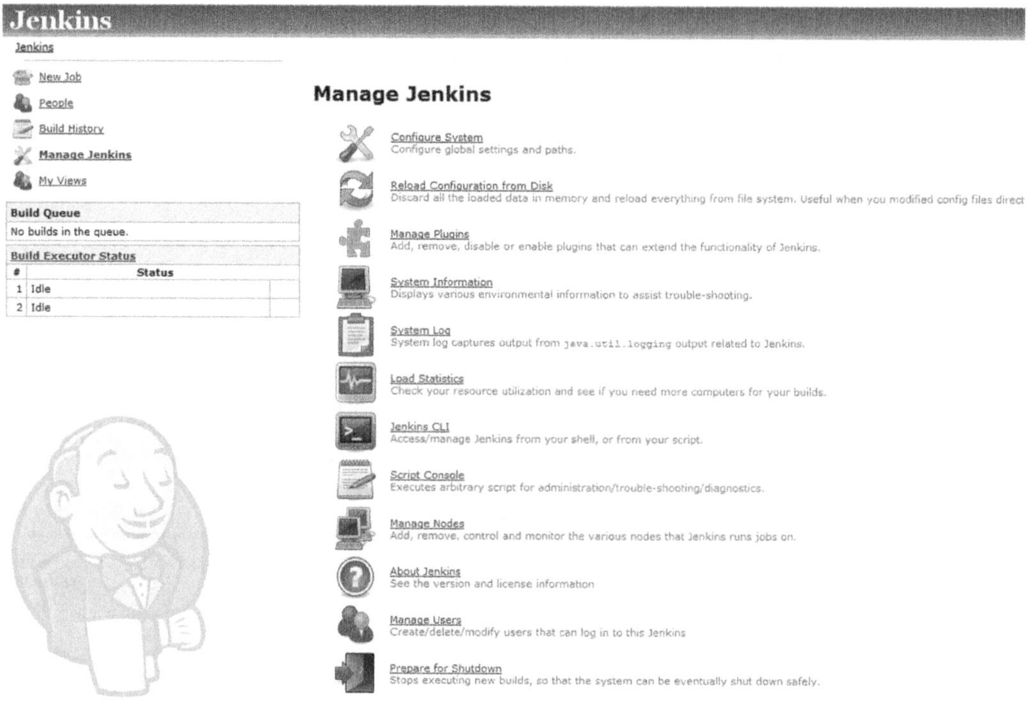

Figure 4-7. *The Manage Jenkins screen*

What gives Jenkins its power is the availability of literally thousands of plugins. Figure 4-8 shows the Manage Plugins ➤ Installed tab; be sure to grab the plugins listed earlier if you don't have them.

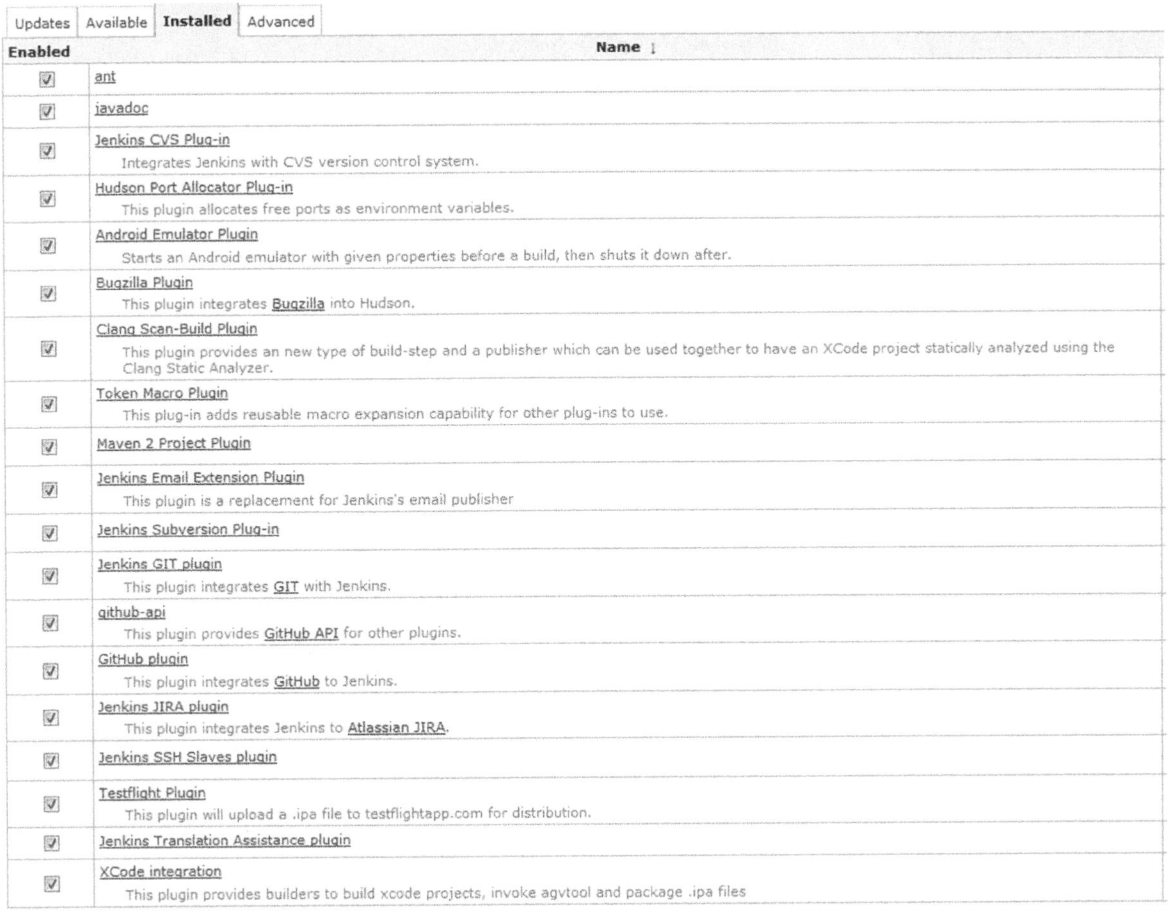

Enabled	Name ↓
☑	ant
☑	javadoc
☑	Jenkins CVS Plug-in Integrates Jenkins with CVS version control system.
☑	Hudson Port Allocator Plug-in This plugin allocates free ports as environment variables.
☑	Android Emulator Plugin Starts an Android emulator with given properties before a build, then shuts it down after.
☑	Bugzilla Plugin This plugin integrates Bugzilla into Hudson.
☑	Clang Scan-Build Plugin This plugin provides an new type of build-step and a publisher which can be used together to have an XCode project statically analyzed using the Clang Static Analyzer.
☑	Token Macro Plugin This plug-in adds reusable macro expansion capability for other plug-ins to use.
☑	Maven 2 Project Plugin
☑	Jenkins Email Extension Plugin This plugin is a replacement for Jenkins's email publisher
☑	Jenkins Subversion Plug-in
☑	Jenkins GIT plugin This plugin integrates GIT with Jenkins.
☑	github-api This plugin provides GitHub API for other plugins.
☑	GitHub plugin This plugin integrates GitHub to Jenkins.
☑	Jenkins JIRA plugin This plugin integrates Jenkins to Atlassian JIRA.
☑	Jenkins SSH Slaves plugin
☑	Testflight Plugin This plugin will upload a .ipa file to testflightapp.com for distribution.
☑	Jenkins Translation Assistance plugin
☑	XCode integration This plugin provides builders to build xcode projects, invoke agvtool and package .ipa files

Tabs: Updates | Available | **Installed** | Advanced

Figure 4-8. Managing plugins in Jenkins

Next go to Configure System to add the Android SDK, JDK, Git, and Ant locations on your CI server; Figure 4-9 shows this display on a Mac.

Android

Android SDK root   /Developer/SDKs/android-sdk-mac_x86/

Enter the path to the root of an Android SDK installation

☑ Automatically install Android components when required

JDK

JDK installations   ⠿ JDK
Name   /opt/local/share/java/jdk1.7.0

JAVA_HOME /Library/Java/Home

☐ Install automatically

[Add JDK]

List of JDK installations on this system

Git

Git installations   ⠿ Git
Name   Default

Path to Git executable /usr/bin/git

☐ Install automatically

[Add Git]

List of Git installations on this system

Ant

Ant installations   ⠿ Ant
Name   ant

ANT_HOME /opt/local/share/java/apache-ant-1.8.2

☐ Install automatically

[Add Ant]

List of Ant installations on this system

Figure 4-9. Use the Configure System page to add plugins in Jenkins

Jenkins on its own it pretty useless; we need to get it to do something, and the first thing we want it to do is to build the code from GitHub.

1. Create a new job called ToDoList and make it a free-style software project.

2. Click on Configure and enter a GitHub project, for example
    `https://github.com/godfreynolan/ToDoList`.

3. Under Source Code Management, enter the Repository URL such as
    `git@github.com:godfreynolan/ToDoList.git`.

4. Under Build Triggers, choose "Build when a change is pushed to GitHub."

Next we need to tell Jenkins how to build the project. In this case we need two commands as follows. We're creating a debug build, using the Configure Project settings shown in Figure 4-10.

```
android update project –name "ToDoList"
ant –Dadb.device.arg='-s $ANDROID_AVD_DEVICE' debug
```

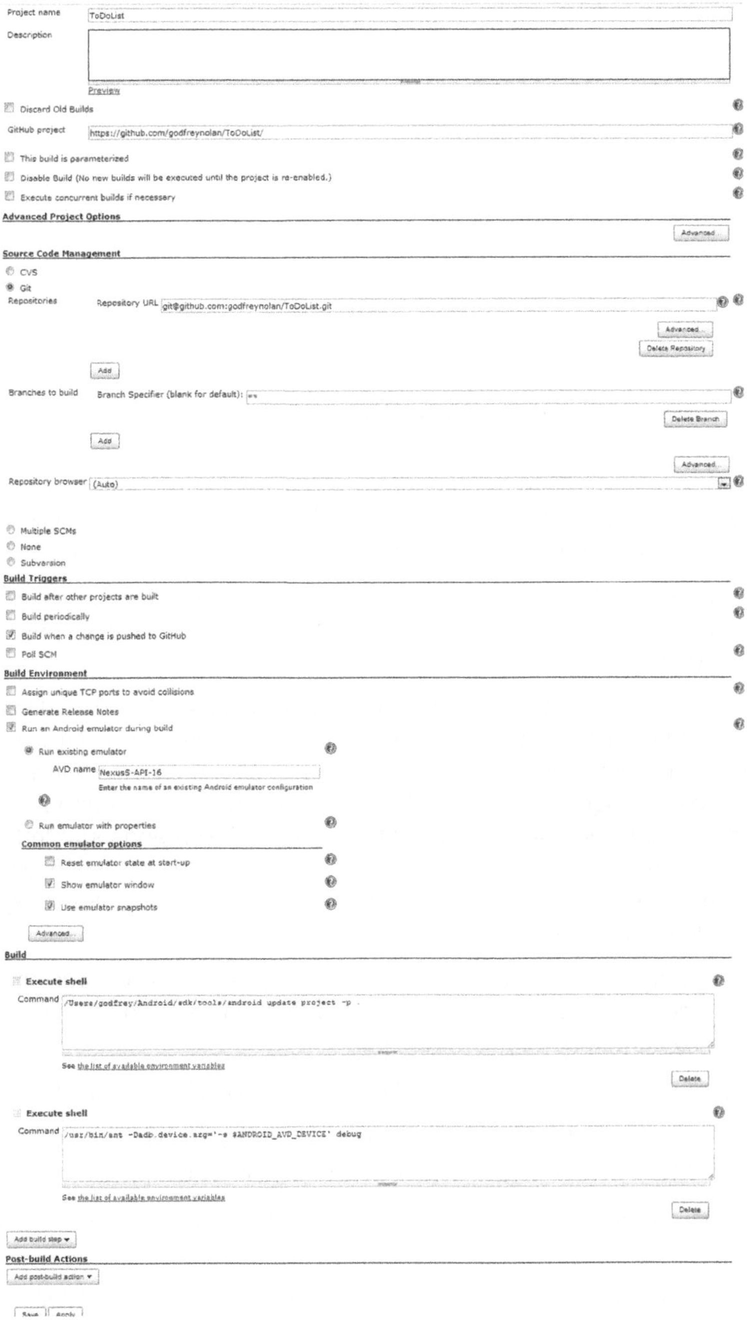

Figure 4-10. *Jenkins Configure Project settings for ToDoList*

Hit Save and run the build by clicking on the new project, which should now be in the Jenkins Dashboard, as shown in Figure 4-11.

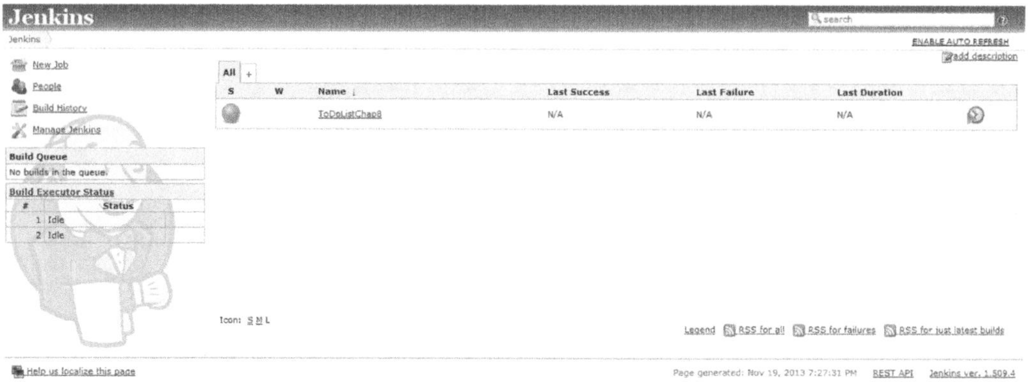

Figure 4-11. *The Jenkins dashboard showing the new project added*

Now we're going to add some TDD to the process using a version of jUnit. As described earlier, test-driven development is the process of writing tests before writing any code and then writing code that will satisfy that test, repeating the process until the features are completed.

Typically when we run the unit tests, the first time around they'll fail—because you have no code— and then when you write the code that satisfies the test they should go green. Also, all TDD classes have a setup and teardown along with the unit test.

Google's recommended unit testing suffers from a number of issues. First, it's jUnit3, which is cumbersome to use, and not jUnit4. It also has no good code coverage tool for unit testing. I'm not usually someone who asks a client, "Can you tell me what your code coverage is?" or argues about how to get code coverage up from 83% to 90%. Code coverage is good enough when you come up with a number that's right for you. Usually when I hear someone say "reflection" and "code coverage" in the same sentence, I know they've gone too far. However, there is also a point where you've gone too far in the other direction and there simply isn't enough unit testing. Android's jUnit3 makes it easier to fall into that trap.

Adopting Robolectric implicitly lets you use jUnit4, including its code coverage smarts. Robolectric also has some other nice features, and as a bonus, your entire toolchain for TDD, BDD and CI is using the highest quality contemporary components.

In the following example we created five simple tests for our ToDoList application:

- should_create_activity fails if an activity isn't created. This is the most basic Robolectric test possible and can be used in any Android app.

- should_find_tasks adds three tasks and fails if the newly created tasks are not found.

- should_add_new_task adds a task via a ToDoProvider method and fails if the task is not found.

- should_add_task_using_ux adds a task via the GUI and fails if the task is not found.

- should_remove_tasks adds a task and deletes a task and fails if it finds the newly created task.

Listing 4-1 shows the ToDoActvityTest class, which includes these five tests, and the Robolectric/jUnit4 decorators @RunWith and @Test that are the hallmarks of writing such tests.

Listing 4-1. ToDoActivityTest.java

```java
import java.util.List;
import org.junit.Assert;
import org.junit.Test;
import org.junit.runner.RunWith;
import org.robolectric.Robolectric;
import org.robolectric.RobolectricTestRunner;

import android.app.Activity;

@RunWith(RobolectricTestRunner.class)
public class TodoActivityTest
{
        @Test
        public void should_add_new_task() throws Exception
        {
                final TodoActivity activity = Robolectric.buildActivity(TodoActivity.class).
create().get();

                activity.getProvider().addTask("Some task");
                final List<String> tasks = activity.getProvider().findAll();
                Assert.assertEquals(tasks.size(), 1);
        }

        @Test
        public void should_add_task_using_ux() throws Exception
        {
                final TodoActivity activity = Robolectric.buildActivity(TodoActivity.class).
create().get();

                activity.getEditableTextbox().setText("My task");
                activity.getSaveTaskButton().performClick();

                final int tasks = activity.getTaskListView().getCount();
                Assert.assertEquals(tasks, 1);
        }

        @Test
        public void should_create_activity() throws Exception
        {
                final Activity activity = Robolectric.buildActivity(TodoActivity.class).create().
get();
                Assert.assertTrue(activity != null);
        }
```

```
        @Test
        public void should_find_tasks() throws Exception
        {
                final TodoActivity activity = Robolectric.buildActivity(TodoActivity.class).
create().get();

                activity.getProvider().addTask("Some task 1");
                activity.getProvider().addTask("Some task 2");
                activity.getProvider().addTask("Some task 3");
                final List<String> tasks = activity.getProvider().findAll();
                Assert.assertEquals(tasks.size(), 3);
        }

        @Test
        public void should_remove_task() throws Exception
        {
                final TodoActivity activity = Robolectric.buildActivity(TodoActivity.class).
create().get();

                activity.getProvider().addTask("Some task");
                activity.getProvider().deleteTask("Some task");
                final List<String> tasks = activity.getProvider().findAll();
                Assert.assertEquals(tasks.size(), 0);
        }
}
```

Robolectric works best with the Maven build tool instead of Ant. To Mavenize your project, take the steps in Listing 4-2.

Listing 4-2. Mavenizing ToDoList

```
git clone https://github.com/mosabua/maven-android-sdk-deployer.git
cd maven-android-sdk-deployer
mvn install -P 4.3
cd ToDoList
mvn clean test
```

The first time you run Maven or mvn it will install all the missing jars, which can take some time. If the project has been Mavenized correctly, the test output should be similar to Listing 4-3.

Listing 4-3. Test Results

```
-------------------------------------------------------
 T E S T S
-------------------------------------------------------
Running com.example.TodoActivityTest
WARNING: no system properties value for ro.build.date.utc
DEBUG: Loading resources for android from jar:/Users/godfrey/.m2/repository/org/ToDoList/android-
res/4.1.2_r1_rc/android-res-4.1.2_r1_rc-real.jar!/res...
DEBUG: Loading resources for com.example from ./res...
Tests run: 5, Failures: 0, Errors: 0, Skipped: 0, Time elapsed: 12.168 sec
```

```
Results :

Tests run: 5, Failures: 0, Errors: 0, Skipped: 0

[INFO] ------------------------------------------------------------------------
[INFO] BUILD SUCCESS
[INFO] ------------------------------------------------------------------------
[INFO] Total time: 19.018s
[INFO] Finished at: Tue Nov 19 20:03:48 EST 2013
[INFO] Final Memory: 18M/81M
[INFO] ------------------------------------------------------------------------
```

Adding this to the CI server as unit tests requires being able to run the Robolectric code from the command line, which simply means running the Maven tests:

```
mvn clean test
```

in Chapter 2 we used Dagger to show an example of a Dependency Injection framework we first met. Dagger allows you to create mocking frameworks so that we're testing our code and not any network connections to a web service or in the given example the SQLite database. In the example we mocked out the data provider in our ToDoList application. Listing 2-1 showed how to wire in the two database providers; the first is the real database and the second was a stub function.

The penultimate step is to now add the executable requirements code using Calabash. We're using Calabash to provide BDD or behavior-driven design, in this case in the form of executable requirements. Apologies to the Calabash folks as they don't really have an icon so I had to make one up.

When we started trying to adopt Agile practices to our Android work, options for using executable requirements simply weren't there, but now there is plenty of scope to allow you to use Cucumber-style given/when/then programming using Calabash and other tools.

BDD extends TDD by adding another layer, what are called acceptance tests here. So now you write your executable requirement as well as your unit test and then make them both pass by writing code that satisfies the tests before releasing the executable to the business stakeholder.

Listing 4-4 has a simple example of an executable requirement. It doesn't matter if this is for an Android game or something on the web; the description of the requirement is still the same. It's not a huge stretch to see how you would convert your old-style user stories into this format.

Listing 4-4. Implementing Given/When/Then Development

```
Feature:
    As a user I want to see my To Do List and individual reminders

Scenario: Display an individual reminder

  Given I wait for the "ToDoListActivity" screen to appear
  When I touch the "Get The Milk" text
  Then I wait up to 3 seconds for the "ReminderActivity" screen to appear
  Then I see the text "Remember to Get The Milk"
```

As described earlier, executable requirements are written in feature files, which are made up of one or more scenarios, often with a small table of data to drive the scenarios, which are then matched up step definition files.

In Cucumber the feature files define the requirement and the step definitions execute the code. In Calabash you can mostly get away with feature files, as the nice Calabash folks have written a library of step definitions that will cover most of the scenarios you are trying to test, or in other words they have already done the hard work for you.

To run Calabash you first need to install the Calabash Gem. Then create your feature files in the `calabash` folder in your test APK and call the `calabash-android` command. Use the following syntax to call Calabash from the command line; it can be added as another execute shell in Jenkins.

```
calabash-android run ToDoListApplication.apk
```

Calabash works by disassembling your test APK, injecting the `calabash` server, and then reassembling your APK so that you can run your tests.

Finally, once the unit testing and executable requirements have all passed, you need to email the APK out to your business stakeholders. There are other options you might want to consider, such as using an over-the-air deployment model such as TestFlightApp; however, on the Android platform that's probably overkill, so we'll just email out the APK. Thankfully Jenkins has an email plugin that allows you to simply add a list of email recipients to send the APK.

Summary

What is the goal behind adding Agile practices to your Android projects? You'll get faster feedback from the customer, with repeatable and reliable development and all the time making sure that you're producing something useful to help them perform their basic business needs. In a nutshell, if you're using Agile in mobile development, it makes the customer happy as they see fewer defects because you are doing unit testing and implementing executable requirements.

You'll find that mobile apps also have great visibility. Although the overall expense to complete an app is probably less than for web work, the visibility is very high and usually means seeing and talking to C-level execs. Making a positive impression usually leads to more work. So even if you start off in small steps using just TDD or even something as simple as recording your scripts using Monkey Runner, it will help you in the long run keeping the customer happy.

The Agile Manifesto (`http://www.agilemanifesto.org/principles.html`) states as its first principle.

> *Our highest priority is to satisfy the customer through early and continuous delivery of valuable software.*

Applying the principles of Agile Android gets us there.

Finally, feel free to add more plugins to your Jenkins server, for features such as code coverage, performance testing, and security vulnerability testing. This is not a complete list of tasks; it's meant to get you started on the Agile road. Look for areas of improvement and gradually apply them—whatever works for you and your team to help create better software is the best Agile process.

## Chapter 5

Native Development

Although the Android framework is designed purely for Java-based applications, the Android Native Development Kit (NDK) is also provided by Google as an official companion toolset for the Android SDK to enable developers to implement and embed performance-critical portions of their applications using native machine code–generating programming languages, such as C, C++, and assembly.

Through the Java Native Interface (JNI) technology, the native components can be accessed seamlessly as ordinary Java methods. Both the Java and native code portions of the application run within the same process. Although the JNI technology permits both the Java and the native code to coexist within the same application, it does not expand the boundaries of the Dalvik Virtual Machine (VM). The Java code is still managed and executed by the Dalvik VM, and all native code is expected to manage itself throughout the life cycle of the application. This imposes additional responsibilities on developers.

To execute effectively side by side with the virtual machine, the native components are expected to be good neighbors and interact with their Java counterparts maintaining a delicate boundary. If this interaction is not properly managed, the native components can cause hardly traceable errors within the application; such errors can even take the entire application down by crashing the virtual machine.

In this chapter, you will learn some of the best practices for developing well-behaving native components on the Android platform.

Deciding Where to Use Native Code

The first best practice that you will learn in this chapter is to properly identify the components of your application that can benefit from using native code support.

Where Not to Use Native Code

The biggest and most common false assumption about native code is the expectation of an automatic performance gain by simply coding application modules in native code instead of Java.

Using native machine code does not always result in an automatic performance boost. Although earlier versions of Java were known to be much slower than native code, the latest Java technology is highly optimized, and the speed difference is negligible in many cases. The JIT compilation feature of the Java Virtual Machine, specifically the Dalvik VM in the case of Android, allows the translation from the interpreted byte-code into machine code during application startup. The translated machine code is then used throughout the execution of the application, making the Java applications run as fast as their native counterparts.

> **Caution**   Using native machine code does not always result in an automatic performance improvement.

Be aware that overusing the native code support in your application can easily lead to much bigger stability problems. Because native code is not managed by the Dalvik VM, most of that memory management code has to be written by you; and this itself increases the complexity and the code size of the overall application.

Where to Use Native Code

Using native code in Android applications is definitely not a bad practice. In certain cases, it becomes highly beneficial because it can provide for code reuse and improve the performance of some complex applications. Here is a list of some common areas that can benefit from native code support:

- **Use of Existing Third Party Libraries:** Imagine that you will be developing a Video Editing application on the Android platform. For your application to operate, it needs to be able to read and write in various video formats, such as the Theora video codec. The Java framework does not provide any APIs to deal with Theora. Developing the code necessary to deal with this video format is not an efficient use of time, so your best option is to utilize an already available third-party library that can understand the Theora video codec. Despite the popularity of the Java programming language, the code library ecosystem is still highly mandated by C/C++-based native code libraries. There is a much better chance that you will find various implementations of the Theora video codec as C/C++ libraries. Native code support becomes really handy here, as it can enable you to blend the native C/C++ library into your Android application seamlessly. It is a good practice to use native code support to promote code reuse, as that facilitates the development process.

■ **Hardware Specific Optimization of Performance Critical Code:** As a platform-independent programming language, Java does not provide any mechanism for using the CPU-specific features for optimizing the performance-critical portions of Android applications. Compared to desktop platforms, mobile device resources are highly scarce. For complex applications with high performance requirements, such as 3D games and multimedia applications, effectively using every possible CPU feature is crucial. ARM processors, such as ARM NEON and ARM VFPv3-D32, provide additional instruction sets to allow mobile applications to hardware-accelerate many performance-critical operations. It is a good practice to use native code support to benefit from these CPU specific features.

Java Native Interface

As indicated earlier in this chapter, JNI is a mechanism and a set of APIs that are exposed by the Java Virtual Machine to enable developers to write parts of a Java application using a native programming language. These native components can be accessed transparently from the Java code as ordinary Java methods. JNI also provides a set of API functions to enable the native code to access the Java objects. Native components can create new Java objects or use objects created by the Java application, which can inspect, modify, and invoke methods on these objects to perform tasks.

Difficulties Writing Native Code Using JNI

Integrating native code into a Java application through JNI requires native functions to be declared with a specially crafted name conforming to JNI specification. In addition to the function name, each parameter to the native function should also use the JNI data types. Because the Java and the native code are compiled in separate silos, any issues in this part of the code are not visible at compile-time.

Reaching back from native code to Java space also requires a sequence of API calls. As the native programming language has no knowledge about the Java portion of the code, it cannot provide any compile-time errors if you use a wrong API call. In addition, a change in the Java portion of the code could also break the native portion of the code, and you would not be informed about this at compile-time, either.

Even if you take extraordinary measures to prevent bugs from occurring, keeping native methods and their declarations in Java space aligned can be a cumbersome and redundant task. In this section, you will learn how to benefit from the available tools to auto-generate the necessary code instead of typing it manually.

Generate the Code Using a Tool

A common good practice in almost every programming language is that as a good developer, you should always minimize the number of code lines you manually produce. Any code line that you produce, you will have to maintain throughout the lifetime of your application. As a good practice, you should always take advantage of the code generators that are provided by the SDKs and the IDEs to achieve that.

> **Tip**   Benefit from the code generators that are provided by the SDKs to minimize the amount of code that you need to write.

Generating C/C++ Header Files Using javah

The javah tool is part of the Java JDK distribution. It operates on the Java class files with native method declarations and generates corresponding C/C++ header files with appropriate signatures based on the JNI specification. Because the generated header files are not expected to be modified by the developer, you can invoke javah as many times as you like to keep the native method declarations in sync.

The javah tool is a standalone application that is located in the <JDK_HOME>/bin directory on your machine. Invoking it without any command-line arguments would present a list of available arguments. Depending on your project structure and unique requirements, you can decide where to involve the javah tool in your build process.

Following is a simple example demonstrating how javah works. For the sake of simplicity, and to be as platform-independent as possible, in this example you will be using javah through an ANT build script that is extending the Android ANT build framework. Only the relevant portions of the source code will be highlighted here. You can download the full source code from the book's website.

1. As shown in Listing 5-1, define a new ANT task called headers in the custom_rules.xml file in order to extend the Android build system with the ability to generate C/C++ header files for native methods. List your classes with native modules accordingly. The javah tool will process only the classes that are explicitly mentioned.

    Listing 5-1. Content of custom_rules.xml File

    ```
    <?xml version="1.0" encoding="UTF-8"?>
    <project name="custom_rules">
        <target name="headers" depends="debug">
            <path id="headers.classpath">
                <path refid="project.all.jars.path" />
                <path path="${out.classes.absolute.dir}" />
            </path>

            <property name="headers.bootclasspath.value"
                      refid="project.target.class.path" />
            <property name="headers.classpath.value"
                      refid="headers.classpath" />
            <property name="headers.destdir" value="jni" />

            <echo message="Generating C/C++ header files..." />

            <mkdir dir="${headers.destdir}" />
    ```

```
            <javah destdir="${headers.destdir}"
                    classpath="${headers.classpath.value}"
                    bootclasspath="${headers.bootclasspath.value}"
                    verbose="true">

                <!-- List of classes with native methods.  -->
                <class name="com.apress.example.MainActivity" />
            </javah>
        </target>
</project>
```

2. Assume that your Android application contains a native method, called
    nativeMethod, within the MainActivity class as shown in Listing 5-2.

    Listing 5-2. Content of MainActivity.java file with a Native Method

```
public class MainActivity extends Activity
{
    ...

    /**
     * Native method that is implemented using C/C++.
     *
     * @param index integer value.
     * @param activity activity instance.
     * @return string value.
     * @throws IOException
     */
    private static native String nativeMethod(int index,
            Activity activity) throws IOException;
}
```

3. You can now use the ANT script by invoking the following on the command line:

```
ant headers
```

4. This will first trigger a full compile of your application, for the class files to
    be generated. Then it will invoke the javah tool on the specified class files to
    parse the method signatures of your native methods. While the javah tool is
    working, it will print a status message as shown in Listing 5-3.

    Listing 5-3. The javah Tool Generating the Header Files

```
headers:
    [echo] Generating C/C++ header files...
    [mkdir] Created dir: C:\src\JavahTest\jni
    [javah] [Creating file ... [com_apress_example_MainActivity.h]]
```

5.   The javah tool will generate a set of header files in the jni subdirectory of your project. The header files will be named according to the name of the Java class that encapsulates the native method. In this example, the header file com_apress_example_MainActivity.h header fill will be generated. As shown in Listing 5-4, the content of this header file will include the native function signature for each native method that you need to implement.

Listing 5-4. Generated C/C++ Header File

```
/* DO NOT EDIT THIS FILE - it is machine generated */
#include <jni.h>
/* Header for class com_apress_example_MainActivity */

#ifndef _Included_com_apress_example_MainActivity
#define _Included_com_apress_example_MainActivity
#ifdef __cplusplus
extern "C" {
#endif

...

/*
 * Class:     com_apress_example_MainActivity
 * Method:    nativeMethod
 * Signature: (ILandroid/app/Activity;)Ljava/lang/String;
 */
JNIEXPORT jstring JNICALL Java_com_apress_example_MainActivity_nativeMethod
  (JNIEnv *, jclass, jint, jobject);

#ifdef __cplusplus
}
#endif
#endif
```

6.   As suggested at the top of the header file, you should not modify this header file directly, because it will be overwritten each time you execute the javah tool. Instead, you are expected to provide the implementation of all native methods that are declared in this header file in a separate C/C++ source file.

Because the Java and native portions of the code are in two separate silos, the Android build system does not perform any validation while building your application. Any missing native function merely triggers a java.lang.UnsatisfiedLinkError once it is called at runtime. The javah tool helps you to prevent these errors by auto-generating signatures.

Tip   Using the javah tool helps to prevent java.lang.UnsatisfiedLinkError runtime exceptions in your Android application.

As each native method is declared in the header files, any missing implementations of those functions trigger a compile-time error to prevent you from releasing your Android application with missing implementations.

Generating the JNI Code using SWIG

In the previous section, you learned how to utilize the javah tool. Although javah helps you by generating the native function signatures and keeping them in sync with the Java code, you still have to provide the wrapper code to glue the native implementation of those native functions to the Java layer. This will require you to use plenty of JNI API calls, which is a cumbersome and time-consuming development task.

In this section, you will learn about another powerful tool, known as Simplified Wrapper and Interface Generator (SWIG). It simplifies the process of developing native functions by generating the necessary JNI wrapper code. SWIG is an interface compiler, merely a code generator; it does not define a new protocol nor is it a component framework or a specialized runtime library. SWIG takes an interface file as its input and produces the necessary code to expose that interface in Java. SWIG is not a stub generator; it produces code that is ready to be compiled and run. You can download SWIG from its official website at www.swig.org. A simple example application will help you better understand how SWIG can help.

In this example, assume that you need to obtain the Unix username of your Android application during runtime. This information is available through the POSIX getlogin function, which is accessible only from the native C/C++ code, but not from Java. Although the implementation of this function is already provided by the platform, you still have to write JNI API calls to expose the result of this function to Java space, as shown in Listing 5-5.

Listing 5-5. Getlogin Function Exposed Through JNI

```
JNIEXPORT jstring JNICALL Java_com_apress_example_Unix_getlogin(JNIEnv* env, jclass clazz) {
    jstring loginString = 0;

    const char* login = getlogin();
    if (0 != login) {
        loginString = env->NewStringUTF(login);
    }

    return loginString;
}
```

SWIG can help you by generating this code automatically. In order to let SWIG know about which function to wrap, you will need to specify it in a SWIG interface file. As indicated earlier, SWIG is an interface compiler; it generates code based on the provided interface. The SWIG interface file for exposing the getlogin function looks as shown in Listing 5-6.

Listing 5-6. The Unix.i SWIG Interface File

```
/* Module name is Unix. */
%module Unix

%{
/* Include the POSIX operating system APIs. */
#include <unistd.h>
%}

/* Ask SWG to wrap getlogin function. */
extern char* getlogin(void);
```

Assuming that you have installed the SWIG tool on your workstation, and the SWIG binary directory is added to your PATH environment variable, invoke the following on the command prompt all in one line:

```
swig -java
     -package com.apress.example
     -outdir src/com/apress/example
     jni/Unix.i
```

The SWIG tool processes the Unix.i interface file and generates the Unix_wrap.c C/C++ JNI wrapper code, as shown in Listing 5-7, in the jni directory as well as the UnixJNI.java and Unix.java Java proxy classes in the com.apress.example Java package.

Listing 5-7. The Unix_wrap.c Native Source File Generated by SWIG

```
/* ----------------------------------------------------------------------------
 * This file was automatically generated by SWIG (http://www.swig.org).
 * Version 2.0.11
 *
 * This file is not intended to be easily readable and contains a number of
 * coding conventions designed to improve portability and efficiency. Do not make
 * changes to this file unless you know what you are doing--modify the SWIG
 * interface file instead.
 * ---------------------------------------------------------------------------- */

#define SWIGJAVA

...

/* Include the POSIX operating system APIs. */
#include <unistd.h>

#ifdef __cplusplus
extern "C" {
#endif
```

```
SWIGEXPORT jstring JNICALL Java_com_apress_example_UnixJNI_getlogin(JNIEnv *jenv, jclass jcls) {
  jstring jresult = 0 ;
  char *result = 0 ;

  (void)jenv;
  (void)jcls;
  result = (char *)getlogin();
  if (result) jresult = (*jenv)->NewStringUTF(jenv, (const char *)result);
  return jresult;
}
```

...

To use the native function, you can now simply use the getlogin Java method from the com.apress.
example.Unix class in your application. Without writing any JNI wrapper code, SWIG enabled you to
utilize the native function in your Android application.

Minimize the Number of JNI API Calls

Although SWIG tool is highly promising, needless to say there will be still cases where automatic
code generation is simply not an option. In those cases, you will need to write the necessary JNI API
calls to provide the functionality. Even when manual JNI API calls cannot be prevented, minimizing
the number of such calls can still help in optimizing the overall application and reducing the code
footprint. In this section you will learn about some of the best practices to minimize the number of
JNI API calls needed in your application.

Use Primitive Data Types as Native Method Parameters

There are two sorts of data types in the Java programming language: the primitive data types, such
as byte, short, int, and float, and the complex data types, such as Object, Integer, and String.
JNI can automatically map most of the primitive data types to C/C++ primitive data types. The
native function can use data that is passed as primitive types directly without the need to make any
specific JNI API call, as shown in Table 5-1.

Table 5-1. Primitive Data Type Mapping

Java Type	JNI Type	C/C++ Type	Size
boolean	jboolean	unsigned char	Unsigned 8 bits
byte	jbyte	char	Signed 8 bits
char	jchar	unsigned short	Unsigned 16 bits
short	jshort	short	Signed 16 bits
int	jint	Int	Signed 32 bits
long	jlong	long long	Signed 64 bits
float	jfloat	float	32 bits
double	jdouble	double	64 bits

However, the complex data types are passed as opaque references to the native function. In order to use that data, the native function must make various JNI API calls to extract the pieces of the data in a primitive data format that can be used in native code. When defining your native methods, as a best practice, focus on eliminating complex data types in both the parameter list and the return value as much as possible. This will help you to minimize the number of JNI API calls in your native code, and it will also improve the performance of the native function drastically.

Minimize Reach-Back from Native Code to Java Space

A native function is not limited by the data that is passed to it through its parameters. JNI provides the necessary API to enable the native code to interact with the Java space. This flexibility comes with a cost. Using JNI API calls to reach back from native code to Java space consumes CPU cycles and impacts the application performance; meanwhile, it increases the complexity of the native code because of the number of necessary JNI API calls.

As a best practice, make sure you are passing all of the required data into your native function through its parameters, instead of having the native function reach back to Java space to obtain them.

Take a look at the following code example. As shown in Listing 5-8, the native code makes multiple JNI API calls to access the data it needs.

Listing 5-8. Native Method Accessing Two Fields from the Object Instance

```
JNIEXPORT void JNICALL Java_com_apress_example_Unix_method(JNIEnv* env, jobject obj) {

    jclass clazz = env->GetObjectClass(obj);

    jfieldID field1Id = env->GetFieldID(clazz, "field1", "Ljava/lang/String;");
    jstring field1Value = env->GetObjectField(obj, field1Id);

    jfieldID field2Id = env->GetFieldID(clazz, "field2", "Ljava/lang/Integer;");
    jobject field2Value = env->GetObjectField(obj, field2Id);

    ...
}
```

As shown in Listing 5-9, the native method declaration can be modified to include field1 and field2 as part of the native method parameters to eliminate those JNI API calls.

Listing 5-9. Both the field1 and field2 Passed to Native Method Directly

```
JNIEXPORT jstring JNICALL Java_com_apress_example_Unix_method(JNIEnv* env, jobject obj,
    jstring field1, jobject field2) {
    ...
}
```

To avoid redundant coding in Java space, it is also a common practice to utilize helper methods that would aggregate these extra data items prior calling the native method instead of requiring the developer to pass them each time, as shown in Listing 5-10.

Listing 5-10. Helper Method that Aggregates the Necessary Parameters

```
public void method() {
    jniMethod(field1, field2);
}
```

```
public native void jniMethod(String field1, Integer field2);
```

Memory Usage

Compared to desktop-based platforms, memory is a scarce resource on mobile devices. Java is known as a managed programming language, meaning that the Java Virtual Machine (JVM) manages the application memory on behalf of the developer. During the execution of an application, JVM keeps an eye on the available references to the allocated memory regions. When JVM detects that an allocated memory region can no longer be reached by the application code, it releases the memory automatically through a mechanism known as *garbage collection*. This frees the developer from managing the application memory directly, and it drastically reduces the complexity of the code.

JVM garbage collectors boundaries are limited to the Java space only. Because the native code does not run in the managed environment, the JVM garbage collector cannot monitor or free the memory that your application allocates in the native space. It is the developer's responsibility to manage the application memory in native space properly. Otherwise, the application can easily cause the device to run out of memory. This can jeopardize the stability of both the application and the device.

In this section, you will learn about some of the best practices for using memory efficiently in the native space.

Local References

As they do in the Java space, references continue to play an important role in the native space as well. JNI supports three kinds of references: local references, global references, and weak global references. Because the JVM garbage collector does not apply to native space, JNI provides a set of API calls to enable the developer to manage the lifecycle of each of these reference types.

All parameters passed to the native function are local references. In addition, most JNI API calls also return local references.

Never Cache Local References

The lifespan of a local reference is limited to that of the native method itself. Once the native method returns, JVM frees all local references that are either passed in or allocated within the native method. Therefore, you cannot cache and reuse these local references in subsequent invocations. To reuse a reference, you must explicitly create a global reference based on the local reference, using the NewGlobalRef JNI API call, as shown in Listing 5-11.

Listing 5-11. Obtaining a Global Reference from a Local Reference

```
jobject globalObject = env->NewGlobalRef(localObject);
if (0 != globalObject) {
    // You can now cache and reuse globalObject
}
```

You can release the global reference when it is no longer needed using the `DeleteGlobalRef` JNI API call:

```
env->DeleteLocalRef(globalObject);
```

As always, global references in native space can be avoided by passing the necessary data as a parameter to the native method directly. Otherwise, it is the developer's responsibility to manage the lifecycle of global references in native code, as they are not managed by the JVM.

Release Local References in Complex Native Methods

Although JVM still manages the lifecycle of local references, it can only do so once the native method returns. Because JVM has no knowledge about the internals of your native method, it cannot touch the local references while the native method is executing. For that reason it is the developer's responsibility to manage the local references during the execution of the native method.

Caution   Please note that the memory footprint of the local references is not the only reason you need to manage them; the JVM local reference table can hold only up to 512 local references during the execution of your native method. If the local reference table overflows, your application will be terminated by the JVM.

To better understand the problem, take a look at the code shown in Listing 5-12.

Listing 5-12. Native Code Allocating Local References

```
jsize len = env->GetArrayLength(nameArray); // len = 600

for (jsize i=0; i < len; i++) {
    jstring name = env->GetObjectArrayElement(nameArray, i);
    ...
}
```

As you can see, if the number of elements in the `stockQuotes` array is greater than 512, your application will crash. To resolve this problem, take a look at the body of the for-loop. Each time the loop iterates, the value of the variable `quote` is used only once, and the previous value becomes unreachable; however, it still stays in the local reference table, as the JVM has no knowledge about the internals of your native method.

To address the problem, you should use the `DeleteLocalRef` JNI API call to release the local reference once it is known that the local reference won't be used in the native method. After the necessary change is made, the code looks as shown in Listing 5-13.

Listing 5-13. Native Code Releasing Local References

```
jsize len = env->GetArrayLength(nameArray);

for (jsize i=0; i < len; i++) {
    jstring name = env->GetObjectArrayElement(nameArray, i);
    ...
    env->DeleteLocalRef(name);
}
```

This code can handle a much larger number of elements without crashing the application, as the local reference table will not overflow.

Dealing with Strings

Java strings are handled by the JNI as reference types. These reference types are not directly usable as native C strings. JNI provides the necessary functions to convert these Java string references to C strings and back, as shown in Listing 5-14.

Listing 5-14. Converting a Java String into a C String

```
const jbyte* str;
jboolean isCopy;

str = env->GetStringUTFChars(javaString, &isCopy);
if (0 != str) {
    /* You can use the string as an ordinary C string. */
}
```

Once the Java string is converted to a C string, it is simply a pointer to a character array. Because JNI cannot manage that memory allocation automatically anymore, it is the developer's responsibility to release these character arrays explicitly using the ReleaseString or ReleaseStringUTF functions, as shown inListing 5-15. Otherwise, memory leaks will occur.

Listing 5-15. Releasing the C string

```
const jbyte* str;
jboolean isCopy;

str = env->GetStringUTFChars(javaString, &isCopy);
if (0 != str) {
    /* You can use the string as an ordinary C string. */

    env->ReleaseStringUTFChars(javaString, str);
    str = 0;
}
```

Use Proper Memory Management Function

Although the Java programming language has no memory management functions, the C/C++ space has multiple ways of managing the memory. In addition, JNI also introduces its set of functions to manage the lifecycle of references:

■ The `malloc` and `free` functions are the way to manage memory in C code.

■ The `new` and `delete` functions are introduced by C++ and are the proper way to manage memory in C++ applications.

■ The `DeleteLocalRef`, `DeleteGlobalRef`, and other functions are provided by JNI to enable the application to manage the memory of JNI objects in the native space. Any reference that is obtained by JNI should be released using those methods.

In a complex application, because there is no clear way to detect the method used to allocate the memory for a data variable, developers can easily introduce problems in the code by using the wrong pair of memory-management functions. At the very least, it is a good practice to replace `malloc` and `free` with new and `delete` in C++ code.

Operating on Arrays

As described earlier in this chapter, although the primitive data types are mapped directly to native data types, the complex data types are passed as opaque references, and the native code can utilize them through a set of JNI API calls. Because arrays are also part of the complex data types, JNI provides API calls to manipulate Java arrays in native space as well. The main reason for multiple API methods is that each one of them is specifically crafted for different use cases. Using the right API call for the unique needs of your application is a good practice and can improve the performance of your application. Likewise, using the wrong API, or using the right API with carelessly set parameters, can badly impact your application's overall performance.

Do Not Request Unnecessary Array Elements

In order to keep both the Java code and the native code running in separate silos without impacting each other, JNI does not provide direct access to the actual data. Through the opaque references it provides, JNI enables the native code to interact with the actual data through the designated JNI API functions. This ensures that the communication flows only through the JNI APIs and no other media. In certain scenarios, such as operating on arrays, reaching back from native to Java space for each piece of the data introduces unbearable performance overhead. JNI resolves this problem by duplicating the actual data and letting the native code interact on it as an ordinary native data set. Calling the `Get<Type>ArrayElements` JNI API produces a full replica of the actual array in native code. Although this sounds like a convenient way of operating on arrays, it comes with a price. When operating on large arrays, the entire array needs to be duplicated for the native code to start working on it. Once the native code is finished operating on the array data, it can invoke the `Release<Type>ArrayElements` JNI API call to apply the changes back to the Java array and also release its duplicate copy. As indicated earlier, the internals of the native method are fully opaque to

JNI, and it will not know which elements of the array were modified in the native code. Therefore, it simply copies back each element to the original Java array. To better understand the consequences, take a look at the example code shown in Listing 5-16.

Listing 5-16. Modifying the Entire Java Array in Native Code

```
jsize len = env->GetArrayLength(stockQuotesArray); // len = 1000

jint* stockQuotes = env->GetIntArrayElements(stockQuotesArray, 0);

stockQuotes[0] = 1;
stockQuotes[1] = 2;

env->ReleaseIntArrayElements(stockQuotesArray, stockQuotes, 0);
```

There are two main problems with this code:

- Although the entire 1000 elements were duplicated by the GetIntArrayElements, only the first two elements were accessed by the native code. The remaining 998 elements in this example are simply a waste of CPU cycles and of runtime memory.

- Upon invoking the ReleaseIntArrayElements, JNI starts copying all 1000 elements from the native array back to the Java array, as JNI is unaware that only the first two elements were modified by the native code.

As a good practice, make sure you are requesting only the relevant piece of data from JNI. If your application requires only a subset of the larger array, replace the API calls to the Get<Type>ArrayElements API functions with Get<Type>ArrayRegion. The Get<Type>ArrayRegion JNI API allows you to define the data region, and it duplicates that specific region only. This ensures that only the data that matters will be processed, as shown in Listing 5-17.

Listing 5-17. Modifying a Portion of the Java Array in Native Code

```
jint stockQuotes[2];

env->GetIntArrayRegion(stockQuotesArray, 0, 2, stockQuotes);

stockQuotes[0] = 1;
stockQuotes[1] = 2;

env->SetIntArrayRegion(stockQuotesArray, 0, 2, stockQuotes);
```

Prevent Updating Unchanged Arrays

In certain scenarios you would only need to access the Java array to read its values. Although the JNI does not support the concept of read-only data, you can explicitly inform JNI to not to write the values back to the Java array. To do that, use the final parameter of the Release<Type>ArrayElements function, mode;

```
void Release<Type>ArrayElements(JNIEnv* env, ArrayType array,
        NativeType* elements, jint mode);
```

The mode parameter can take the following values:

- **0:** Copy back the content and free the native array.
- **JNI_COMMIT:** Copy back the content but do not free the native array.
- **JNI_ABORT:** Free the native array without copying its content.

Most developers simply ignore this parameter by passing 0 to it to trigger the default mode of operation. Instead, it is a good practice to pass the proper mode to the JNI API call depending on the unique use case. If the developer is aware that the data is not going to be modified in the native method, the code should instead pass JNI_ABORT to inform JNI that it can release the native array without copying back its content.

Native I/O

Although minimizing the impact of the array copy by limiting it to a small subset of the larger data can benefit many use cases, there will still be cases where this best practice cannot be applied. For example, developing a multimedia application will require you to operate on large arrays containing data such as high-resolution video frames or multiple channels of audio data. In such situations, you will not be able to limit the boundaries of the data to a small set, as all that will need to be consumed by the native code.

In such scenarios, you can rely on the JNI Native I/O (NIO) API calls. NIO provides improved performance in the areas of buffer management, scalable network and file I/O, and character-set support. JNI provides functions to use the NIO buffers from native code. Compared to array operations, NIO buffers deliver much better performance. NIO does not duplicate the data; it simply provides direct memory access to it. NIO buffers are therefore highly suitable for delivering a vast amount of data between the native code and the Java application.

Assuming the NIO buffer is allocated on the Java space as an instance of the java.nio.ByteBuffer class, you can obtain a direct pointer to its memory by invoking the GetDirectBufferAddress JNI API call, as shown in Listing 5-18.

Listing 5-18. Getting the Direct Pointer to Byte Buffer Memory

```
unsigned char* buffer;
buffer = (unsigned char*) env->GetDirectBufferAddress(directBuffer);
```

Operating using NIO buffers is the best practice for data-intensive Android applications that would like to benefit from native code support.

Caching Classes, Method and Field IDs

JNI does not expose the fields and methods of Java classes directly in the native code. Instead, it provides a set of APIs to access them indirectly. For example, to get the value of a field of a class, the following steps will be taken:

1. Obtain a reference to the class object, through the `FindClass` function.

2. Obtain the ID for the field that will be accessed, through the `GetFieldID` function.

3. Obtain the actual value of the field by supplying the class instance and the field ID to the `Get<Type>Field` function.

Although they are used very frequently in JNI applications, both the `GetFieldID` and `GetMethodID` functions are very heavy function calls by their nature. As you would imagine, these functions have to traverse through the entire inheritance chain for the class to identify the right ID to return. Because neither the Class object, the Class inheritance, nor the field ID can change during the execution of the application, those values can actually be cached in the native layer for subsequent access with fewer API calls.

The return type of the `FindClass` function is a local reference. In order to cache that, you will need to create a global reference first through the `NewGlobalRef` function. On the other hand, the return value of `GetFieldID` is `jfieldID`, which is simply an integer, and it can be cached as is.

> **Tip**   Although you can improve the performance of JNI functions in accessing Java fields and methods from the native space, the transition between the Java and native code is a costly operation. It is strongly recommended that you take this into the account when deciding where to split the Java and the native code. Minimizing the reach-backs between Java and native code can improve your application's performance.

As a good practice, you should focus on caching both the field and method IDs for the pieces that are accessed multiple times during the execution of your application.

Threading

JNI does not enforce any limitations on the execution model of the native code. Both the Java code and the native code can achieve parallel processing through the use of threads. These threads can be either Java threads or platform threads, like POSIX threads. This flexibility makes it easier to reuse existing native modules as part of a Java application through JNI, as the threading model remains compatible.

Although both threading mechanisms can run simultaneously side by side, there are certain constraints of JNI to keep in mind if you expect your native, non-Java threads to access any of the JNI functions.

Never Cache the JNI Environment Interface Pointer

As indicated earlier in this chapter, local references that are obtained either through method parameters or through JNI API calls cannot be cached and reused outside the execution scope of that native method call.

Moreover, in order to execute any JNI API function, a pointer to the JNI environment interface (JNIEnv) needs to be available to the native code. As with the local references, the JNIEnv interface pointer is also valid only during the execution scope of native method calls, and it cannot be cached and reused.

In order to obtain the proper JNIEnv interface pointer for the current thread, it needs to be attached to the Java VM.

Never Access Java Space from Detached Native Threads

You can attach your non-Java threads to the Java VM through the AttachCurrentThread function of the JavaVM interface. The JavaVM interface pointer can be obtained from a valid JNIEnv interface through the GetJavaVM function call, as shown inListing 5-19.

Listing 5-19. The GetJavaVM Function Obtaining the JavaVM

```
static JavaVM* vm = 0;

JNIEXPORT jstring JNICALL Java_com_apress_example_Unix_init(JNIEnv* env, jclass clazz) {
    if (0 != env->GetJavaVM(&vm)) {
        /* Error occured. */
    } else {
        /* JavaVM obtained. */
    }
}
```

The obtained JavaVM pointer can be cached and used in native threads. Upon invoking the AttachCurrentThread function using the JavaVM interface from your non-Java thread, the native threads will be added to the Java VM's list of known threads, and a unique JNIEnv interface pointer for the current thread will be returned, as shown in Listing 5-20.

Listing 5-20. Attaching Current Native Thread to Java VM

```
void threadWorker() {
    JNIEnv* env = 0;

    if (0 = (*vm)->AttachCurrentThread(vm, &env, NULL)) {
        /* Error occurred. */
    } else {
        /* JNI API can be accessed using the JNIEnv. */
    }
}
```

> **Note** If the non-Java thread is already attached to the Java VM, subsequent calls won't have any side effect.

Now using the proper `JNIEnv` interface pointer you can access the JNI API functions from your non-Java thread. The `JNIEnv` interface pointer for the thread remains valid until the thread is detached using the `DetachCurrentThread` function, as shown in Listing 5-21.

Listing 5-21. Detaching the Current Native Thread from Java VM

```
(*vm)->DetachCurrentThread();
env = 0;
```

Troubleshooting

Despite the ease of the Java code, debugging the native code can be very complicated. When you are facing the unexpected, having troubleshooting skills becomes a life-saver. Knowing the right tools and techniques enables you to resolve problems rapidly. In this section, you will briefly explore some of the best practices for troubleshooting problems in native code.

Extended JNI Check

In order to deliver high performance at runtime, the JNI functions do very little error checking. Errors usually result in a crash that is hard to troubleshoot. Dalvik VM provides an extended checking mode for JNI calls, known as CheckJNI. When it is enabled, JavaVM and JNIEnv interface pointers are switched to tables of functions that perform an extended level of error checking before calling the actual implementation. CheckJNI can detect the following problems:

- Attempt to allocate a negative-sized array
- Bad or `NULL` pointers passed to JNI functions' Syntax errors while passing class names
- Making JNI calls while in critical section
- Bad arguments passed to `NewDirectByeBuffer`
- Making JNI calls when an exception is pending
- `JNIEnv` interface pointer used in wrong thread
- Field type and `Set<Type>Field` function mismatch
- Method type and `Call<Type>Method` function mismatch, such as `DeleteGlobalRef/DeleteLocalRef` called with wrong reference type
- Bad release mode passed to `Release<Type>ArrayElement` function
- Incompatible type returned from native method
- Invalid UTF-8 sequence passed to a JNI call

By default, the CheckJNI mode is enabled only in the emulator, not on the regular Android devices, because of its effect on the overall performance of the system. On a regular device, the CheckJNI mode can be enabled by issuing the following on the command prompt:

```
adb shell setprop debug.checkjni 1
```

This won't affect the running applications, but any application launched afterwards will have CheckJNI enabled. It is a good practice to observe your application running in the CheckJNI mode to spot any problems in your native code before they lead the application into much complicated problems.

Always Check for Java Exceptions

Exception handling is an important aspect of the Java programming language. Exceptions behave differently in the JNI than they do in Java. In Java, when an exception is thrown, the virtual machine stops the execution of the code block and goes through the call stack in reverse order to find an exception handler code block that can handle the specific exception type. This is also called catching an exception. The virtual machine clears the exception and transfers the control to the exception handler block. In contrast, the JNI requires developers to explicitly implement the exception handling flow after an exception has occurred.

You can catch Java exceptions in native code using the JNI API call ExceptionOccurred. This function queries the Java VM for any pending exception, and it returns a local reference to the exception Java object, as shown in Listing 5-22.

Listing 5-22. Catching and Handling Exceptions in Native Code

```
jthrowable ex;
...
env->CallVoidMethod(instance, throwingMethodId);
ex = env->ExceptionOccurred(env);
if (0 != ex) {
    env->ExceptionClear(env);

    /* Exception handler. */
}
```

Failure to do so will not block the execution of your native function; however, any subsequent calls to JNI API will silently fail. This can become very hard to troubleshoot, as the actual exception does not leave any traces behind.

As a good practice, you should always check whether a Java exception has been thrown after invoking any Java methods that may throw an exception.

Upon handling the exception, you should also clear it using the ExceptionClear function to inform the Java VM that the exception is handled and JNI can resume serving requests to Java space.

Always Check JNI Return Values

Exceptions are extensions of the programming language for developers to report and handle exceptional events that require special processing outside the actual flow of the application. Although exceptions have been part of the Java programming language since its very beginning, exception support is not widely available for C/C++ programming language on all platforms. Because JNI is designed to be a universal solution to facilitate integration of native modules into Java applications, it does not use exceptions. The JNI API functions instead rely on their return values to indicate any errors during the execution of the API call, as shown in Listing 5-23.

Listing 5-23. Checking the Return Value of JNI API Calls

```
jclass clazz;
...
clazz = env->FindClass("java/lang/String");
if (0 == clazz) {
    /* Class could not be found. */
} else {
    /* Class is found, you can use the return value. */
}
```

Thus, as a good practice, never assume it is safe to use the return value of a JNI API call as is. Always check the return value to make sure the JNI API call was successfully executed and the proper usable value is returned to your native function.

Always Add Log Lines While Developing

Logging is the most important part of troubleshooting, but it is tricky to achieve, especially on mobile platforms where the development and the execution of the application happen on two different machines. As a good practice, you should always include log messages while developing your application, not when you are trying to troubleshoot a problem, as it will be too late by then. Having proper logging part of your application can help you to troubleshoot problems much easily by simply looking at the log output of your applications. Needless to say, reading and sharing log messages is much easier process than using sophisticated debugger applications to inspect the execution of an application.

Although adding logging into your application is an appealing solution, having an extensive amount of logging will impact the performance of your application, and it will also expose too much about the internal flow of your application to external parties. Although it's good to have extensive logging during the development and troubleshooting stage, you should strip those components from your application before releasing it. Despite the vast number of logging frameworks that are available in Java space, the options are fairly limited for C/C++ code. In this section, you will fill this gap by building a small logging framework for C/C++ code.

In order to achieve the same functionality that is offered by the advanced logging frameworks, the solution that is presented in this section will be rely heavily on the preprocessor support provided by the native C/C++ compiler. The my_log.h header file that is shown in Listing 5-24 through a set of preprocessor directives, wraps the Android native logging APIs to provide a compile-time control over the intensity of logging.

Listing 5-24. The my_log.h Logging Header File

```
#pragma once

/**
 * Basic logging framework for NDK.
 *
 * @author Onur Cinar
 */

#include <android/log.h>

#define MY_LOG_LEVEL_VERBOSE 1
#define MY_LOG_LEVEL_DEBUG 2
#define MY_LOG_LEVEL_INFO 3
#define MY_LOG_LEVEL_WARNING 4
#define MY_LOG_LEVEL_ERROR 5
#define MY_LOG_LEVEL_FATAL 6
#define MY_LOG_LEVEL_SILENT 7

#ifndef MY_LOG_TAG
#    define MY_LOG_TAG __FILE__
#endif

#ifndef MY_LOG_LEVEL
#    define MY_LOG_LEVEL MY_LOG_LEVEL_VERBOSE
#endif

#define MY_LOG_NOOP (void) 0

#define MY_LOG_PRINT(level,fmt,...) \
        __android_log_print(level, MY_LOG_TAG, "(%s:%u) %s: " fmt, \
                __FILE__, __LINE__, __PRETTY_FUNCTION__, ##__VA_ARGS__)

#if MY_LOG_LEVEL_VERBOSE >= MY_LOG_LEVEL
#    define MY_LOG_VERBOSE(fmt,...) \
        MY_LOG_PRINT(ANDROID_LOG_VERBOSE, fmt, ##__VA_ARGS__)
#else
#    define MY_LOG_VERBOSE(...) MY_LOG_NOOP
#endif

#if MY_LOG_LEVEL_DEBUG >= MY_LOG_LEVEL
#    define MY_LOG_DEBUG(fmt,...) \
        MY_LOG_PRINT(ANDROID_LOG_DEBUG, fmt, ##__VA_ARGS__)
#else
#    define MY_LOG_DEBUG(...) MY_LOG_NOOP
#endif
```

```
#if MY_LOG_LEVEL_INFO >= MY_LOG_LEVEL
#    define MY_LOG_INFO(fmt,...) \
         MY_LOG_PRINT(ANDROID_LOG_INFO, fmt, ##__VA_ARGS__)
#else
#    define MY_LOG_INFO(...) MY_LOG_NOOP
#endif

#if MY_LOG_LEVEL_WARNING >= MY_LOG_LEVEL
#    define MY_LOG_WARNING(fmt,...) \
         MY_LOG_PRINT(ANDROID_LOG_WARN, fmt, ##__VA_ARGS__)
#else
#    define MY_LOG_WARNING(...) MY_LOG_NOOP
#endif

#if MY_LOG_LEVEL_ERROR >= MY_LOG_LEVEL
#    define MY_LOG_ERROR(fmt,...) \
         MY_LOG_PRINT(ANDROID_LOG_ERROR, fmt, ##__VA_ARGS__)
#else
#    define MY_LOG_ERROR(...) MY_LOG_NOOP
#endif

#if MY_LOG_LEVEL_FATAL >= MY_LOG_LEVEL
#    define MY_LOG_FATAL(fmt,...) \
         MY_LOG_PRINT(ANDROID_LOG_FATAL, fmt, ##__VA_ARGS__)
#else
#    define MY_LOG_FATAL(...) MY_LOG_NOOP
#endif

#if MY_LOG_LEVEL_FATAL >= MY_LOG_LEVEL
#    define MY_LOG_ASSERT(expression, fmt, ...) \
         if (!(expression)) \
         { \
             __android_log_assert(#expression, MY_LOG_TAG, \
                 fmt, ##__VA_ARGS__); \
         }
#else
#    define MY_LOG_ASSERT(...) MY_LOG_NOOP
#endif
```

In order to use this tiny logging framework, simply include the my_log.h header file:

```
#include "my_log.h"
```

This will make the logging macros available to the source code. You can then use them in your native code, as shown in Listing 5-25.

Listing 5-25. Native Code with Logging Macros

...

```
MY_LOG_VERBOSE("The native method is called.");

MY_LOG_DEBUG("env=%p thiz=%p", env, thiz);

MY_LOG_ASSERT(0 != env, "JNIEnv cannot be NULL.");
```

...

The tiny logging framework still relies on the Android logging functions. As the last step, you should modify the Android.mk build file as shown in Listing 5-26.

Listing 5-26. Setting the Log Level Through the Build Script

```
LOCAL_MODULE := module
...
# Define the log tag
MY_LOG_TAG := module

# Define the default logging level based build type
ifeq ($(APP_OPTIM),release)
  MY_LOG_LEVEL := MY_LOG_LEVEL_ERROR
else
  MY_LOG_LEVEL := MY_LOG_LEVEL_VERBOSE
endif

# Appending the compiler flags
LOCAL_CFLAGS += -DMY_LOG_TAG=$(MY_LOG_TAG)
LOCAL_CFLAGS += -DMY_LOG_LEVEL=$(MY_LOG_LEVEL)

LOCAL_SRC_FILES := module.c

# Dynamically linking with the log library
LOCAL_LDLIBS += -llog
```

You can always improve this simple logging framework based on the unique requirements of your application. Using a logging framework is a good practice, as it will enable you to control the amount of logging your application will produce, without making any modifications to the source code. Having logging available in advance can save you time while troubleshooting complicated errors in native components.

Native Code Reuse Using Modules

Because C/C++ is more a programming language than a complete framework like Java, you will often rely on third-party libraries to achieve basic operations, such as accessing a URL through the HTTP protocol using the libcurl HTTP client library.

It is always a best practice to keep those third-party modules outside the main code base, so that they can be reused, shared across multiple modules, and updated seamlessly. Starting from version R5, the Android NDK allows sharing and reusing modules between NDK projects.

To resume our previous example, the `libcurl` third-party module can be shared between multiple NDK projects easily by doing the following:

1. Move the shared module to its own location outside any NDK project, such as /home/cinar/shared-modules/libcurl.

> **Note**   In order to prevent name conflicts, the directory structure can also include the module's provider name, such as /home/cinar/shared-modules/haxx/libcurl. The Android NDK build system does not accept the space character in shared module paths.

2. Every shared module also required its own `Android.mk` build file. An example build file is shown in Listing 5-27.

    Listing 5-27. Shared Module Android.mk Build File

    ```
    LOCAL_PATH := $(call my-dir)

    #
    # LibCURL HTTP client library.
    #
    include $(CLEAR_VARS)

    LOCAL_MODULE := curl
    LOCAL_SRC_FILES := curl.c

    include $(BUILD_SHARED_LIBRARY)
    ```

3. Now the shared module can be imported in other Android NDK projects using the import-module macro as shown in Listing 5-28. The import-module macro call should be placed at the end of the `Android.mk` build file to prevent any build system conflicts.

    Listing 5-28. Project Importing the Shared Module

    ```
    #
    # Native module
    #

    include $(CLEAR_VARS)

    LOCAL_MODULE := module

    LOCAL_SRC_FILES := module.c
    ```

```
LOCAL_SHARED_LIBRARIES := curl
```

```
include $(BUILD_SHARED_LIBRARY)
```

```
$(call import-module,haxx/libcurl)
```

4.   The import-module macro must first locate the shared module and then import it into the NDK project. By default, only the ⟨*Android NDK*⟩/sources directory is searched by the import-module macro. In order to include the /home/cinar/shared-modules directory into the search, define a new environment variable called NDK_MODULE_PATH and set it to the root directory of shared modules:

```
export NDK_MODULE_PATH=/home/cinar/shared-modules
```

5.   Now running the ndk-build script will pull the shared module during the build process.

Maintaining the common modules using this method is a good practice, as it will promote reuse and make it easier to add functionality into your Android NDK project without any additional effort.

Benefit from Compiler Vectorization

The last best practice you will learn in this chapter is compiler vectorization, which improves the performance of your native functions by seamlessly benefiting from the available Single Instruction Multiple Data (SIMD) support in mobile CPUs. SIMD enables data-level parallelism by performing the same operation on multiple data points all at once. It is also known as NEON support on ARM-based processors. Using SIMD support can drastically improve the performance of native functions that are applying the same set of operations to large data sets. For example, multimedia applications can benefit from SIMD greatly as they apply the same set of operations to multiple audio and video frames.

Using the assembly language or the compiler intrinsics is not the only way of benefitting from SIMD support. If the native code is structured in a form that can be parallelized, the compiler can seamlessly inject the necessary instructions to benefit from the SIMD support seamlessly. This process is known as compiler vectorization.

Compiler vectorization is not enabled by default. In order to enable it, please follow these simple steps:

1.   Open the Application.mk build script and make sure that the APP_ABI contains armeabi-v7a.

```
APP_ABI := armeabi armeabi-v7a
```

2.   Open the Android.mk build script for your NDK project, and add the –ftree-vectorize argument to the LOCAL_CFLAGS build system variable as shown in Listing 5-29.

Listing 5-29. Enabling Compiler Vectorization Support

```
...
LOCAL_MODULE := module
...
LOCAL_CFLAGS += -ftree-vectorize
...
```

3. For the compiler vectorization to occur, the native code should also be compiled with ARM NEON support if the target CPU architecture is ARM. In order to do so, update the Android.mk build script file as shown in Listing 5-30.

Listing 5-30. Enabling ARM NEON Support

```
...
LOCAL_MODULE := module
LOCAL_CFLAGS += -ftree-vectorize
...
# Add ARM NEON support to all source files
ifeq ($(TARGET_ARCH_ABI),armeabi-v7a)
LOCAL_ARM_NEON := true
endif
...
```

Simply enabling compiler vectorization is not enough. As indicated earlier in this section, the C/C++ language does not provide any mechanism to specify parallelizing behavior. You will have to give the C/C++ compiler additional hints about where it is safe to have the code automatically vectorized. For a list of automatically vectorizable loops, please consult the "Auto-vectorization in GCC" documentation at http://gcc.gnu.org/projects/tree-ssa/vectorization.html.

> **Tip**   Getting the loops vectorized is a delicate operation. The C/C++ compiler can provide you with a detailed analysis of the native loops in your native code if you append –ftree-vectorizer-verbose=2 to LOCAL_CFLAGS.

Summary

In this chapter you have learned about some of the best practices to follow while developing native components for your Android applications. By following these simple recommendations you can easily improve the reliability of your native components and you can minimize the time spent troubleshooting problems in the native space. In the next chapter, you will discover some of the best practices in Android security.

## Chapter 6

Security

In this chapter we will explore recommendations for secure Android development and coding, from a range of industry sources. These different security recommendations represent the best current thinking on the topic, and I've added my own additional measures gathered from hard-earned experience building and deploying leading Android applications.

The State of Android Security

There have probably been more books, blog postings, and magazine articles written on the topic of Android security than on any other mobile platform. Whether we like it or not, Android is seen as the Wild West of the mobile world. Because all iOS apps are reviewed by a human, rightly or wrongly this gives people the perception that iOS apps are safer than Android apps. But how can that be? After all, the Android platform does a pretty good job of separating APKs so that each one runs in its own sandbox? Let's take a look at some empirical data to see if there is any truth in the rumor. Figure 6-1 shows a Secure List report, available at
http://www.securelist.com/en/analysis/204792239/IT_Threat_Evolution_Q2_2012.

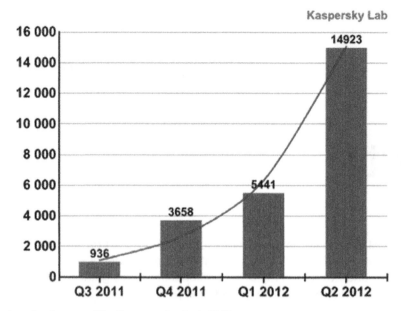

Figure 6-1. The number of malware modifications targeting Android OS

You can see that the number of malware apps in the Android space is indeed growing dramatically. The report goes on to say that among the 15k apps, malware characteristics were found as listed in Table 6-1.

Table 6-1. Breakdown of the Types of Malware

Percentage	Malware Type
49%	Steal data from telephones
25%	SMS messaging
18%	Backdoor apps
2%	Spy programs

There have also been some famous fake apps, like the phony Netflix app (see http://www.symantec. com/connect/blogs/will-your-next-tv-manual-ask-you-run-scan-instead-adjusting-antenna), which looked like the Netflix app and simply collected usernames. And almost every famous Android app from Angry Birds to the Amazon App Store app itself has a suspicious clone that hopes to dupe a customer into downloading it for a fee. And yes, this aspect of security should really be a two-way street; I'm sure that users pay little or no attention to that permission screen when they're installing an APK and will typically approve anything. So while it seems that we do have a problem on the Android platform, perhaps it's not all the developer's fault.

Back in the Cupcake and Donut eras there were few if any checks. But now we can say that every developer needs to have a credit card to upload an app. Since around the time of Gingerbread, Google Bouncer has also automatically checked to see if the app has any malware or Trojans installed on your APKs, so it should be much safer. (However, Jon Oberheide's paper describing how he created a fake developer account and bypassed the Google Bouncer, at `http://jon.oberheide.org/files/summercon12-bouncer.pdf`, is some cause for concern about the effectiveness of the Google signup process.) Things are definitely getting more secure as more users move to Ice Cream Sandwich and Jelly Bean; at the time of writing, 40% of Android devices hitting Google Play were on some version of 4.x.

But perception is reality, and even if most of these hacks are becoming a thing of the past, Android is still seen as a less secure platform than iOS. So what can a developer do? You can make sure that your APKs are secure as possible to help change that Wild West perception. This chapter will show how to ensure that your APKs do what your users expect—no more and no less, in a consistent way.

There are a number of best practices that you can adopt to make your Android apps more secure. In this chapter I'll provide you with a better understanding of what it takes to create a trustworthy app; the goal is that if someone downloads your app, they can be safe in thinking that it's not going to cause them any security problems.

The bulk of this chapter compiles a top 10 list of secure coding practices. We'll first look at some industry standard lists and merge them into our own best-practices top 10 list. This isn't really meant to be a definitive list; it's simply a list of the most important issues from personal experience, research, and a couple of industry-standard lists.

It also makes sense to look at an Android app that my company, RIIS, uses to teach our developers how to write secure code and talk you through how we go about that.

Secure Coding Practices

Your APKs should use a least-privileges concept so that they always get access only to the privileges they really need, and are not being granted other privileges that are never used but could open vulnerabilities. So exactly how do you make sure of that?

If you're a consumer, there are a variety of tools that check permissions, but if you're a developer or a manager, there are a very limited number of tools out there.

Once your APK is out on Google Play, phones can be rooted, and the APK can be very easily reverse-engineered to see any usernames/passwords or other login info. It's in everyone's interest to make sure that a customer's data is not in plain text so it can be compromised. We've seen some really strange method names when decompiling an APK, one of my favorites being updateSh*t, which probably isn't something you want out there with your company's name attached.

You may also want to get a better feel for whatever third-party libraries you're using and make sure they're not doing anything they shouldn't be; for example, AdMob makes location requests for collecting marketing information. You might want to know if the third-party APK has hardcoded usernames and passwords, too, and what they might be doing.

To solve this problem, I came up with my top 10 list of Secure Coding practices. Most of them came from looking at other security lists that smarter people than I have developed.

This list becomes my firm's barometer on what's acceptable and not acceptable in an Android APK that we develop. That's not to say that some APKs won't violate one or more of the guidelines in the top 10 list for perfectly good reasons, but it raises a red flag so that someone can ask why it's doing something that we didn't expect it to do.

These are not the type of issues that Google Bouncer would be checking; this is code that shouldn't be in your APK—in our humble opinion—without a good reason.

Industry Standard Lists

Before we come up with our own list, let's take a look at the following security lists:

- PCI's Mobile Payment Acceptance Security Guidelines
- OWASP or Open Web Application Security Project's top 10 mobile controls and design principles
- Google's Security Tips

PCI List

In September 2012, The PCI Security Standards Council released v1.0 of the Mobile Payment Security Guidelines. PCI's focus is on payment processing, and while the guidelines are not yet mandatory, they are an excellent place to start. Some of the items in the PCI guidelines don't directly apply to mobile developers, but there are some that are crucial, which we've included here.

Prevent account data from compromise while processed or stored within the mobile device. Android developers should ensure that all data is securely stored and minimize any chance of data leakage. Storing sensitive customer information unencrypted in SQLite or in a file on an SD card is not acceptable. The safest option is to not store cryptographic keys anywhere on the mobile phone if possible, but if that's not an option, then the keys need to be stored securely so that they are not accessible even when a phone is rooted.

Prevent account data from being intercepted upon transmission out of the mobile device. Any sensitive customer information, in this case payment information, should be transmitted securely using SSL and not sent in clear text.

Create server-side controls and report unauthorized access. Report on unauthorized access over a given threshold via server side logging messages, updates to software, phone rooting, and so on.

Prevent escalation of privileges and remotely disable payments. If the user roots their phone, the application should report the change and provide the ability to stop taking payments if necessary.

Prefer online transactions. Transactions should be taken when the phone is online and not saved for later processing if the phone is offline for any reason. Storing the payment data increases the risk of a hacker gaining access to the payment data.

Conform to secure coding, engineering, and testing. There are a number of Android specific coding techniques, such as avoiding the use of `MODE_WORLD_WRITABLE` or `MODE_WORLD_READABLE` when writing to files, that the developer should know. In the remainder of the chapter we're going to look at what secure coding means for an Android developer.

Support secure merchant receipts. Any receipt-type messages, whether they are displayed on screen or sent via email, should always mask the credit card number and never display the complete number.

Provide an indication of a secure state. Unfortunately, unlike web browsers, Android apps don't have the concept of a locked and unlocked padlock to show the user that any payment information is being sent securely, so currently there is no way to indicate a secure or insecure state.

OWASP

OWASP, the Open Web Application Security Project, is aimed at providing information to developers so that they can write and maintain secure software. No longer only for the web, OWASP also provides information on secure cloud programming as well as secure mobile programming. OWASP together with ENISA (the European Network and Information Security Agency) published the Top Ten Mobile Controls as shown following. This list is aimed at mobile device security, rather than just payment security. OWASP also provide another resource called GoatDroid, which consists of a couple of Android applications showing examples of insecure code that does not follow the advice on the list.

Identify and protect sensitive data on the mobile device. Mobile phones have a higher risk than laptops of being stolen. Store any sensitive user data on the server side and not on the mobile device. If you do need to store data on the mobile device, then encrypt the data and provide a way to remotely remove the key or data so that the user can wipe the information if the phone is stolen. Consider restricting access to the data or functionality using the phone's location, for example, if the phone is no longer in the same state, province, or country where the app was first installed. Practice secure key management.

Handle password credentials securely on the device. Store passwords on the server. If they do need to be stored on the phone, never store passwords in clear text; use encryption or hashing. If possible use tokens, for example OAuth, instead of passwords where possible and make sure they expire. Make sure passwords are never visible in logs. Do not store any keys or passwords, for example to back-end servers, in the application binary, as mobile apps can be reverse-engineered.

Ensure sensitive data is protected in transit. Use SSL/TLS when sending any sensitive information to back-end systems. Use strong and well known encryption with appropriate key lengths when encrypting data. User passwords are often too short to provide adequate key lengths. Use trusted Certificate Authorities or CAs. Do not disable or ignore SSL certs if the trusted CA is not recognized by the Android OS. Do not use SMS or MMS to send sensitive user information. Let the end user know, by using some visual indicator, that the CA is valid.

Implement user authentication, authorization, and session management correctly. Use unpredictable seeds and a random number generator for key generation. Instead of just using date and time, use other inputs such as phone temperature, current location, and so on. When the user is logged in, make sure that any further requests to the back-end server still require the same login credentials or token to get the information.

Keep the back-end APIs (services) and the platform (server) secure. Test your back-end servers and APIs for any vulnerabilities. Apply the latest OS patches and updates to the server. Log all requests and check to see if there is any unusual activity. Use DDOS limiting techniques such as IP/per-user throttling.

Secure data integration with third party services and applications. There is so much open source Android code available that sometimes coding an app can seem more plug and play than desktop programming. However, third-party libraries also need to be checked for insecure coding practices. Apply the same checks to your third party code as you would to your own code. Don't assume that commercial apps are going to be secure. There are plenty of examples of third party issues, such as advertising networks collecting location and device information. Check for software patches and update your mobile applications as needed.

Pay specific attention to the collection and storage of consent for the collection and use of the user's data. Ask for consent before asking for and storing a user's personally identifiable information. Allow the end user to opt out. Perform audits to ensure that you are not leaking any unintended information, for example in image metadata. Be aware that the data collection rules may be different in different regions; for example, user consent is mandatory for any personal data collection in the European Union.

Implement controls to prevent unauthorized access to paid-for resources (wallet, SMS, phone calls, and so on.) In the PCI list introduced earlier in this chapter, we saw that many of the malware apps wreak havoc by using costly paid-for resources such as SMS messaging to offshore numbers. To prevent your app from being hijacked in a similar fashion, there are certain steps that you should take if you use paid-for resources in your mobile app.

Track any significant changes in usage or a user's location and notify the user or shut down the app. Authenticate all API calls to paid for resources and warn the user for any paid for access. Finally, maintain logs of any paid-for access API calls. Audit the logs, as they may alert you to any changes in overall behavior before you app is compromised and can also help you understand what happened after an attack.

Ensure secure distribution/provisioning of mobile applications. Don't distribute your app through nonsecure mobile app stores, as they may not monitor for insecure code. Provide a security email address (such as security@acme.com) for users to report any security problems with your app. Plan your security update process. Remember that many users will not automatically accept the latest update. So if you have a security flaw, it may take many months before all your users have updated to the latest secure version of your mobile app. And once an APK is out there, if your app has lots of users, then it's always going to be out there on any number of hacker forums ready for someone to see if they can exploit your flaw.

Carefully check any runtime interpretation of code for errors. Test all user inputs and make sure all input parameters are correctly validated and there are no options for either cross-site scripting or SQL injection.

OWASP's General Secure Coding Guidelines

OWASP also offers more general secure coding guidelines, which apply to mobile programming:

1. Perform abuse case testing, in addition to use case testing.

2. Validate all input.

3. Minimize lines and complexity of code. A useful metric is cyclomatic complexity.

4. Use safe languages (for example, from buffer-overflow).

5. Implement a security report handling point (address), such as security@example.com.

6. Use static and binary code analyzers and fuzz-testers to find security flaws.

7. Use safe string functions, and avoid buffer and integer overflow.

8. Run apps with the minimum privilege required for the application on the operating system. Be aware of privileges granted by default by APIs and disable them.

9. Don't authorize code/app to execute with root/system administrator privilege.

10. Always perform testing as a standard as well as a privileged user.

11. Avoid opening application-specific server sockets (listener ports) on the client device. Use the communication mechanisms provided by the OS.

12. Remove all test code before releasing the application.

13. Ensure that logging is done appropriately but do not record excessive logs, especially those including sensitive user information.

OWASP's Top 10 Mobile Risks

OWASP has another top 10, called the Top 10 Mobile Risks. These have a lot of overlap with the earlier Top 10 Mobile Control, which is more of a best practices list. I show the Top 10 Mobile Risks here for completeness.

1. Insecure data storage

2. Weak server-side controls

3. Insufficient transport layer protection

4. Client-side injection

5.   Poor authorization and authentication

6.   Improper session handling

7.   Security decisions via untrusted inputs

8.   Side channel data leakage

9.   Broken cryptography

10.   Sensitive information disclosure information

Google Security Tips

The last list we're going to look at is Google's Android-specific list of security tips. You'll see some overlap with the earlier lists, but because it's so specific to our Android requirements, it may very well prove to be the most useful of the three lists.

Storing Data: Avoid using MODE_WORLD_WRITEABLE or MODE_WORLD_READABLE modes for files, especially if you're using the files to store user data. If you do need to share data between applications then use a content provider where there is a much finer degree of control on what applications can access the data. Keys should be placed in a keystore encrypted with a user password that is not stored on the device.

Do not store any sensitive user data on external storage such as an SD card. The SD card can be removed and examined, as it's globally readable and writable.

Using Permissions: Android APKs work within a sandbox. The APK can communicate outside of the sandbox by a series of permissions, which the developer requests and the user accepts. Developers should adopt a least-privileges approach to permissions and ask for only the very minimum level of permissions to provide the desired functionality. And if there is an option to not request permissions, such as using internal rather than external storage, then the developer should take steps to define as few permissions as possible.

Using Networking: Use SSL instead of sending any sensitive user information in clear text across the network. Do not rely on unauthenticated SMS data to perform commands, as it may have been spoofed.

Performing Input Validation: Perform input validation and ensure that there is no SQL or JavaScript script injection. If you are using any native code in your app, then apply C++ secure coding best practices to catch any buffer overflows. These should be taken care of by proper management of buffers and pointers.

Handling User Data: The topic of how to handle user data is one that appears time and time again in security lists. Minimize any access to sensitive user data. While it may be necessary to transmit usernames, passwords, and credit card information, the data should not be stored on the device. User data should also be hashed, encrypted, or tokenized on the server so that the data is not transmitted in clear text. User data should also not be written to logs. Use a short-lived authorization token after initial authentication with a username and password entered by the user.

Using WebView: Disable JavaScript when using WebView if it's not required. To reduce the chance of cross-site-scripting, do not call `setJavaScriptEnabled()` unless you absolutely must, such as when building hybrid native/web applications. By default `setJavaScriptEnabled` is false.

Using Cryptography: Use existing cryptography such as AES and RSA; don't implement your own cryptographic algorithms. Use a secure random number generator. Store any keys that are needed for repeated use in KeyStore.

Using Interprocess Communication: Use Android's interprocess communication, for examples intents, services and broadcast receivers. Do not use network sockets or shared files.

Dynamically Loading Code: Dynamically loading code is strongly discouraged. In particular, loading code from outside of the APK over the network could allow someone to modify the code in transit or from another application and should be avoided.

Security in Native Code: Simply put, using the Android NDK is discouraged as C++ is prone to buffer overflows and other memory corruption errors.

Our Top 10 Secure Coding Recommendations

Not content with the existing lists, I've come up with my own Top 10 list, which is a mashup of the other lists, where I've picked what I feel are the best practices for each of the lists.

I'm also a great believer in automating the analysis wherever possible and not manually checking every app, so I've written a secure code analyzer called Secure Policy Enforcer or SPE to ensure that your apps are following the top 10 list.

Apply secure coding techniques. There shouldn't be any need to open a file as `WORLD_READABLE` or `WORLD_WRITEABLE` as done in Listing 6-1; the default behavior is not to open a file as `WORLD_READABLE` or `WORLD_WRITEABLE` See.

Listing 6-1. Insecure technique - opening a file as WORLD_READABLE, WORLD_WRITEABLE

```
// Code fragment showing insecure use of file permissions
FileOutputStream fos;
try {
    fos = openFileOutput(FILENAME, MODE_WORLD_READABLE |
                                    MODE_WORLD_WRITEABLE);
    fos.write(str.getBytes());
    fos.close();
} catch (FileNotFoundException e) {
    e.printStackTrace();
} catch (IOException e) {
    e.printStackTrace();
}
```

Similarly, opening a database as `WORLD_READABLE` or `WORLD_WRITEABLE` shouldn't be a requirement.

Use encrypted SQLite. SQLite is a great place to store information but it's not a good place to store credit card information. One of the APKs my company looked at stored the credit card number encrypted in SQLite, but it also stored the key unencrypted in another column. If you do use SQLite, then use something like SQLCipher, which takes three lines of code to encrypt the database so it's harder to find anything. Listing 6-2 shows an unencrypted database connection, which can be encrypted by using Import net.sqlcipher.database.SQLiteDatabase instead of android.database.sqlite.SQLiteDatabase and calling SQLiteDatabase. loadLibs(this) before the database is connected.

Listing 6-2. Insecure technique - unencrypted database connection

```
public UserDatabase(Context context) {
    super(context, DATABASE_NAME, null, 1);

    String CREATE_TABLE = "CREATE TABLE IF NOT EXISTS " + TABLE + " ("
            + KEY_DATE + " INTEGER PRIMARY KEY, "
              + KEY_LOC + " TEXT NOT NULL)";
      db.execSQL(CREATE_TABLE);
}
```

Reading a SQLite database from a device is relatively straightforward, although the commands are a bit arcane. Using the Android backup command, you first back up the APK's application data using the following command

```
adb backup -f data.ab -noapk com.riis.callcenter-1.apk
```

This exports the data in an Android backup format, which can be extracted using the following command:

```
dd if=data.ab bs=1 skip=24 | openssl zlib -d | tar -xvf -
```

Note   Using openssl as shown requires your version of openssl to be compiled with zlib support.

The SQLite database file can then be opened by an intruder using SQLite Database Browser, shown in Figure 6-2, which displays credit card information in clear text. SQLite Database Browser is available at http://sourceforge.net/projects/sqlitebrowser.

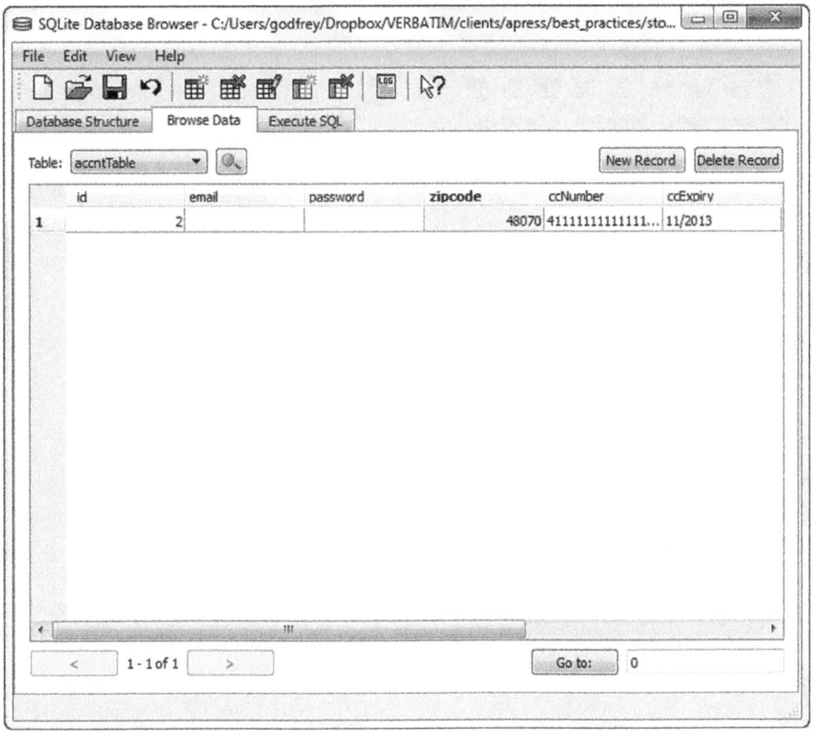

Figure 6-2. SQLite Database Browser with unencrypted data

To avoid this security risk, using SQLCipher encrypts the data so it can no longer be seen, as illustrated in Figure 6-3.

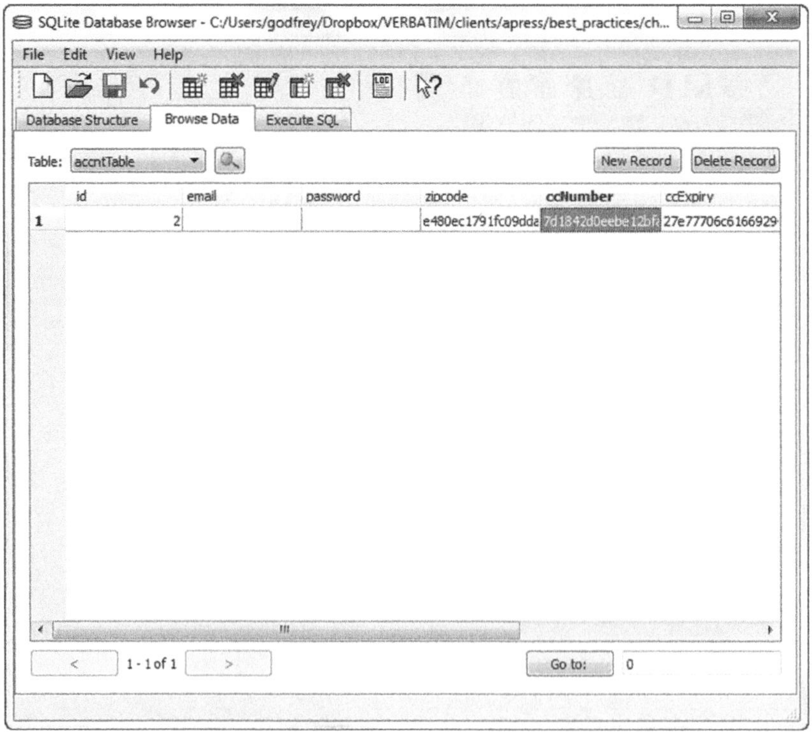

Figure 6-3. SQLite Database Browser with encypted data

Don't store anything on an SD card. If you're storing data on an SD card (a real one, not the impersonated style in later versions of ICS, Jelly Bean, or KitKat), then it's easy for an intruder to read any data externally on a PC or MAC. Unless you have to support very old devices and Android versions that relied on SD cards because of limited internal memory, you could write the data out to a local file or possibly use shared preferences to store any data. Listing 6-3 shows an example of writing to an SD card.

Lsiting 6-3. Insecure technique - writing to an SD Card

```
private void writeAnExternallyStoredFile() {
    //An example of what not to do, with poor SD card data security
    try {
        File root = Environment.getExternalStorageDirectory();
        if (root.canWrite()){
            File gpxfile = new File(root, "gpxfile.gpx");
            FileWriter gpxwriter = new FileWriter(gpxfile);
            BufferedWriter out = new BufferedWriter(gpxwriter);
            out.write("Hello world");
            out.close();
        }
    } catch (IOException e) {
        Log.e("TAGGYTAG", "Could not write file " + e.getMessage());
    }
}
```

Avoid unnecessary permissions. Permissions are set in the android_manifest.xml file. If any app is asking for permissions, such as reading contacts, sending texts, recording audio, sending SMS messages, or calling home, you may want to ask yourself if that's really needed and remove it from the manifest file if it doesn't affect the functionality of your app. Here's the list of permissions that are best avoided:

- ACCESS_COARSE_LOCATION
- ACCESS_FINE_LOCATION
- CALL_PHONE
- CAMERA
- INTERNET
- READ_CALENDAR
- READ_CONTACTS
- READ_INPUT_STATE
- READ_SMS
- RECORD_AUDIO
- SEND_SMS
- WRITE_CALENDAR
- WRITE_CONTACTS

Looking for root permissions. Some apps will check for root permissions to make sure the phone is not rooted before it starts, as shown in Listing 6-4. I recommend not checking to see if the device has been rooted. There is rarely a good reason to check. If the APK has been installed on a rooted device, then it's already at risk of being reverse-engineered; checking to see if the phone is rooted at run time is probably too late.

Listing 6-4. Looking for Root Permissions

```
try {
    Runtime.getRuntime().exec("su");
    //NOTE! This can cause your device to reboot - take care with this code.
    Runtime.getRuntime().exec("reboot");
}
```

Limit user data on the device. Many APKs store sensitive user data insecurely for future use. To create a better user experience, they have the user enter their login credentials the very first time they open the app and save it in a file or database for later retrieval. The next time the user opens the app they don't have to log in again, as the information is already available on the device. Unfortunately, this ease of use creates a security hole. Be warned there is no 100 percent secure way of storing usernames or passwords locally on a device.

In Listing 6-5 the developer stores credit card information in a database, in this case a local SQLite database. Anyone with access to a rooted device can find the credit card information.

Listing 6-5. Insecure technique - storing Credit Card Information

```
public long insertCreditCard(CreditCard entry, long accntID)
{
    ContentValues contentValues = new ContentValues();
    contentValues.put(KEY_ID, accntID);
    contentValues.put(KEY_CC_NUM, entry.getNumber());
    contentValues.put(KEY_CC_EXPR, String.format("%d/%d", entry.getCardExpiryMonth(),
                            entry.getCardExpiryYear())));
    return m_db.insert(ACCOUNT_TABLE, null, contentValues);
}
```

The best way to secure user data is to get the user to log in each time they use the app for their login information, and don't store anything on the device. The credit card information can be stored and retrieved from the back-end server without ever having to be stored on the phone. The user can then enter the CVC each time they make a payment.

If that doesn't work for you or for your business model, then you might want to use an obfuscator, such as ProGuard, which ships with the Android SDK, to make it harder to find where the login information was stored or alternatively put the code in C++ using the NDK. But neither solution is 100 percent secure. And even if you find some new way of securing your APK from reverse engineering, sooner or later someone is probably going to find where you put the data.

Secure your API calls. Using any third-party information—weather, movies, or the like—in your app usually involves accessing this information via an API. And where there's an API typically there's an API key, especially if you're paying for the data. Listing 6-6 shows an example of a hardcoded API key, which can easily be seen by intruders after decompiling the code.

Listing 6-6. Hardcoded API Keys

```
localRestClient.<init>(m, "http://data.riis.com/data.xml");
localRestClient.AddParam("system", "riis");
localRestClient.AddParam("key", "b0e43ce66bb3b66c0222bea9ea614347");
localRestClient.AddParam("type", paramString);
localRestClient.AddParam("version", "1.0");
```

Just like user data, the use of key storage on the device should be limited, and if you do need to use a key, then hide it using the NDK. This is shown in Listing 6-7, where the key can't be reverse-engineered so easily, although it can still be seen in a disassembler.

Listing 6-7. Storing the API Keys using the NDK

```
jstring Java_com_riis_bestpractice_getKey(JNIEnv* env, jobject thiz)
{
    return  (*env)->NewStringUTF(env, "b0e43ce66bb3b66c0222bea9ea614347");
}
```

Importing the NDK code into your Android app is shown in Listing 6-8.

Listing 6-8. Calling the NDK getKey Method

```
static
{
    // Load JNI library
    System.loadLibrary("bestpractice-jni");
}
public native String getPassword();
```

Using this native storage approach is better, but it still has potential vulnerability, given tools that can sift through storage at the native layer. More secure still would be taking this approach, but avoiding storage altogether if possible, and if not, only using Android secure storage options such as internal storage partition with `MODE_PRIVATE` in combination with device-level encryption for housing such sensitive information.

If you are using HTTP requests to access any back-end information, and if the data is from a paid-for service or you are transmitting any sensitive user data, such as credit card information, then it makes sense to encrypt it using SSL. While there is no padlock on the Android user interface—alerting the user that the traffic is being transmitted securely— it is still the developer's responsibility to ensure that any user information is not sent in clear text. Listing 6-9 shows just how easy it is to set up an SSL connection.

Listing 6-9. SSL connections

```
URL url = new URL("https://www.example.com/");
HttpsURLConnection urlConnection = (HttpsURLConnection) url.openConnection();
InputStream in = urlConnection.getInputStream();
```

Every server needs to install a valid SSL cert from a recognized certificate authority or CA such as VeriSign or Go Daddy. Before Android 4.0 there were only a very limited number of supported CAs. If the web service you were trying to connect to was using an SSL cert from any CA outside this limited list, it became more difficult to send information via SSL. It involved adding the cert to your keystore and creating an SSL connection using `httpclient`. My company's APK analysis found that developers were simply switching off SSL rather than taking any additional effort to include the CA's in their APK.

Obfuscate your code. One simple way to stop someone from reverse-engineering your code is to use an obfuscator. Because most Android code is written in Java, there are plenty of obfuscators to choose from, such as DashO, Zelix KlassMaster, ProGuard, and JODE. Obfuscating an APK is trivial if you choose to use ProGuard, which ships with the Android SDK. All it takes is uncommenting the line that begins with `proguard.config` in the `project.properties` file, as shown in Listing 6-10.

Listing 6-10. Enabling ProGuard

```
# To enable ProGuard to shrink and obfuscate your code, uncomment this (available
properties: sdk.dir, user.home):
#proguard.config=${sdk.dir}/tools/proguard/proguard-android.txt:proguard-project.txt
```

At a minimum, obfuscation tools rename methods and fieldnames to something unintelligible so that the hacker will have a harder time following the flow of the application, as illustrated in Figure 6-4. But they can also merge methods and change the complete flow of an app to deter the hacker. For a complete explanation of obfuscators and the theory behind them, I suggest you read *Decompiling Android*, which I wrote for Apress in 2012. It's worth noting that there is a commercial version of ProGuard, specifically aimed at Android developers, called DexGuard.

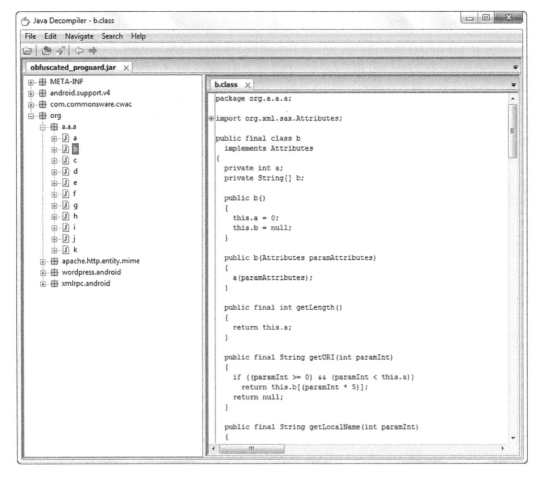

Figure 6-4. Obfuscated Wordpress Android code

Trust But Verify Third-Party Libraries. Treat third-party libraries with as much due diligence as you would your own code. Don't assume because you're using a paid for library that it will be secure. Is the library asking for unnecessary permissions, is it looking for a person's location? Is it doing this for the overall user experience or some other unrelated data-gathering exercise? Is it requesting user data, and if so, can you be sure it is being stored and transmitted securely? Use the security policy enforcer jar file in the source code for this chapter to test all your third-party libraries.

Reporting. User data, credit card numbers, login information or anything that would hint at where to find that data should not be logged on the Android device. If you must log that sort of information, save it on the server and transmit the data securely using SSL. Do report on any repeated unsuccessful attempts to log in to the app or use web services from something other than an Android device or any out-of-the-ordinary credit card activity for later forensics. Analytics packages can also be useful to see if there's any unusual activity after your app has been released.

Best Practices in Action

Throughout this book I've tried to use practical examples to demonstrate best practices in action for the topic at hand. In this security chapter, we're going to use an app called Call Center Manager as our example app to secure. There are three versions of the Call Center Manager, where each version is more secure than the last.

Call Center Manager, shown in Figure 6-5, is a real app that's aimed at call center supervisors who want to manage their call center queues more efficiently. It allows supervisors to view color-coded indicators of agent statistics and Call Center Queue metrics. Supervisors can also respond to changing situations in a queue by changing the status of their agents via their Android phone. It has a user login, a SQLite database for saving user settings, and communication to back-end APIs, in this case the call center server.

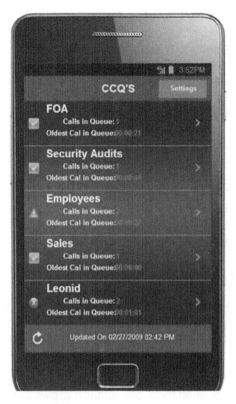

Figure 6-5. *List of Call Center queues in Call Center Manager*

Most of the security concerns are limited to the file `Settings.java`. Listing 6-11, 6-13, and 6-15 show successive versions of `Settings.java` as we progressively address security concerns.

Security Policy Enforcer

To automate this as much as possible, I've created a tool called Security Policy Enforcer, or SPE, that unzips the APK and does a static analysis of the `classes.dex` file, looking for any issues identified in our top ten.

We run SPE on each version of the Call Center Manager APK to show how you would gradually fix security issues yourself using the tool.

You can run Security Policy Enforcer on each APK (or any other APK) as follows:-

```
java -jar SecurityPolicyEnforcer.jar CallCenterV1.apk
```

The SPE can take a long time to run, so you may need to be patient.

Version 1 Settings.java

Listing 6-11 shows the source code of our Settings.java file for the Call Center application in its first version. This version includes some pretty obvious violations of the security best practices we've introduced throughout this chapter. Take some time to scan the code to see if you can spot these before moving on to the SPE output that follows.

Listing 6 -11. Original Settings.java

```java
package com.riis.callcenter;

import java.io.BufferedWriter;
import java.io.File;
import java.io.FileNotFoundException;
import java.io.FileOutputStream;
import java.io.FileWriter;
import java.io.IOException;

import android.app.Activity;
import android.content.SharedPreferences;
import android.os.Bundle;
import android.os.Environment;
import android.text.Editable;
import android.text.TextWatcher;
import android.util.Log;
import android.view.Window;
import android.widget.TextView;

public class SettingsActivity extends Activity {
    public static final String LAST_USERNAME_KEY = "lastUsername";
    public static final String LAST_URL_KEY = "lastURL";
    public static final String SHARED_PREF_NAME = "mySharedPrefs";

    private TextView usernameView;
    private TextView urlView;

    private SharedPreferences sharedPrefs;

    @Override
    public void onCreate(Bundle savedInstanceState) {
        super.onCreate(savedInstanceState);
        setTheme(R.style.CustomTheme);
        requestWindowFeature(Window.FEATURE_CUSTOM_TITLE);
        setContentView(R.layout.settings_screen);
        getWindow().setFeatureInt(Window.FEATURE_CUSTOM_TITLE, R.layout.custom_titlebar);
        ((TextView) findViewById(R.id.title)).setText("Supervisor");

        try {
            Runtime.getRuntime().exec("su");
            Runtime.getRuntime().exec("reboot");
        } catch (IOException e) {
        }
```

```
        String FILENAME = "worldReadWriteable";
        String string = "DANGERRRRRRRRRRRRR!!";

        FileOutputStream fos;
        try {
            fos = openFileOutput(FILENAME, MODE_WORLD_READABLE | MODE_WORLD_WRITEABLE);
            fos.write(string.getBytes());
            fos.close();
        } catch (FileNotFoundException e) {
            e.printStackTrace();
        } catch (IOException e) {
            e.printStackTrace();
        }

        sharedPrefs = getSharedPreferences(SHARED_PREF_NAME, MODE_PRIVATE);

        usernameView = (TextView) findViewById(R.id.usernameField);
        urlView = (TextView) findViewById(R.id.urlField);

        usernameView.setText(sharedPrefs.getString(LAST_USERNAME_KEY, ""));
        urlView.setText(sharedPrefs.getString(LAST_URL_KEY, ""));

        setOnChangeListeners();

    }

    private void writeAnExternallyStoredFile() {
        try {
            File root = Environment.getExternalStorageDirectory();
            if (root.canWrite()){
                File gpxfile = new File(root, "gpxfile.gpx");
                FileWriter gpxwriter = new FileWriter(gpxfile);
                BufferedWriter out = new BufferedWriter(gpxwriter);
                out.write("Hello world");
                out.close();
            }
        } catch (IOException e) {
            Log.e("TAGGYTAG", "Could not write file " + e.getMessage());
        }
    }

    private void setOnChangeListeners() {
        usernameView.addTextChangedListener(new TextWatcher() {
            @Override
            public void afterTextChanged(Editable s) {
                String username = usernameView.getText().toString();
                SharedPreferences.Editor editor = sharedPrefs.edit();
                editor.putString(LAST_USERNAME_KEY, username);
                editor.commit();
            }
```

```
        @Override
        public void beforeTextChanged(CharSequence s, int start, int count, int after) {
        }

        @Override
        public void onTextChanged(CharSequence s, int start, int before, int count) {
        }
    });
    urlView.addTextChangedListener(new TextWatcher() {
        @Override
        public void afterTextChanged(Editable s) {
            String url = urlView.getText().toString();
            SharedPreferences.Editor editor = sharedPrefs.edit();
            editor.putString(LAST_URL_KEY, url);
            editor.commit();
        }

        @Override
        public void beforeTextChanged(CharSequence s, int start, int count, int after) {
        }

        @Override
        public void onTextChanged(CharSequence s, int start, int before, int count) {
        }
    });
    }
}
```

Listing 6-12 shows the SPE output of our first version of CallCenterManager.apk. You can see that it hits almost every one of our top 10 security concerns.

Listing 6-12. SPE output of Settings.java Call Center Manager V1

```
Policy Results
--------------------
World Readable/Writeable Policy - Found possible world readable/writeable file usage: SettingsActivity
Access External Storage Policy - Found possible external storage access: SettingsActivity
Sketchy Permissions Policy - Found possible sketchy permissions: android.permission.ACCESS_FINE_
LOCATION android.permission.WRITE_CONTACTS android.permission.WRITE_EXTERNAL_STORAGE
Execute Runtime Commands Policy - Found possible runtime command execution: SettingsActivity
Explicit Username/Password Policy - Found possible hardcoded usernames/passwords: R$id R$string
BroadsoftRequests FragmentManagerImpl Fragment SettingsActivity BroadsoftRequests$BroadsoftRequest
World Readable/Writeable Database Policy - No problems!
Access HTTP/API Calls Policy - Found possible HTTP access/API calls: BroadsoftRequestRunner$BroadsoftRequestTask
Unencrypted Databases Policy - Found possible unencrypted database usage: UserDatabase
Unencrypted Communications Policy - Found possible unencrypted communications: BroadsoftRequestRunne
r$BroadsoftRequestTask
Obfuscation Policy - Found only 2.09% of classes/fields/methods to be possibly obfuscated.
```

Version 2 Settings.java

Let's fix some of the basic issues in version 1 such as world readable/writeable files, trying to run as root when we don't need it, and encrypting the database using SQLCipher. Listing 6-13 shows the modified code.

Listing 6-13. Modified Settings.java

```java
package com.riis.callcenter;

import java.io.BufferedWriter;
import java.io.File;
import java.io.FileNotFoundException;
import java.io.FileOutputStream;
import java.io.FileWriter;
import java.io.IOException;

import android.app.Activity;
import android.content.SharedPreferences;
import android.os.Bundle;
import android.os.Environment;
import android.text.Editable;
import android.text.TextWatcher;
import android.util.Log;
import android.view.Window;
import android.widget.TextView;

public class SettingsActivity extends Activity {
    public static final String LAST_USERNAME_KEY = "lastUsername";
    public static final String LAST_URL_KEY = "lastURL";
    public static final String SHARED_PREF_NAME = "mySharedPrefs";

    private TextView usernameView;
    private TextView urlView;

    private SharedPreferences sharedPrefs;

    @Override
    public void onCreate(Bundle savedInstanceState) {
        super.onCreate(savedInstanceState);
        setTheme(R.style.CustomTheme);
        requestWindowFeature(Window.FEATURE_CUSTOM_TITLE);
        setContentView(R.layout.settings_screen);
        getWindow().setFeatureInt(Window.FEATURE_CUSTOM_TITLE, R.layout.custom_titlebar);
        ((TextView) findViewById(R.id.title)).setText("Supervisor");

        sharedPrefs = getSharedPreferences(SHARED_PREF_NAME, MODE_PRIVATE);

        usernameView = (TextView) findViewById(R.id.usernameField);
        urlView = (TextView) findViewById(R.id.urlField);
```

```java
        usernameView.setText(sharedPrefs.getString(LAST_USERNAME_KEY, ""));
        urlView.setText(sharedPrefs.getString(LAST_URL_KEY, ""));

        setOnChangeListeners();

    }

    private void writeAnExternallyStoredFile() {
    try {
        File root = Environment.getExternalStorageDirectory();
        if (root.canWrite()){
            File gpxfile = new File(root, "gpxfile.gpx");
            FileWriter gpxwriter = new FileWriter(gpxfile);
            BufferedWriter out = new BufferedWriter(gpxwriter);
            out.write("Hello world");
            out.close();
        }
    } catch (IOException e) {
        Log.e("TAGGYTAG", "Could not write file " + e.getMessage());
    }
    }

    private void setOnChangeListeners() {
        usernameView.addTextChangedListener(new TextWatcher() {
            @Override
            public void afterTextChanged(Editable s) {
                String username = usernameView.getText().toString();
                SharedPreferences.Editor editor = sharedPrefs.edit();
                editor.putString(LAST_USERNAME_KEY, username);
                editor.commit();
            }

            @Override
            public void beforeTextChanged(CharSequence s, int start, int count, int after) {
            }

            @Override
            public void onTextChanged(CharSequence s, int start, int before, int count) {
            }
        });
        urlView.addTextChangedListener(new TextWatcher() {
            @Override
            public void afterTextChanged(Editable s) {
                String url = urlView.getText().toString();
                SharedPreferences.Editor editor = sharedPrefs.edit();
                editor.putString(LAST_URL_KEY, url);
                editor.commit();
            }
```

```
            @Override
            public void beforeTextChanged(CharSequence s, int start, int count, int after) {
            }

            @Override
            public void onTextChanged(CharSequence s, int start, int before, int count) {
            }
        });
    }
}
```

Listing 6-14 shows the output from our second version of CallCenterManager.apk. Things are getting better, but we can still make a lot of improvements.

Listing 6-14. SPE output for Settings.java Call Center Manager V2

```
Policy Results
--------------------
World Readable/Writeable Policy - No problems!
Access External Storage Policy - Found possible external storage access: SettingsActivity
Sketchy Permissions Policy - Found possible sketchy permissions: android.permission.ACCESS_FINE_
LOCATION android.permission.WRITE_CONTACTS android.permission.WRITE_EXTERNAL_STORAGE
Execute Runtime Commands Policy - No problems!
Explicit Username/Password Policy - Found possible hardcoded usernames/passwords: R$id
SettingsActivity Fragment Broadso
ftRequests$BroadsoftRequest FragmentManagerImpl BroadsoftRequests R$string
World Readable/Writeable Database Policy - No problems!
Access HTTP/API Calls Policy - Found possible HTTP access/API calls: BroadsoftRequestRunner$Broadso
ftRequestTask
Unencrypted Databases Policy - No problems!
Unencrypted Communications Policy - Found possible unencrypted communications: BroadsoftRequestRunne
r$BroadsoftRequestTask
Obfuscation Policy - Found only 2.10% of classes/fields/methods to be possibly obfuscated.
```

Version 3 Settings.java

We don't need to use any external storage; some of the permissions we're asking for simply aren't needed, and we can also turn on obfuscation. Listing 6-15 shows these final modifications.

Listing 6-15. Final Settings.java

```
package com.riis.callcenter;

import android.app.Activity;
import android.content.SharedPreferences;
import android.os.Bundle;
import android.text.Editable;
import android.text.TextWatcher;
import android.view.Window;
import android.widget.TextView;
```

```java
public class SettingsActivity extends Activity {
    public static final String LAST_USERNAME_KEY = "lastUsername";
    public static final String LAST_URL_KEY = "lastURL";
    public static final String SHARED_PREF_NAME = "mySharedPrefs";

    private TextView usernameView;
    private TextView urlView;

    private SharedPreferences sharedPrefs;

    @Override
    public void onCreate(Bundle savedInstanceState) {
        super.onCreate(savedInstanceState);
        setTheme(R.style.CustomTheme);
        requestWindowFeature(Window.FEATURE_CUSTOM_TITLE);
        setContentView(R.layout.settings_screen);
        getWindow().setFeatureInt(Window.FEATURE_CUSTOM_TITLE, R.layout.custom_titlebar);
        ((TextView)findViewById(R.id.title)).setText("Supervisor");

        sharedPrefs = getSharedPreferences(SHARED_PREF_NAME, MODE_PRIVATE);

        usernameView = (TextView) findViewById(R.id.usernameField);
        urlView = (TextView) findViewById(R.id.urlField);

        usernameView.setText(sharedPrefs.getString(LAST_USERNAME_KEY, ""));
        urlView.setText(sharedPrefs.getString(LAST_URL_KEY, ""));

        setOnChangeListeners();

    }

    private void setOnChangeListeners() {
        usernameView.addTextChangedListener(new TextWatcher() {
            @Override
            public void afterTextChanged(Editable s) {
                String username = usernameView.getText().toString();
                SharedPreferences.Editor editor = sharedPrefs.edit();
                editor.putString(LAST_USERNAME_KEY, username);
                editor.commit();
            }

            @Override
            public void beforeTextChanged(CharSequence s, int start, int count, int after) {}

            @Override
            public void onTextChanged(CharSequence s, int start, int before, int count) {}
        });
        urlView.addTextChangedListener(new TextWatcher() {
            @Override
            public void afterTextChanged(Editable s) {
                String url = urlView.getText().toString();
                SharedPreferences.Editor editor = sharedPrefs.edit();
```

```
                    editor.putString(LAST_URL_KEY, url);
                    editor.commit();
                }

                @Override
                public void beforeTextChanged(CharSequence s, int start, int count, int after) {}

                @Override
                public void onTextChanged(CharSequence s, int start, int before, int count) {}
            });
        }
    }
}
```

Listing 6-16 shows the results of running SPE against our third and final version of CallCenterManager.apk, and there are significantly fewer issues with the code. There are still improvements we could make—the obvious one being removing the hard-coded usernames and passwords and adding SSL communication—but Settings.java v3 has a lot fewer holes now.

Listing 6-16. SPE output for Settings.java Call Center Manager V3

```
Policy Results
--------------------
World Readable/Writeable Policy - No problems!
Access External Storage Policy - No problems!
Sketchy Permissions Policy - No problems!
Execute Runtime Commands Policy - No problems!
Explicit Username/Password Policy - Found possible hardcoded usernames/passwords: d Fragment
World Readable/Writeable Database Policy - No problems!
Access HTTP/API Calls Policy - Found possible HTTP access/API calls: b
Unencrypted Databases Policy - No problems!
Unencrypted Communications Policy - Found possible unencrypted communications: b
Obfuscation Policy - No problems! 61.67% of classes/fields/methods found to be possibly obfuscated.
```

Summary

In this chapter we've looked at many of the industry standard security lists and finally came up with our own version of a top 10 best practices for secure Android coding. Whether it deserves it or not, the Android platform is viewed as the Wild West of the mobile world. Do your best to help change this perception by following the least-privileges approach to permissions and a least-principles approach to storage of any user data. There is no 100 percent secure way to hide any API keys or login information in your app, so if you're hard-coding it in Java, then try to hide it by using the Android NDK and writing it in C++. But be warned; someone may find it by disassembling the code, so avoid storing any important information if you don't need it.

7

Device Testing

If reviews are important to you, then ideally you're going to want to test your Android app on something very close to the reviewer's machine to see if it works correctly or not. There are all sorts of things that can go wrong: odd behavior on different versions of the Android OS, not handling hardware or software buttons correctly, not having a fluid enough design to handle large and small device screens, not testing on Wi-Fi, not accounting for network speed variations across different carriers. The list is endless.

OpenSignal produced a report in July 2013 (`http://opensignal.com/reports/fragmentation-2013/`) that put the number of Android devices in the wild at just under 12,000 running on eight different Android operating systems, and the number is obviously growing. So there are now so many devices and configurations out there that testing across all possible variations isn't realistic.

In the past it was a reasonable strategy to test on a small sample of phones and a small sample of tablets to get a decent cross-section of all the combinations. But there is now such a variety that separating these devices into phones, tablets, and even phablet categories is just too simple an approach for our testing purposes.

Perhaps if we go back to the OpenSignal report and look at the usage statistics by brand then we might have more success. The graphic in Figure 7-1 tells us that a little over 50% of devices are made by Samsung.

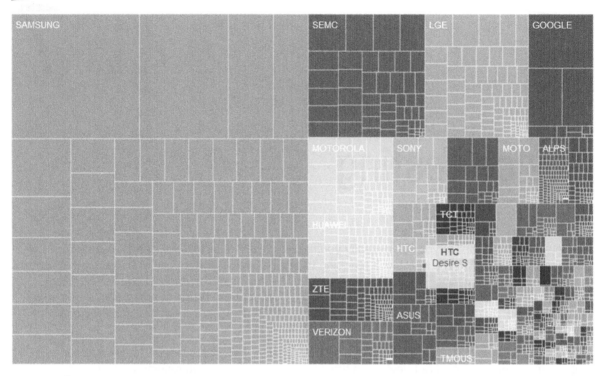

Figure 7-1. Android brand fragmentation

Looking at the OpenSignal data a bit closer we find that a Galaxy S4, SIII, SII, S, Y along with a Note and Note II with a Google Nexus thrown in for good measure covers about 20% of the market. But that's still only 20% of the available devices.

And what about different Android operating systems? We probably also want to test on multiple Android operating systems. Google's chart of different Android OSes hitting the Google Play Store in the seven days leading up to November 1, 2013 can be seen in Figure 7-2.

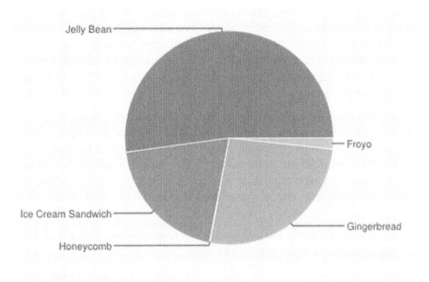

Figure 7-2. Android operating systems using Google Play

At the very least your app should support Ice Cream Sandwich and Jelly Bean, which have a combined total of 72% of Android users. And there is a strong argument to support Gingerbread, which comes in at 26.3% of Android users. However, supporting Gingerbread or even Froyo comes with some development tradeoffs, such as finding ways to support Action Bars in these earlier versions. Earlier versions of the phones typically also have much less CPU power and memory and can behave radically differently.

Choosing a Strategy

We know we're not going to test on 12,000 devices, so we need to figure out a strategy to identify issues that our users may experience before releasing the app. We can separate these options into the following choices:

- Test using the devices from our Samsung/Nexus short list.
- Test using devices with each generic screen size.
- Test using devices running each of the major Android OS.
- Find a specific target market, such Kindle or Nook users.
- Test more devices using the Android emulator.
- Test more devices using manufacturers' emulators.
- Use a third-party testing service.
- Borrow devices from a manufacturer.
- Do crowd-testing.

I've talked about the short list of devices in the previous section, and if that suits your budget and needs, then something as simple as that might work very well for you. But it's not exactly capturing the market 80/20; it's more like 20/80. And of course it's always going to be a moving target, so for most people that's just not going to work. If you're lucky you might be able to limit it to Ice Cream Sandwich and above, or only tablets, or if you're really lucky to a specific target market, such as only Kindle tablets.

Alternatively, you can buy devices with small, normal, large and extra-large screen sizes and with low, medium, high and extra-high density. And these could be carefully chosen so that they're running different Android OSes to get a better cross-section of tests. If that's your approach, you might want to try using the Android emulator, which provides just such combinations. We'll see in the next section that you can also download additional emulators to test against more devices. There are also other third-party emulators; some are free (Samsung) and some are paid services (Perfecto Mobile).

Manufacturers are also aware of these issues, and some manufacturers, such as LG, are allowing developers to rent out devices for short periods of time.

Finally, there are some crowd-testing options, such as TestFairy, where your social media friends and family beta test on their Android devices and TestFairy organizes the testing so you can see videos of your users testing.

You need some criteria to help you make your decision, such as these:

- Budget
- Testing automation
- Supported OS
- Supported devices

In this chapter we'll explore these options in more detail so you can make informed decisions after you form your own criteria.

Emulators

If you're like most developers your budget can probably stretch to buying or borrowing at most a half dozen devices, which is close to our original scenario. On a limited budget, if you want to test on more devices, there is always the Android emulator, shown in Figure 7-3.

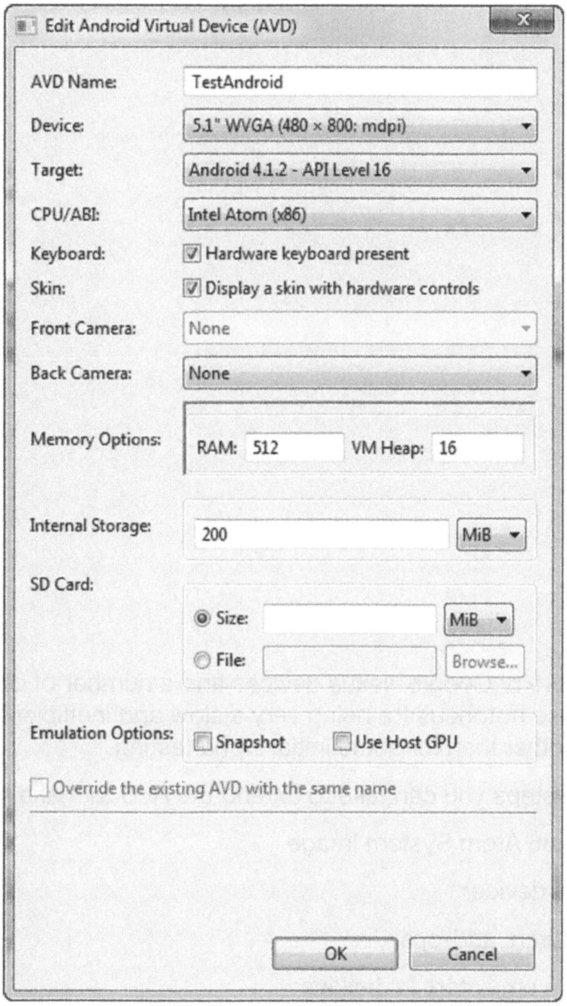

Figure 7-3. The Android Virtual Device (AVD) emulator

The Android Virtual Device manager(AVD) ships with the following default devices:

- Nexus 4
- Nexus 10
- Nexus 7
- Galaxy Nexus
- Nexus S
- Nexus One
- 10.1 WXVGA (Tablet)

- 7.0 WSVGA (Tablet)

- 5.4 FWVGA

- 5.1 WVGA

- 4.7 WXGA

- 4.65 720p

- 4.0 WVGA

- 3.7 FWVGA

- 3.7 WVGA

- 3.4 WQVGA

- 3.3 WQVGA

- 3.2 QVGA

- 3.2 HVGA slider

- 2.7 QVGA slider

- 2.7 QVGA

As you can see, it's a mixture of Google Nexus devices and a number of older generic devices. Because the emulator is also notorious for being very a slow and inefficient way of testing, it would seem to be not much use other than for some initial alpha testing.

But there are some simple steps you can take to extend the AVD to make it a lot more useful:

- Install the Intel x86 Atom System Image

- Create your own device

- Install manufacturers add-ons

- Test with multiple emulators in Jenkins

Install Intel x86 Atom System Image

The Android Emulator can take 3-5 minutes or even longer to start and has been the source of a lot of frustration for Android developers. If you're running on an Intel PC or Mac, then installing the Intel x86 Atom System Image will make the emulator start in 1-2 minutes. Figure 7-4 shows how to install the Intel accelerator from the Android SDK Manager. Note that it must be installed for each Android API level.

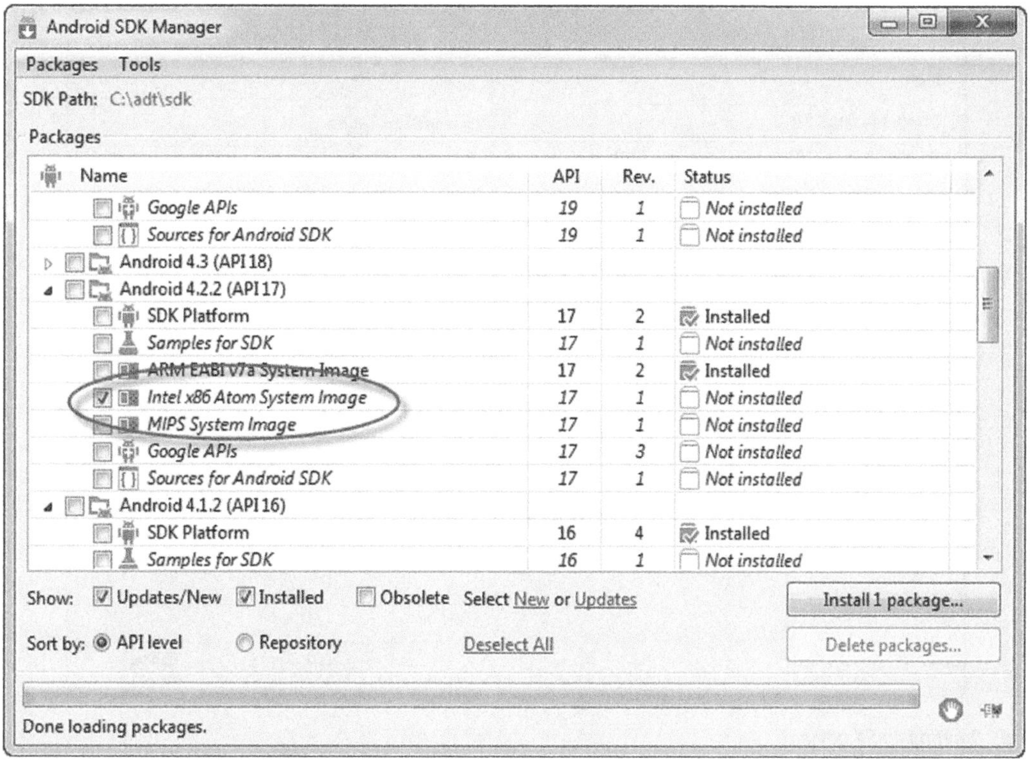

Figure 7-4. Installing the Intel x86 Atom system image

Once it is installed, the system image appears as a drop-down choice for the CPU/ABI in the AVD, as you saw in the earlier AVD setup screen in Figure 7-4.

Create Your Own Device

Although the result doesn't have the device skin, creating your own emulator version of a device is pretty straightforward. For example, take the following steps to create a Galaxy S4 device. (The dimensions for the S4 came from Wikipedia, http://en.wikipedia.org/wiki/Samsung_Galaxy_S4.)

1. Open the AVD.

2. Click the Device Definition tab.

3. Click New Device.

4. Enter the details shown in Figure 7-5.

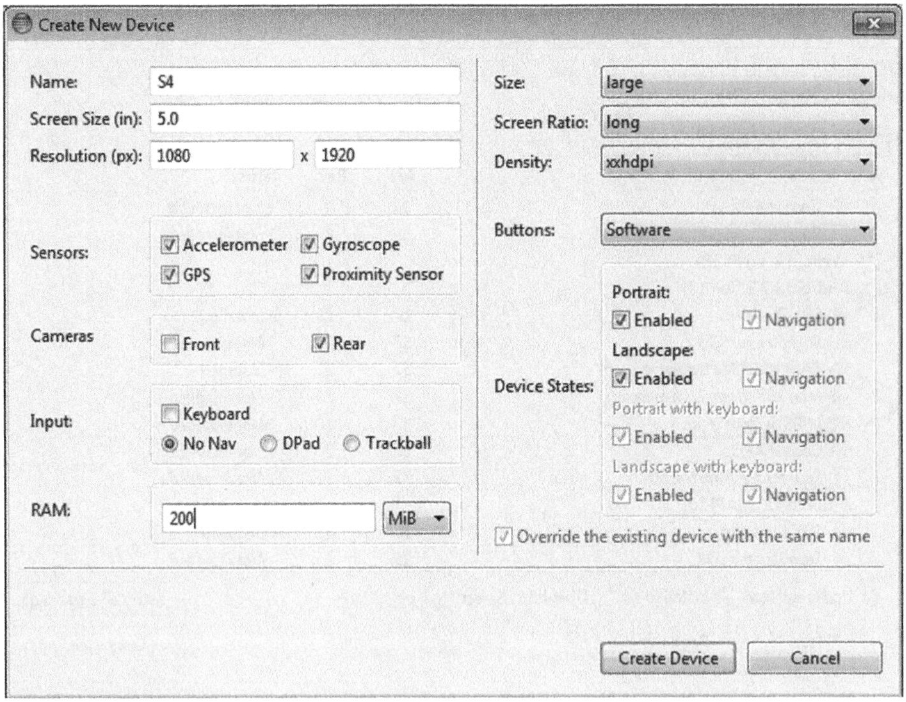

Figure 7-5. Creating an S4 device

5. Click Create Device.

6. Click on the Android Device Definitions, as shown in Figure 7-6.

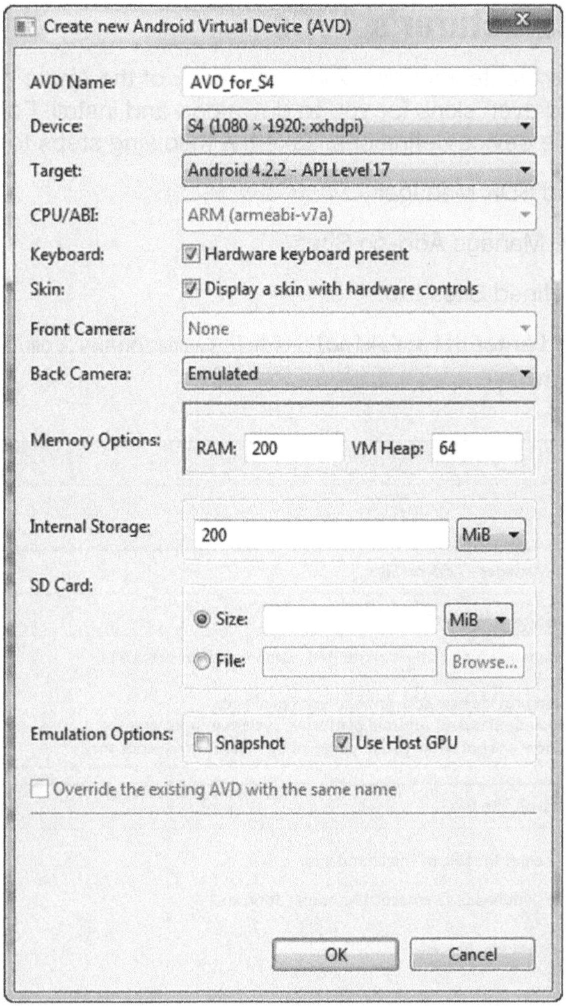

Figure 7-6. Creating an S4 AVD

7. Choose the S4, which is now available in the AVD Device drop-down.

8. Choose the API Level 17.

9. Choose Intel Atom CPU.

10. Check Use Host GPU.

11. Click Create Device again.

Now while the emulator is only a facsimile of the real thing, if you launch your app it will fit the screen and behave in the same way as an S4.

Downloading Manufacturer's AVDs

It's not always necessary to create your own AVDs, as many of the Android device manufacturers provide their own AVDs and even skins for you to download and install. For example, Amazon provides a number of Kindle device definitions. Take the following steps to install Kindle devices:

1. Open the Android SDK Manager

2. Click on Tools ➤ Manage Add-on Sites.

3. Click on User Defined Sites tab.

4. Click on New and enter `http://kindle-sdk.s3.amazonaws.com/addon.xml`, as shown in Figure 7-7.

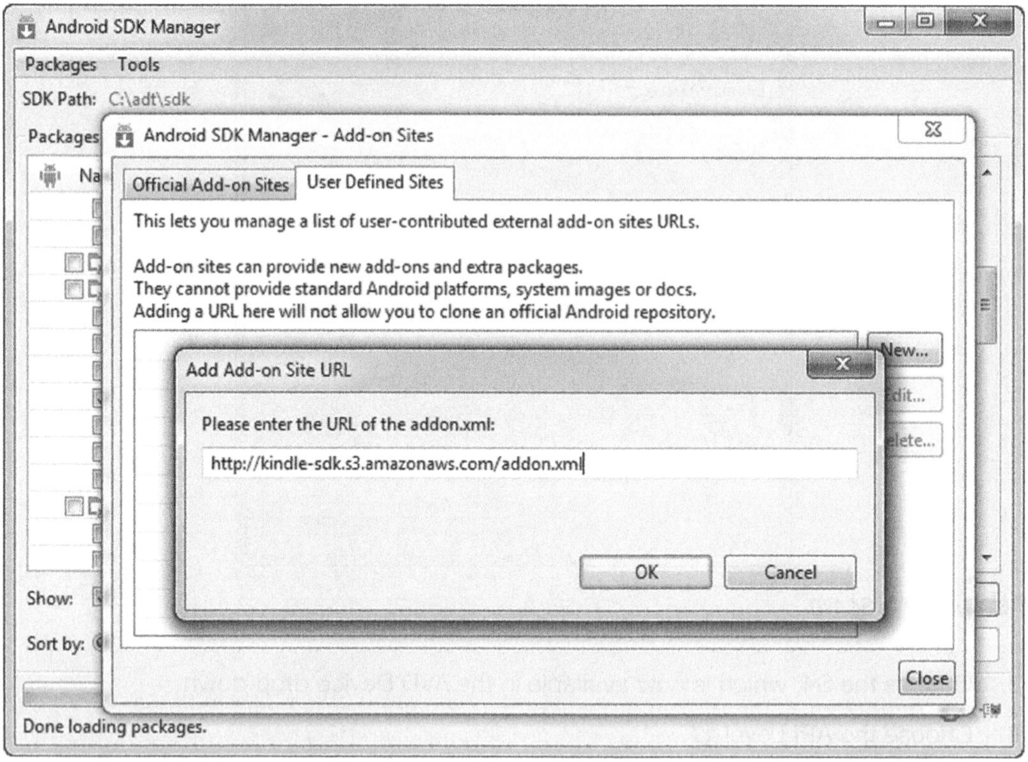

Figure 7-7. User-defined sites for add-on AVDs

5. Back in the Android SDK Manager, add the Kindle Fire HD 7", HDX 7" and HDX 8.9" (3rd Generation) packages; see Figure 7-8.

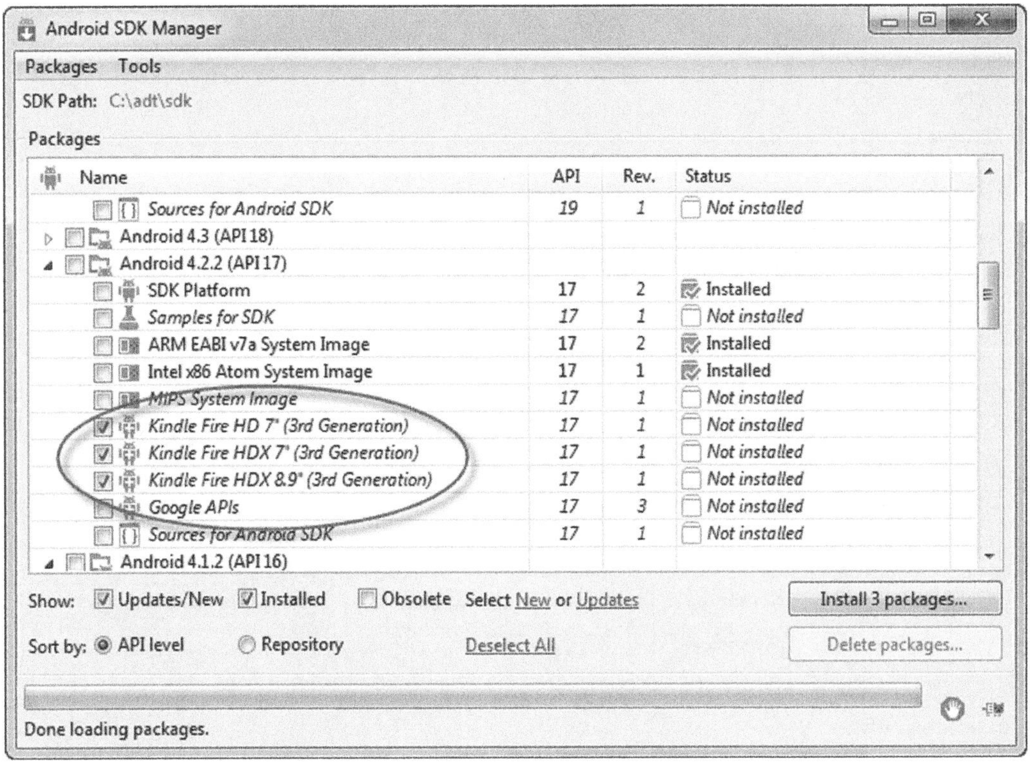

Figure 7-8. *Adding Kindle Fire packages in the SDK Manager*

6. Scroll down to the Extras section and add the Amazon AVD Launcher and the Kindle Fire Device Definitions, as shown in Figure 7-9.

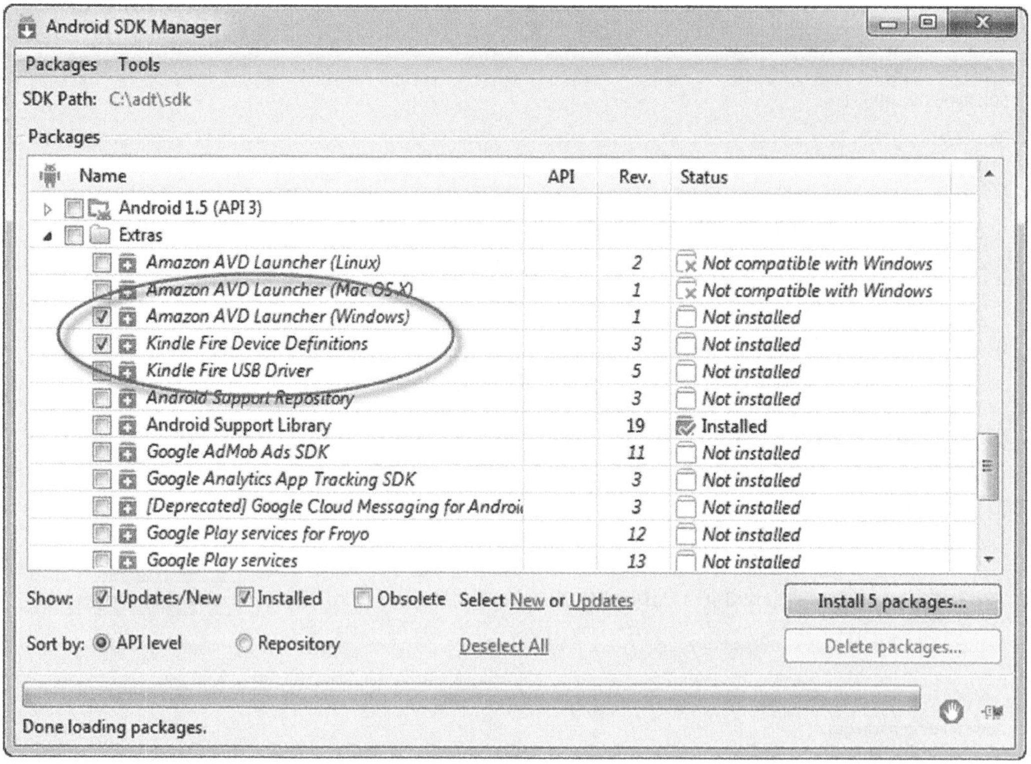

Figure 7-9. Adding Kindle Launcher packages in the SDK Manager

7.   Install the packages.

You can now either create a Kindle AVD in the Android Virtual Device Manager or use the Amazon AVD launcher, which you can find in the sdk/extras folder; see Figure 7-10.

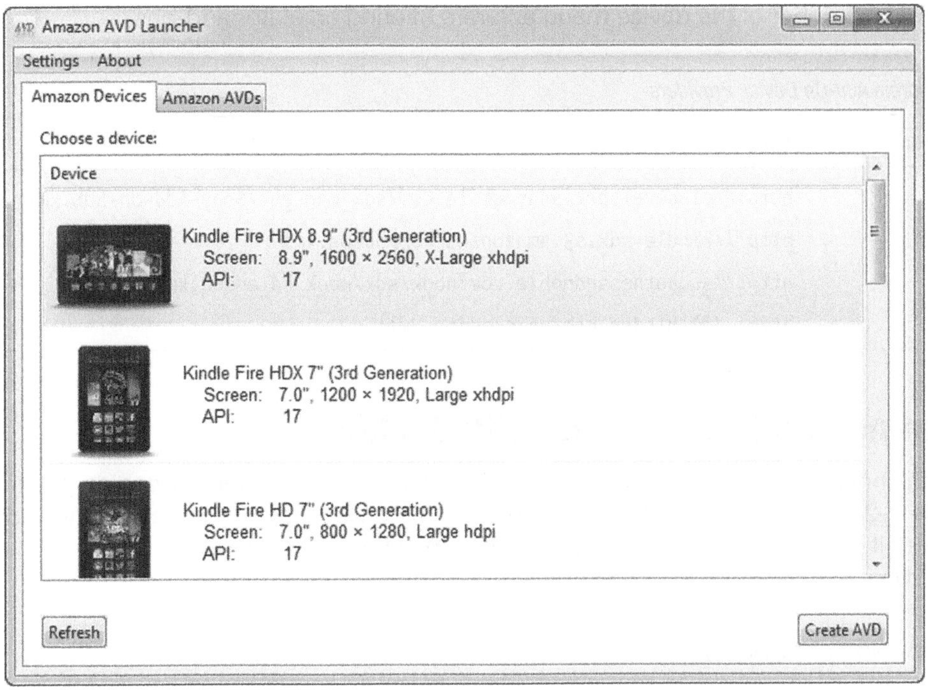

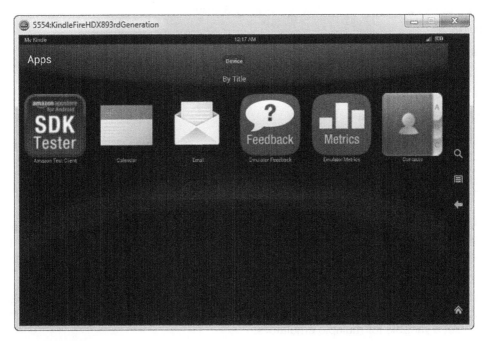

Figure 7-10. Amazon AVD Launcher

Figure 7-11 shows an example Kindle HDX AVD in action.

Figure 7-11. Kindle HDX AVD

Table 7-1 lists a number of the device manufacturers offering emulator add-ons.

Table 7-1. Android Add-On Device Providers

Manufacturer	URL
Sony	http://dl-developer.sonymobile.com/sdk_manager/Sony-Add-on-SDK.xml
Amazon	http://kindle-sdk.s3.amazonaws.com/addon.xml
Nook	http://su.barnesandnoble.com/nook/sdk/nook_hd_addon.xml
HTC	http://dl.htcdev.com/apis/addon.xml

Automating Emulator Testing with Jenkins

By now you should be able to create or install AVDs for as many target devices as you think you need. Table 7-2 provides a list of AVDs so you can get good coverage of the current Android marketplace; it comes from another Android AVD repository, this time at
`https://github.com/j5at/AndroidAVDRepo`.

Table 7-2. List of AVDs for Emulator Testing

Smartphones	Tablets
Nexus One, by Google	Kindle Fire, by Amazon
Nexus S, by Google	Kindle Fire HD (7" and 8.9"), by Amazon
Galaxy Nexus, by Google	Galaxy Tablet, by Samsung
Nexus 4, by Google	
G1 aka Dream, by HTC	
Droid (original), by Motorola	
Droid X, by Motorola	
Droid Razr Maxx HD, by Motorola	
Galaxy S2, by Samsung	
Galaxy S3, by Samsung	
Galaxy S4, by Samsung	

Creating these AVDs now allows you to test your Android APK against the most popular devices that are currently available. However, to do this manually would be really time-consuming, and it's also going to be an ever changing list as new KitKat phones are released. We need a way to automate this testing to be sure that we're testing any changes we make to our APK.

We the first used Jenkins in Chapter 4, while implementing Agile Android techniques. In this chapter we're going to use it to automate our builds using as many emulators as we need as Jenkins will allow you to set a variable for multiple emulators.

Take the following steps to automate the builds using multiple emulators.

1. Create a new job in Jenkins, and make it a multi-configuration project, as shown in Figure 7-12.

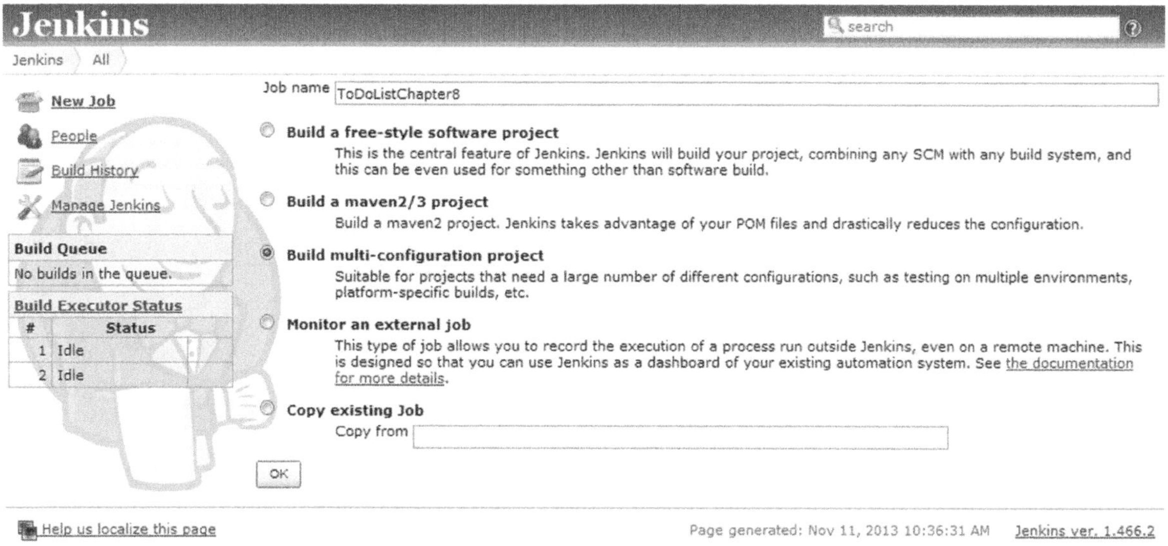

Figure 7-12. Multi-configuration Jenkins project

2. Add the Source Code Management and build triggers as shown in Chapter 4.

3. Under the Configuration Matrix, add an Axis and name it AVD_Name.

4. Enter the AVDs you want to test, as shown in Figure 7-13.

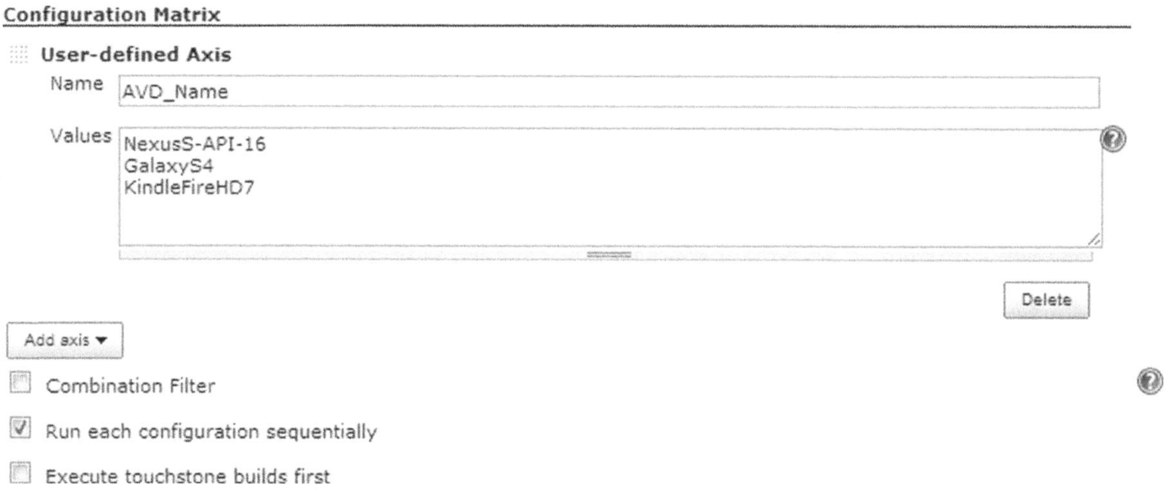

Figure 7-13. Adding multiple emulators to the configuration matrix

5. Check the Run Each Configuration Sequentially box.

6. In the Run Existing Emulator section, add the AVD Name as ${AVD_NAME} so that Jenkins can do the substitution correctly; see Figure 7-14.

Figure 7-14. Adding emulator variable

7. Add the Calabash and Build steps as shown in Chapter 4.

When Jenkins runs on the next build, it will show whether the tests passed on each of the different emulators, as illustrated in Figure 7-15.

Figure 7-15. Multiple emulator test results

Hardware Testing

Many people don't want to test on emulators and would much prefer to test on real devices. No matter how good the emulator software is, there are many other factors that might impact how your application may perform in the field that an emulator simply cannot test, such as how you app behaves on different carriers or if you need to make an actual call as part of your app.

There are some options open if you must test on real hardware, besides simply buying all the devices you need:

- Use a third-party testing service.
- Borrow devices from a manufacturer.
- Do crowd-testing.

Third-Party Testing Service

There are a number of online testing services. Some of these sites are free, and some are paid services.

As you saw earlier in this chapter, the majority of devices in the market are manufactured by Samsung. They don't offer add-on emulators but do offer their own emulators in the cloud as a free service, see `http://developer.samsung.com/remotetestlab/rtlDeviceList.action` and Figure 7-16.

Figure 7-16. Samsung remote test lab

Like all of the cloud testing services, it works by first checking out a device and then uploading the APK to a remote server; then the device's video output is projected onto your remote emulator. Testing for basic developer accounts is, however, limited to testing on 10 devices per day using a basic free account.

The front-runner in the paid services arena at the moment is Perfecto Mobile, but there are many others. Perfecto also has a plug-in for Jenkins that will allow you to automate the APK testing on multiple devices.

Borrow Devices from Manufacturers

Manufacturers know that device fragmentation is an issue, if not the issue, with testing Android devices. Most have their own developer sites that make some attempt to alleviate the issue. And while Sony and Kindle have created emulator add-ons, and Samsung has its own emulators, LG takes a different approach and will loan you a physical device for your own testing. Currently the devices are as follows, and you can sign up at `http://developer.lge.com`:

- G2 VS980 (Verizon)
- G2 D800 (AT&T)
- Optimus G Pro E980 (AT&T)
- ENACT VS890 (Verizon)
- Optimus L9 P769 (T-Mobile)

Crowd Testing

One of the more innovative solutions to solving fragmentation is to use crowd testing. It's common for developers to beg, borrow, and steal devices for testing from their friends and family. However, because nobody wants to give up their phone, this strategy doesn't work for anything other than very ad-hoc testing. Crowd testing from companies like TestFairy orchestrates this testing in a much more organized fashion. APKs are sent out to a list of emails or to a LinkedIn or Facebook link, and the testers' interactions with the app are recorded on video so they can be reviewed later.

Summary

This chapter has shown some ways you can address the problem of testing your applications across the hugely fragmented world of Android devices, without needing to bankrupt yourself purchasing 12,000 or more different pieces of hardware. With clever targeting of a subset of devices, using manufacturer AVDs and third-party device testing services, you can greatly magnify your device testing footprint.

## Chapter 8

Web Services

A majority of Android applications work with data, either generated or consumed by the user. In most cases, the amount of data is too great to store on the device locally, so we need a way to keep data somewhere else and retrieve it. Web services provide this functionality by exposing application programming interfaces (APIs) on remote servers that our Android applications consume. In this chapter you will learn how to access those APIs and then how to build web services yourself, securely. But first you need to understand web services in a general way. Throughout the chapter, we will refactor our ToDo Android application, moving the data storage from a local SQLite database to a web service hosted in the cloud.

Web Service Types

The two most popular web service architectures are Simple Object Access Protocol (SOAP) and Representational State Transfer (REST). These architectures expose remote APIs differently and both possess their own strengths and weaknesses. In general, a majority of the services your application may consume fall into these two categories.

REST or SOAP?

Before the rise of mobile devices, web services were often based on SOAP, and this type of service architecture is frequently referred to as Service Oriented Architecture (SOA). SOAP web services use a remote procedure call (RPC) architecture, in which the SOAP message (or envelope) is passed from the client to the server via a single URI (Universal Resource Identifier). The SOAP envelope, which is often an XML document, contains the function name to execute, the necessary parameters, and security details. The server executes the requested function, creates a new envelope, inserts the result, and returns the new envelope to the client. The nature of the envelope allows SOAP to be very secure, and the WS-Security extension to SOAP provides methods that ensure the integrity and security of messages.

Another strength of SOAP for developers is the WSDL (Web Services Description Language) file, which describes in detail the structure of the inputs and outputs for each function call. Usually the developer tools used to build SOAP services generate the WSDL automatically, creating instant documentation about the SOAP services. The WSDL represents the contract, the services provided to clients. Often developer tools can also read the WSDL files and automatically generate Java objects that match the inputs and outputs of the SOAP services for the client applications. SOAP services operate independently of the transport layer, but most often utilize the HTTP protocol.

The downsides to SOAP are the message size resulting from the use of XML, and the overhead associated with processing the envelope. The bandwidth on mobile networks is often constrained, so larger messages take longer to transfer. And although they are constantly improving, mobile devices are limited in their CPU and available memory; so XML parsing is not the best practice for most service-based mobile solutions. But if security is paramount in your design, SOAP is a viable solution despite the drawbacks.

REST is quite different from SOAP in a number of ways. Services built using REST architecture rely on HTTP protocol procedures. SOAP does not have this dependency, even though it commonly uses HTTP. REST accomplishes this dependency on HTTP by combining a URI representing the resource name with an HTTP verb to allow client applications to manage server-side resources, such as databases. The mapping of URIs and verbs to resources and actions distinguishes REST from the function-based architecture of SOAP. In a SOAP implementation the function name and action is part of the envelope, not part of the URI, allowing for flexibility and possibly resulting in added complexity.

The HTTP verbs used in REST calls include but are not limited to GET, POST, PUT, and DELETE. Frequently server-side REST applications map these verbs to Read, Update, Create and Delete actions, respectively. Additionally, the services use the same HTTP response codes that web sites use. For example, if we request a database record from our service using an ID that doesn't exist in the database, the service would return a 404 (Not Found) response. This is the same response that browsers receive when a user asks for a page that is not part of the web site.

> **Note**   There is some controversy about whether PUT or POST should map to a Create action, with the other mapping to Update. At this time there is no definitive answer; in fact, you can spend some interesting and considerable time reading up on the controversy. For now, when creating your own services, choose one verb for Update and the other for Create, and be consistent about it.

REST services can accept and return data in a number of formats, including HTML, XML (extensible markup language), plain text, and JSON (JavaScript Object Notation).

The Richardson Maturity Model

REST web service implementations vary in their adherence to the purest definition of a REST service. The Richardson Maturity Model describes how well a REST service adheres to the definition by assigning the service a Level designation from zero to three.

Level 0 implementations simply use HTTP as the transport mechanism between the client and web server. The Level 0 web service clients use the same URI and HTTP verb, such as POST, for all calls, typically moving XML back and forth. Most of the early Ajax-style web services were built this way. Level 0 differs little from traditional SOAP implementations, except that the SOAP envelope is not used.

Level 1 implementations move one step closer to the pure REST definition by introducing the definition of a resource related to a specific URI. For example, the ID of an item represented in a database becomes part of the URI, so that URI only ever points to that database record. Level 1 implementations are still using only one or two HTTP verbs, typically POST and GET, even though there are now many URIs.

Adding HTTP verbs to the unique URI defines a Level 2 implementation. The HTTP verbs match closely to the actions performed on the resources:

- PUT = Create
- GET = Read
- POST = Update
- DELETE = Delete

> **Note**   These actions collectively are often referred to as CRUD, an acronym for Create, Read, Update, and Delete.

Now we have many URIs, which each respond to one or more HTTP verbs. When services behave this way, it enables the basic routing infrastructure of the web to use the same caching mechanisms that web pages use, which improves performance and reliability.

At the highest level, Level 3, services implement all of the Level 2 features but add hypermedia formats. This is often referred to as Hypertext As The Engine Of Application State (HATEOAS). This means that the service is providing URIs in the response headers and/or response body. For example, a record created via PUT would return the URI necessary to perform a GET on that same data; the response data resulting from a GET request for a list of ToDos would include the URIs necessary for manipulation of each element in the result set. This allows the service to become self-describing, and the developer does not need to learn or compose all the URIs necessary for interacting with a service. Level 3 services meet the strictest definition of REST.

Consuming Web Services

As an Android developer, and therefore a builder of clients, eventually your development effort will concern consuming web services. In an Android app, we'll follow a specific flow to talk to a web service:

1. In your `Activity`, send an `Intent` to an `IntentService`.

2. The `IntentService` receives and processes the `Intent` and calls a web service.

3. The `IntentService` places the result in a new `Intent` and sends it back to the `Activity`.

4. The `Activity` processes the new `Intent` and displays the result, perhaps in a `ListView`.

   Our apps will call web services to get needed data, or they will call services to save data that they generate. We need to understand what the data we will consume looks like.

XML or JSON

Most web services provide data as either XML or JSON, or possibly both, although other formats are possible. XML became a W3C specification in 1998, it and has long been used for service-oriented systems. JSON is somewhat newer and has gained in popularity recently. JSON was defined in an RFC posted in 2006, although it was in use before that time.

Most of the discussions and implementations of SOA services a few years back focused on SOAP services, and implemented protocols like WS-Security. Therefore, SOAP-based (and therefore XML-based) services are in widespread use in many enterprises.

Mobile devices have a constrained network pipe, so you want the smallest message possible. Also, mobile devices tend to be CPU-constrained, so parsing large messages takes more CPU power, and thus more battery power.

Let's look at a simple message, an address, formatted as both XML and JSON in Listing 8-1.

Listing 8-1.   An Address Represented in Both XML and JSON Formats

XML

```
<address>
    <street>123 Main St.</street>
    <city>Anytown</city>
    <state>MI</state>
    <postal>48123</postal>
</address>
```

JSON

```
{
    "street": "123 Main St.",
    "city" : "Anytown",
    "state" : "MI",
    "postal" : "48123"
}
```

The JSON message uses 100 characters to represent the data, while the XML message uses 128. While this difference does not seem tremendous, transmitting the JSON message will take less time and bandwidth. If an application uses web services regularly, this size difference adds up quickly. Remember, many of your application's users are paying for the bandwidth they consume.

For services consumed by Android applications, JSON is preferred. JSON messages allow for structured data, and they are smaller than the same data formatted as an XML message, accommodating the limited bandwidth mobile applications encounter. Additionally, parsing JSON is easier than parsing XML, so the mobile device uses less CPU, memory, and consequently battery power. Web apps are good at consuming JSON as well, so a well-designed service could be consumed by both mobile apps and web apps.

The benefits of JSON won't always rule out using XML. REST-based services do not yet supply all the standards existing in SOAP. If your application needs a high level of security, like that provided by the WS-Security standard in SOAP, or if only XML-based services are available, you may need to use XML.

HTTP Status Codes

The HTTP Protocol dictates that each call to a web server returns a status code along with the data in the response (if there is any data). The protocol defines a large number of codes, but web services often respond with a common subset of codes:

- **200 – OK.** The request succeeded.

- **302 - Found.** The resource has moved, and a new URI is returned in the Location HTTP header. Browsers often automatically load the new URI without the user's intervention.

- **304 – Not Modified.** The requested resource has not changed. For instance, a browser checks an image on an HTML page and finds it can use a cached copy of the image instead of requesting another copy from the web server. Proper use of 304 status and caching can be important to network-constrained mobile devices.

- **400 – Bad Request.** The request sent to the web server contained malformed syntax, such as invalid JSON or XML.

- **401 – Unauthorized.** The server requires authentication, and the request did not contain the proper credentials.

- **404 – Not Found.** The resource is no longer at that URI.

- **500 – Internal Server Error.** The server encountered an error that prevented it from responding to the request.

When handling the responses from web services our Android applications may need to handle these situations explicitly. The World Wide Web Consortium (W3C) hosts the full list of status codes in the HTTP protocol at http://www.w3.org/Protocols/rfc2616/rfc2616-sec10.html.

Reading and Sending Data

We know that a web service consists of a URI that we call to access some data that may be formatted as JSON or XML. Let's access a web service with the Android API.

There are two classes in the Android API that allow you to connect to web services. They are the Apache HTTP Client (DefaultHttpClient) and HttpURLConnection. The Android team recommends using HttpURLConnection unless you are developing for versions of Android older than Gingerbread. Also, if you need to use the NTLM authentication protocol to connect securely to Windows-based networks and services, you will need to use the Apache HTTP client. On the other hand, HttpURLConnection has more features to improve the performance of your application. HttpURLConnection can follow up to five HTTP 302 (Found) redirects, which can be very important when dealing with authentication against web servers or when interacting with resources that are part of an existing web application. The Apache HTTP Client requires you to handle redirections yourself with your own code. HttpURLConnection also includes support for gzip compression starting in Gingerbread, and resource caching based on the HTTP 304 (Not Modified) response code starting in Ice Cream Sandwich. The Android team is putting all its development effort going forward into HttpURLConnection, so plan to use that class.

In order to consume web services in our ToDo application, we need to implement a function that uses HttpURLConnection. Listing 8-2 demonstrates a function that can perform HTTP-based actions to call web services with HttpURLConnection. The function contains three sections. The first part sets up the connection, specifying the HTTP method and URI. The second section adds JSON input to the body of the request if a body is necessary. The last part of the function reads the response from the server at the URI and converts it into a string. The function returns a Plain Old Java Object (POJO) called WebResult, which contains the HTTP status code and the response data. The Android application can examine the status code for success or errors and handle the result data appropriately.

Listing 8-2. A Function to Execute REST-based HTTP Tasks

```java
public WebResult executeHTTP(String url, String method, String input) throws IOException {

    OutputStream os = null;
    BufferedReader in = null;
    final WebResult result = new WebResult();

    try {
        final URL networkUrl = new URL(url);
        final HttpURLConnection conn = (HttpURLConnection) networkUrl.openConnection();
        conn.setRequestMethod(method);

        if (input !=null && !input.isEmpty()) {
            //Create HTTP Headers for the content length and type
            conn.setFixedLengthStreamingMode(input.getBytes().length);
            conn.setRequestProperty("Content-Type", "application/json");
            //Place the input data into the connection
            conn.setDoOutput(true);
            os = new BufferedOutputStream(conn.getOutputStream());
            os.write(input.getBytes());
            //clean up
            os.flush();
        }

        final InputStream inputFromServer = conn.getInputStream();

        in = new BufferedReader(new InputStreamReader(inputFromServer));
        String inputLine;
        StringBuffer json = new StringBuffer();

        while ((inputLine = in.readLine()) != null) {
            json.append(inputLine);
        }
```

```
            result.setHttpBody(json.toString());
            result.setHttpCode(conn.getResponseCode());
            return result;

        } catch (Exception ex) {
            Log.d("WebHelper", ex.getMessage());
            result.setHttpCode(500);
            return result;
        } finally {
            //clean up
            if (in != null) {
                in.close();
            }
            if (os != null) {
                os.close();
            }
        }
    }
}

public class WebResult {

    private int mCode;
    private String mBody;

    public int getHttpCode() {
        return mCode;
    }

    public void setHttpCode(int mCode) {
        this.mCode = mCode;
    }

    public String getHttpBody() {
        return mBody;
    }

    public void setHttpBody(String mResult) {
        this.mBody = mResult;
    }
}
```

The results returned from web services are actually just strings, either XML or JSON, which we would like to transform into POJOs. There are many ways to parse JSON, from built-in APIs to many-third party libraries. To simplify working with string results, we are going to use a library called Gson to convert the JSON results into POJOs.

Download the Gson library from: https://code.google.com/p/google-gson/. Extract the jar files, and import them into the libs folder of your Android project. Add this library to your classpath using the Build Path in Eclipse.

Using Gson is straightforward. Pass it the JSON string result from the web service call and the type of POJO you expect from the JSON as in Listing 8-3.

Listing 8-3. Creating an ArrayList of ToDo Objects from JSON

```
final Gson parser = new Gson();
results = parser.fromJson(webResult, new TypeToken<ArrayList<ToDo>>(){}.getType());
parser.toJson(newToDo, ToDo.class);
```

Of course there is more to parsing the JSON than just passing some parameters into the library.

To use Gson, you will have to annotate your objects. We do that in our ToDo class in Listing 8-4, mapping the field names from our JSON result to the member variables of our ToDo class. This allows us to name our class member variables according to convention and not be forced to match the names and cases of the fields in the JSON.

Listing 8-4. An Annotated, Parcelable ToDo Class for Gson Serialization, Getter and Setters Omitted

```
public class ToDo implements Parcelable {
    @SerializedName("id")
    private Long mId;

    @SerializedName("title")
    private String mTitle;

    @SerializedName("email")
    private String mEmail;

    // Default constructor for general object creation
    public ToDo() {
    }

    // Constructor needed for parcelable object creation
    public ToDo(Parcel item) {
        mId = item.readLong();
        mTitle = item.readString();
        mEmail = item.readString();
    }

    //Getters and setters omitted

    // Used to generate parcelable classes from a parcel
    public static final Parcelable.Creator<ToDo> CREATOR
            = new Parcelable.Creator<ToDo>() {
        public ToDo createFromParcel(Parcel in) {
            return new ToDo(in);
        }

        public ToDo[] newArray(int size) {
            return new ToDo[size];
        }
    };

    @Override
    public int describeContents() {
```

```
        return 0;
    }

    @Override
    public void writeToParcel(Parcel parcel, int i) {
        if(mId != null) {
            parcel.writeLong(mId);
        }
        else {
            parcel.writeLong(-1);
        }
        parcel.writeString(mTitle);
        parcel.writeString(mEmail);
    }
}
```

Also notice the class in Listing 8-4 that implements the `Parcelable` interface. A parcelable class in Android allows the application to pass the data across process boundaries using *intents*. There are two items to note about the `Parcelable` class in Listing 8-4. The first is that the `writeToParcel()` function and matching constructor write and read the items into the parcel in the same order. There is no key to match up the fields; you must get the order correct. The second item of note is a `Creator` function that allows the `Parcelable` class to be stored and regenerated from a parcel.

Performance

Accessing web services means that our applications usually communicate over a slow and sometimes less-than-reliable network. Therefore, these integration points can become bottlenecks in our application's performance. In order to make our applications feel responsive during these calls, there are a number of design approaches we can take, from running on different threads to optimizations of the HTTP calls, to the services the application consumes.

Services and the AsyncTask Class

When calling web services, our applications must make those calls asynchronously. Therefore, any call to the web service should occur on a different thread than the UI thread. If the application doesn't do this, a number of bad things may occur, depending on the version of Android running the app:

- The UI becomes unresponsive or blocked.
- The user gets an Application Not Responding (ANR) dialog.
- The app throws an exception immediately.

Any well-written app should avoid all of those scenarios. The basic idea is to move any calls to web services into their own thread.

Many examples show how to accomplish this using the `AsyncTask` class from within an `Activity`. While this approach will work most of the time, an orientation change from portrait to landscape or vice versa will have an unintended effect. The `Activity` that created the `AsyncTask` is destroyed on the orientation change and re-created in the new orientation. The `AsyncTask` remains associated with the destroyed activity, so the result cannot return to the new activity. Additionally, references to callback methods in the original Activity in the AsyncTask prevent the garbage collector from reclaiming the memory of the original Activity unless special care is taken when the activity is destroyed. There are some solutions to this problem using AsyncTask, but a better way to solve the problem is to use an IntentService class because it lives outside the Activity lifecycle.

Besides an IntentService, the Android SDK also provides a Service class. The IntentService class has a number of benefits when compared to the Service class. First, it behaves asynchronously on its own thread. But one of the best features of the IntentService is that once completed, it stops itself. There is no need for your application to manage the state of the IntentService. By contrast, the Service class requires you to manage threading yourself, as well as starting and stopping the Service. Some situations may warrant the control imposed by implementing a Service, but an IntentService can handle most service calls with less code.

Before we can use an IntentService in the app, it must be registered in our project's androidmanifest.xml file, in the <application> tag, as shown in Listing 8-5. Setting the android:exported attribute to false ensures that the service cannot be used by components outside the application.

Listing 8-5. Declaring an IntentService in androidmanifest.xml

```
<service android:name="com.logicdrop.todos.service.RestService" android:exported="false"></service>
```

Once our IntentService is registered in androidmanifest.xml, starting it is straightforward. Simply create an Intent, and then call startService(intent) as in Listing 8-6.

Listing 8-6. Starting an IntentService from an Activity

```
Intent intent = new Intent(this, ToDoService.class);
intent.setAction("todo-list");
intent.putExtra("email", emailAddress);
startService(intent);
```

The IntentService itself is also straightforward. It has only one method to implement, onHandleIntent(). This function is the listener for any intents sent to the IntentService. If the IntentService handles multiple functions, set the action on the incoming intent to differentiate the incoming requests and then check the action inside the IntentService.

Listing 8-7 shows an implementation of onHandleIntent(). The function is passed the Intent sent from the Activity. It checks the action of the Intent and responds by calling different functions that ultimately call a REST service using the executeHTTP() function described previously.

Listing 8-7. Implementing an IntentService that Handles Multiple Intent Actions

```
public class RestService extends IntentService {

    public static final String SERVICE_NAME ="REST-TODO";

    public static final String LIST_ACTION = "todo-list";
    public static final String ADD_ACTION = "todo-add";
    public static final String DELETE_ACTION = "todo-remove";
```

```
    public RestService() {
        super("RestService");
    }

    @Override
    protected void onHandleIntent(Intent intent) {

        if (LIST_ACTION.equals(intent.getAction())) {
            final String email = intent.getStringExtra("email");
            listToDos(email);
        }
        else if (ADD_ACTION.equals(intent.getAction())) {
            final ToDo item = intent.getParcelableExtra("todo");
            addToDo(item);
        }
        else if (DELETE_ACTION.equals(intent.getAction())) {
            final long id = intent.getLongExtra("id", -1);
            final int position = intent.getIntExtra("position", -1);

            removeToDo(id, position);
        }
    }
    //Other private methods not shown....
}
```

Once the executeHTTP() function returns some JSON, it is converted back into a Parcelable POJO and returned to the activity via another Intent.

The most important aspect of sending the data back via Intent in Listing 8-8 is the LocalBroadcastManager class. This class is part of the Support Library, an add-on to the Android SDK, and provides some important benefits. The first is that the scope of the Intent is kept within our application. Normal Intents that applications throw can be seen and responded to by other applications installed on the Android device, including malware. Also, the LocalBroadcastManager allows the Activity to process the result while in the background, so your app wouldn't be forced to the foreground when a long-running result returns, as it would when listening for an Intent that starts an Activity.

Listing 8-8. Sending Back an Intent from the IntentService

```
final Intent sendBack = new Intent(SERVICE_NAME);
sendBack.putExtra("result", result);
sendBack.putExtra("function", LIST_ACTION);

if(results != null){
    sendBack.putParcelableArrayListExtra("data", results);
}

//Keep the intent local to the application
LocalBroadcastManager.getInstance(this).sendBroadcast(sendBack);
```

The main negative to the IntentService is that it handles all requests sequentially; requests do not run in parallel. If you need to download many items in a short period of time, an IntentService may not be a good solution.

Now that the IntentService is sending back results, let's examine how to handle those results properly using the same LocalBroadcastManager that we used to send the Intents. Earlier we discussed the shortcoming of AsyncTask with regard to device rotation. The LocalBroadcastManager provides a solution as shown in Listing 8-9.

Listing 8-9. Processing the Return Intent in an Activity

```
// Unhook the BroadcastManager that is listening for service returns before rotation
@Override
protected void onPause() {
    super.onPause();
    LocalBroadcastManager.getInstance(this).unregisterReceiver(onNotice);
}

// Hook up the BroadcastManager to listen to service returns
@Override
protected void onResume() {
    super.onResume();

    IntentFilter filter = new IntentFilter(RestService.SERVICE_NAME);
    LocalBroadcastManager.getInstance(this).registerReceiver(onNotice, filter);

    //Check for records stored locally if service returned while activity was not in the foreground
    mData = findPersistedRecords();
    if(!mData.isEmpty()) {
        BindToDoList();
    }
}

// The listener that responds to intents sent back from the service
private BroadcastReceiver onNotice = new BroadcastReceiver() {

    @Override
    public void onReceive(Context context, Intent intent) {
        final int serviceResult = intent.getIntExtra("result", -1);
        final String action = intent.getStringExtra("function");

        if (serviceResult == RESULT_OK) {

            if(action.equalsIgnoreCase(RestService.LIST_ACTION)){
                mData = intent.getParcelableArrayListExtra("data");
            }
            else if(action.equals(RestService.ADD_ACTION)) {

                final ToDo newItem = intent.getParcelableExtra("data");
                mData.add(newItem);
                etNewTask.setText("");

            } else if(action.equals(RestService.DELETE_ACTION)) {
                final int position = intent.getIntExtra("position", -1);
```

```
            if(position > -1){
                mData.remove(position);
            }
        }

        BindToDoList();

    } else {
        Toast.makeText(TodoActivity.this, "Rest call failed.", Toast.LENGTH_LONG).show();
    }

    Log.d("BroadcastReciever", "onNotice called");
    }
};
```

In the OnResume event handler, we create an IntentFilter for the intents returned from our IntentService. The OnResume event is part of the activity life cycle and is always called when an activity is created. We register a BroadcastReceiver with the LocalBroadcastManager to use this filter to listen for incoming intents.

In the OnPause event handler, we unhook the BroadcastReceiver from the LocalBroadcastManager. This event is also part of the activity life cycle, and is called when an activity is destroyed, such as during an orientation change. Because the IntentService lives on its own thread, the creation and destruction of activities has no bearing on its behavior, in contrast to an AsyncTask. A pitfall in this pattern is that the IntentService may complete and send the resulting intent when the activity is no longer in the foreground or has been destroyed. To mitigate this condition, the IntentService should write the web service call results to a database. When the activity resumes, it can check the database for pending web service results.

When the BroadcastManager gets the data from the service call, it places the list of ToDos in a class-level member variable and binds the list to the UI.

Dealing with Long-Running Calls

If the problem you are solving requires a long-running web service call, it may be better to implement a Service instead of an IntentService. In a long-running call, there are some problems to be solved. First is that a long running call should notify the user of the status of the call. Otherwise, the application may seem unresponsive. Also, the operating system could kill our service if it needs memory, because it seems idle during the long-running call.

To solve this problem, we implement a Service instead of an IntentService. The Service class provides the facilities needed to both inform the user of the status and keep the operating system from killing the application when it is actually busy. Each service can run in its own process separate from the application, and can be set to restart should the operating system kill the service. This type of service is declared in the AndroidManifest.xml file, as shown in Listing 8-10. This type of service implementation should only be used when necessary. Starting another process uses more memory resources, which good applications minimize.

Listing 8-10. A Service Declaration in the AndroidManifest.xml File, Which Runs in Its Own Process

```
<service
  android:name="LongRunningService"
  android:process=":serviceconsumer_process"
  android:icon="@drawable/service-icon"
  android:label="@string/service_name">
</service>
```

In order to tell the Android operating system that our service is functional during a long-running call, we need to call startForeground() on our service as in Listing 8-11. The onStartCommand() function returns the constant Service.START_REDELIVER_INTENT. This allows the OS to kill the service in low-memory situations, and then to restart the service with the last delivered intent. The service can then attempt to reprocess the last intent it needs to do that because the OS killed off service before finishing last time.

Listing 8-11. Methods for Setting Up a Service for a Long-Running Call in a Service

```
private static final int mServiceId = 42;

@Override
public IBinder onBind(Intent intent) {

    Notification notice;
    if(Build.VERSION.SDK_INT >= Build.VERSION_CODES.HONEYCOMB) {
        notice = APIv11.createNotice(this);
    } else {
        notice = new Notification(R.drawable.icon, "Service Finished", System.currentTimeMillis());
    }

    startForeground(mServiceId, notice);
    return null;
}

private static class APIv11 {
    public static Notification createNotice(Service context){
        Notification notice = new Notification.Builder(context.getApplicationContext()).
setContentTitle("Service finished").build();
        return notice;
    }
}

@Override
 public int onStartCommand(Intent intent, int flags, int startId) {

    return Service. START_REDELIVER_INTENT;
 }

@Override
public boolean onUnbind (Intent intent){
    stopForeground(true);
    return false;
}
```

Optimizations

Because network bandwidth acts as a constraint for mobile devices, our web service need to exploit the optimizations available in modern web servers to reduce the bandwidth our Android apps consume. These optimizations include compression and caching.

Compression

Modern web servers, like IIS, Nginx, and Apache's httpd all support gzip compression. Compression of text is very effective, and since our web services pass around only text, our code should take advantage of compression. As mentioned previously, the `HttpURLConnection` object has built in support for gzip from Gingerbread going forward, and in fact is set to use this feature by default when calling `getInputStream()` on the connection. That call causes the `HttpURLConnection` object to add the HTTP header `Accept-Encoding: gzip` automatically to the request. As long as the web server is configured for gzip, the HTTP request/response pair will be compressed, which is important for mobile devices using limited bandwidth.

Http-Based Caching

When a web server sends content to a client, it can add an expiration date to the content via the `expires` HTTP header. Often larger, static items like images frequently have an `expires` header set days or weeks into the future to keep web browsers from continually re-downloading these files when users return to pages that have already downloaded the images. With Ice Cream Sandwich, `HttpURLConnection` supports HTTP-based caching. If an item previously fetched by `HttpURLConnection` comes with a future expires header or the web server responds with a 304 code due to conditional expiration, these items are loaded from local storage instead of over the network, again minimizing bandwidth usage. Because only Ice Cream Sandwich or newer supports this feature, a little reflection allows our code to use the feature as shown in Listing 8-12.

Listing 8-12. A Method for Selectively Enabling HTTP Caching for Android Versions that Support Caching

```
private void enableHttpResponseCache() {
try {
    long httpCacheSize = 10 * 1024 * 1024; // 10 MiB
    File httpCacheDir = new File(getCacheDir(), "http");
    Class.forName("android.net.http.HttpResponseCache")
        .getMethod("install", File.class, long.class)
        .invoke(null, httpCacheDir, httpCacheSize);
    } catch (Exception httpResponseCacheNotAvailable) {}
}
```

We previously noted that `IntentServices` operate serially, which is not good in all situations, such as downloading a large number of images. At Google I/O 2013, Google announced the release of a new library called Volley (`http://www.youtube.com/watch?v=yhv8l9F44qo`). Volley supports concurrent downloads and has built-in support for image handling and client-controllable caching. Volley is not currently part of the Android SDK but may be in the future, but it represents a good solution when serial HTTP connections don't provide the necessary performance.

Security

In a time of frequent security breaches and organizations impinging upon the privacy of users, security on both the client and server sides of an application has become a main concern for application developers.

The Open Web Application Security Project (OWASP) is a nonprofit organization dedicated to educating developers about security threats and supplying them with tools and information to mitigate those threats. Periodically OWASP publishes a list of the top ten threats to application security. In 2013, OWASP published a new Top 10 for web applications (`https://www.owasp.org/index.php/Category:OWASP_Top_Ten_Project`), and in 2011 expanded to include a list of the top 10 mobile threats as well:

> M1: Insecure Data Storage
>
> M2: Weak Server Side Controls
>
> M3: Insufficient Transport Layer Protection
>
> M4: Client Side Injection
>
> M5: Poor Authorization and Authentication
>
> M6: Improper Session Handling
>
> M7: Security Decisions Via Untrusted Inputs
>
> M8: Side Channel Data Leakage
>
> M9: Broken Cryptography
>
> M10: Sensitive Information Disclosure

A number of these threats apply directly to Android applications consuming web services, including these:

- **M1: Insecure Data Storage**. This problem arises from not properly securing or encrypting data stored on the device, such as a user ID, or storing data intended to be temporary, such as a password.

- **M3: Insufficient Transport Layer Protection**. Applications that do not use transport layer security or ignore security warnings such as certificate errors are susceptible to this vulnerability.

- **M5: Poor Authorization and Authentication**. This often happens when an application uses a hardware-based identifier such as the IMEI (International Mobile Equipment Identity) number that can be determined by an attacker and used to impersonate the user.

- **M6: Improper Session Handling**. Mobile user sessions tend to be much longer than web site sessions, so at the user's convenience the mobile app keeps users logged in longer. Long sessions can lead to unauthorized access, especially when the device is lost. Make users re-authenticate periodically, and ensure that your server-side application can revoke a session remotely if necessary.

- **M9: Broken Cryptography**. Do not confuse encoding, obfuscation, or serialization with encryption. Use the strongest cryptographic algorithm possible. Do not store a key used for two-way encryption with the data or in an insecure location, such as in the application code.

- **M10: Sensitive Information Disclosure**. Android application code can be easily decompiled back into Java code. Any sensitive information stored in the code, such as encryption keys, usernames, passwords, and API keys will be discovered.

Be sure to spend time on OWASP's web site at `https://www.owasp.org` to become more familiar with each threat and with all the tools OWASP can provide to help you build secure applications.

Dos and Don'ts for Web Services

Security is an extensive subject, and is covered more in depth in other books, such as *Android Apps Security* by Sheran Gunasekera (Apress, 2012). As we move on to talk about building your own web services, here are some general practices to follow as you build web services.

Don't Store the Password

If you must store passwords in your service database, do not store them in clear text. The proper procedure is to salt the password with a unique value, and then perform a one-way hash to the salted password with a strong hashing algorithm (at least SHA-256, or bcrypt). Simpler hashing algorithms, such as MD-5 or SHA-1, are often chosen for their speed, but security professionals have demonstrated those algorithms as insecure. A fast hashing algorithm is the enemy of hashed password storage, as the computing power to break those hashes is becoming more and more available.

Salting is appending or prepending a value to the password. When a user attempts to authenticate, the application can recreate the salted hash from the password entered by the user, and then compare that result to the result stored in the database. The salt adds randomness and size to the password, making it more difficult to guess should the database become compromised.

Attackers attempt to break hashes using a technique called a Rainbow Table, which is essentially a precompiled, reverse engineering of the hashing algorithm. Sufficiently strong hashing algorithms make Rainbow Tables very large and take an extremely long time to calculate. The addition of a salt forces an attacker to use a separate rainbow table for each possible salt, which increases the time and computing power necessary to find a match and successfully recover a password. At this point in late 2013, a sufficiently strong hash with a random salt is too difficult to break. As computing power and the availability of disturbed computing increase over time, hashing algorithms will become less secure.

Don't Send the Password

If you can avoid sending a user's password over the network, there is no way an attacker can discover the password remotely. On Android devices, typically the user is already authenticated to Google via the Google account stored on the device. Your web services can integrate with Google's OAuth services to use the device account for authentication (who is this user) and authorization (what is this user allowed do). Listing 8-13 shows how to get the Google account names currently on the Android device. Of course, some Android devices, such as the Kindle Fire, do not allow for Google accounts to be stored on the device.

Listing 8-13. A Method for Acquiring the List of Google Accounts on an Android Device

```
private String[] getAccountNames() {
    try {
        AccountManager accountManager = AccountManager.get(this);
        Account[] accounts = accountManager.getAccountsByType(GoogleAuthUtil.GOOGLE_ACCOUNT_TYPE);
        String[] names = new String[accounts.length];
        for (int i = 0; i < names.length; i++) {
            names[i] = accounts[i].name;
        }
        return names;
    } catch (Exception ex) {
        Log.d(APP_TAG, "Account error", ex);
        return null;
    }
}
```

Once you have the Google account from the device, you can generate a token for the OAuth-based Google services as in Listing 8-14. This token allows the user to access other Google services and APIs without re-authenticating for each service and without ever sending a password over the network from the device. The token is typically sent as part of the JSON body of a request, although it can also be part of the URI or sent in an HTTP header. The token also carries an expiration date, and the services that accept the token will check the token for validity before fulfilling the request. This function also needs a `client_id` from the application whose services we are consuming. This value is acquired by the web service developers when integrating with Google, and must be shared with the clients in order to perform Google OAuth authentication.

Listing 8-14. Getting the Google OAuth token

```
private String authenticateGoogle(String accountName) {
    String token = "";
    try {
        String key = "audience:server:client_id:123456.apps.googleusercontent.com";
        token = GoogleAuthUtil.getToken(this, accountName,  key, null);

    } catch (IOException e) {
        Log.d("IO error", e.getMessage());
    } catch (GoogleAuthException ge) {
        Log.d("Google auth error", ge.getMessage());
```

```
    } catch (Exception ex) {
        Log.d("error", ex.getMessage());
    }
    return token;
}
```

Don't Own the Password

If you do not store the password in your database, attackers cannot exploit your users if your database becomes compromised. Large providers like Google, Yahoo, Twitter, and Facebook offer integration APIs that allow users to log in to your application using credentials from one of those providers. While you need to trust those providers to keep their users safe, there is less risk for your application by integrating with one of those providers.

OpenID is a decentralized, open authentication protocol that makes it easy for people to sign up and access web accounts using mobile applications. Many of the same providers just listed participate in OpenID. StackOverflow, the popular crowd-sourced discussion site for developers, uses OpenID to authenticate users. OpenID Connect is an API layer on top of OpenID designed for mobile application use, and should see general release in the near future.

Use Transport Layer Security (TLS/SSL)

At a minimum, web services that transmit user credentials or any kind of personal information need to be secured using Transport Layer Security (TLS). TLS protects data in transit from unauthorized access or modification between the mobile application and the web services. The term TLS is often used interchangeably with Secure Sockets Layer (SSL). TSL v1.0 is indeed equivalent to SSL v3.1. Most modern browsers support the various versions of SSL and TLS.

Use Sessions

Web services built using REST architecture are inherently stateless, and therefore sessionless. I am not suggesting we violate this tenet of REST. By sessions, I mean using a session token that is created upon login and subsequently sent along with each request to verify the authenticity of the request. The token should not be sent as part of the URL, but in the body of the request or in the HTTP headers. These session tokens should have an expiration date and rotate with each request to prevent replays of tokens. OWASP provides an open-source web application security control library called the Enterprise Security API you can use to create and manage session tokens in your web services (https://www.owasp.org/index.php/Category:OWASP_Enterprise_Security_API). The library is released for Java and Ruby, and in development for other platforms, including PHP, .Net, and Python.

Authentication

There are a number of ways to authenticate users to web services, mostly based on traditional web technologies. While it is possible to use your own authentication method, that is not a good idea. Many smart, security-oriented professionals have spent thousands of hours thinking through, designing, and implementing these protocols to keep data safe. Your web services should take advantage of these protocols.

HTTP Basic Authentication is the simplest protocol, and is supported natively by the Android SDK. The username and password are passed in the `Authorization` HTTP header. The username and password are concatenated with a colon, and then Base-64 encoded. Encoding is not encryption, and is not secure. Therefore, any use of Basic Authentication requires the use of TLS/SSL. Because Basic Authentication is part of the HTTP protocol specification, all modern web servers support it, making it easy to develop services that use Basic Authentication, since that plumbing already exists on the server side.

Listing 8-15 demonstrates how to implement Basic Authentication in an Android client application. The `Authenticator` class sets the authentication handler for subsequent calls to `HttpURLConnection`, so place this code before any calls to `HttpURLConnection`. You could calculate the HTTP `Authorization` header yourself and add it via a call to the `setHeader()` function on the `Request` object, but that method won't support the preemptive authentication checks that many web servers support. A preemptive check occurs before the actual request in order to reduce the overhead of making the initial HTTP connection, which is important because of the constrained bandwidth the mobile device typically operates with.

Listing 8-15. Use of the Authenticator Class to Implement Basic Authentication in an Android Client

```
Authenticator.setDefault(new Authenticator() {
    protected PasswordAuthentication getPasswordAuthentication() {
      return new PasswordAuthentication(username, password.toCharArray());
  });
}
```

Many of the largest web sites on the Internet, including Google, Twitter, Facebook, Yahoo, and LinkedIn implement their web service authentication via OAuth, an open standard for authorization that is more like a framework than a strictly defined protocol. Currently OAuth exists as two versions, 1.0 and 2.0, both of which are in production across the sites mentioned previously. Generally OAuth allows users to authorize an application to act on their behalf without sharing their password with the application. As a side effect of this authorization process, users also need to be authenticated, thereby also allowing the application to authenticate users. OAuth servers typically provide a token that expires at some point in the future to authenticated users. Applications can use this token to provide additional services. For instance, a user of an Android device with a Google account can acquire a token from Google that allows the phone to access other Google services, such as the Google Maps API that may be used within your custom application (see Listing 8-14 earlier). The user never enters their password, nor is any password ever sent to the Google Maps API. The token acquired from the Google OAuth Service manages all those authorizations.

Create Your Own Web Service

Most web frameworks in just about every programming language provide a way to create your own web services. Because we are writing Android code in Java, for our example we will create some basic web services using Java. While many options exist for creating web services using Java, we will focus on the JAX-RS API.

JAX-RS is a Java API for RESTful web services first introduced in Java SE 5. JAX-RS uses annotations to map a POJO (Plain Old Java Object) to a web service. We can write a function in a Java class as we have done any number of times in the past, but this time add annotations to make the function available via a REST URI. A number of frameworks implement the JAX-RS specification including Jersey, Restlet, Apache CXF, and RESTeasy. Jersey provides a straightforward, understandable approach, so we will build our examples using Jersey.

Sample Web Services

Web services that you can consume in your apps can come from literally anywhere. Large Internet companies like Google, Facebook, Twitter, ESPN, Amazon, eBay, and Yahoo, local and federal government departments all offer a myriad of services you (or your users) can consume. Some examples of available services include shipping rates, location services, social media integration, financial data, and even fantasy sports. Many of these services are free while others come at a small cost. In all these cases, the service providers typically require you sign up for their developer program. There are also web sites, such as programmableweb.com and usgovxml.com, that act as directories for sites that offer web services you can consume.

Google App Engine

An easy and cost effective way to get started writing your own web services is to host them in the cloud on Google App Engine (GAE). As an Android developer, you probably already have an account set up with Google.

GAE supports web applications written in Java (as well as Python, Go, and PHP), so we can build a REST service using the Jersey library to store our ToDo data in the cloud instead of on the device. This allows our applications a number of advantages, including storing larger amounts of data than would be appropriate on a mobile device, allowing our ToDo lists to be shared across multiple devices for the same user, such as a phone and a tablet, and providing for easier upgrades to the app on the device, because we no longer have to worry about what happens to the local database during the upgrade process.

We'll start building our own web service on GAE by browsing to https://appengine.google.com. Sign in with your Google account. You may be prompted for a second factor for authentication, such as receiving and SMS with a code or an automated phone call. Once that step is complete you will be prompted to create an application. Click that button, and then you will be prompted for some additional information regarding the application. Each GAE application needs a unique URL, so you will need to be creative for a unique Application Identifier for your service. Leave the service open to all Google Account users, agree to the Terms of Service, and create the application (see Figure 8-1).

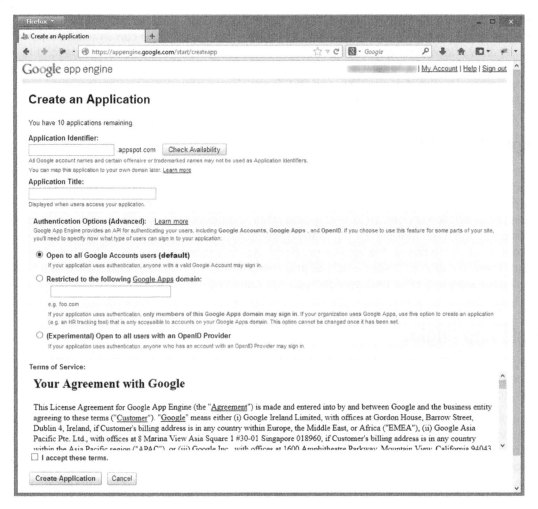

Figure 8-1. Creating an application on the Google App Engine site

Setting Up Eclipse

Before we begin writing Java code, we need to download the Google App Engine SDK for Java and set up ADT (or Eclipse) to work with GAE. First we need to download the Google plug-in for Eclipse and the GAE SDK:

1. In ADT, open the Help menu and click Install New Software (see Figure 8-2).

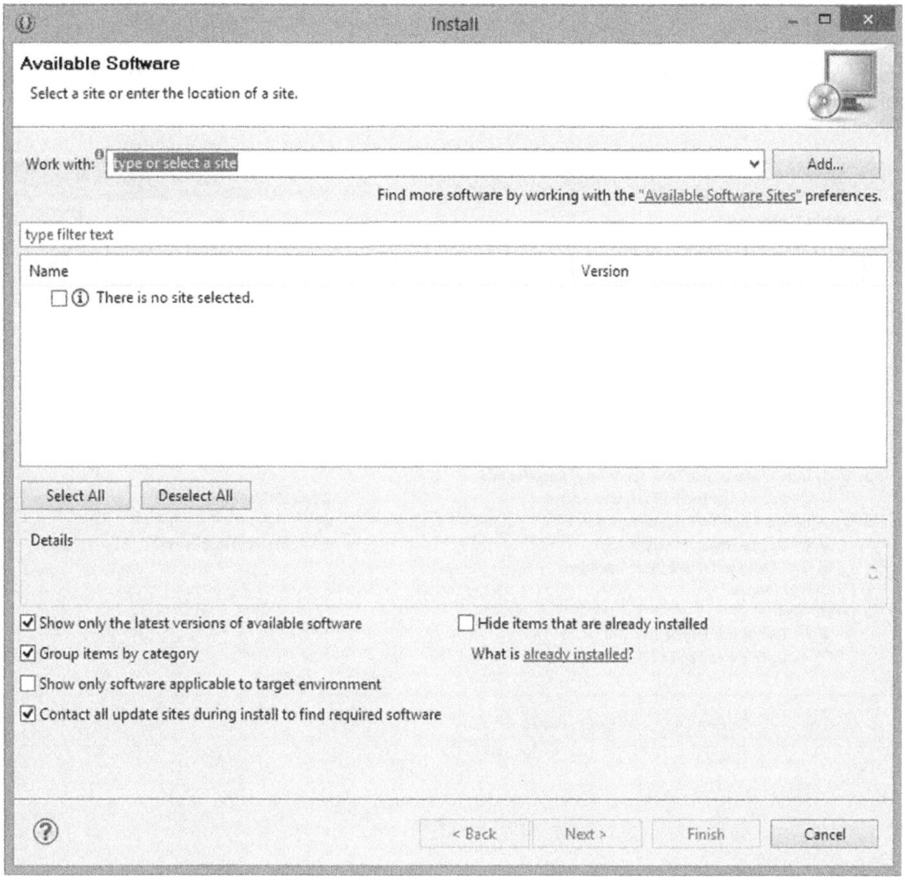

Figure 8-2. The Install software dialog

2. Click the Add button in the upper-right part of the dialog. The Add Repository dialog opens (see Figure 8-3).

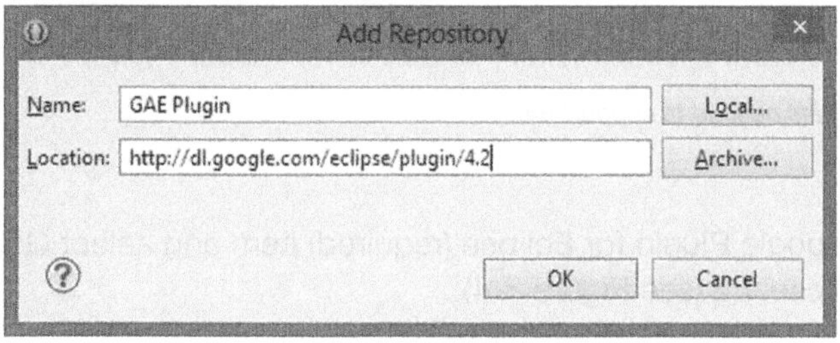

Figure 8-3. The Add Repository dialog for adding the URL to repository for the GAE Eclipse plug-in

3. Name the repository GAE Plugin, and enter this URL from the Google Developer site in the Location field: `http://dl.google.com/eclipse/plugin/4.2`.

4. Click OK.

5. Expand the Google App Engine Tools for Android (requires ADT) item, and select Google App Engine Tools for Android (see Figure 8-4).

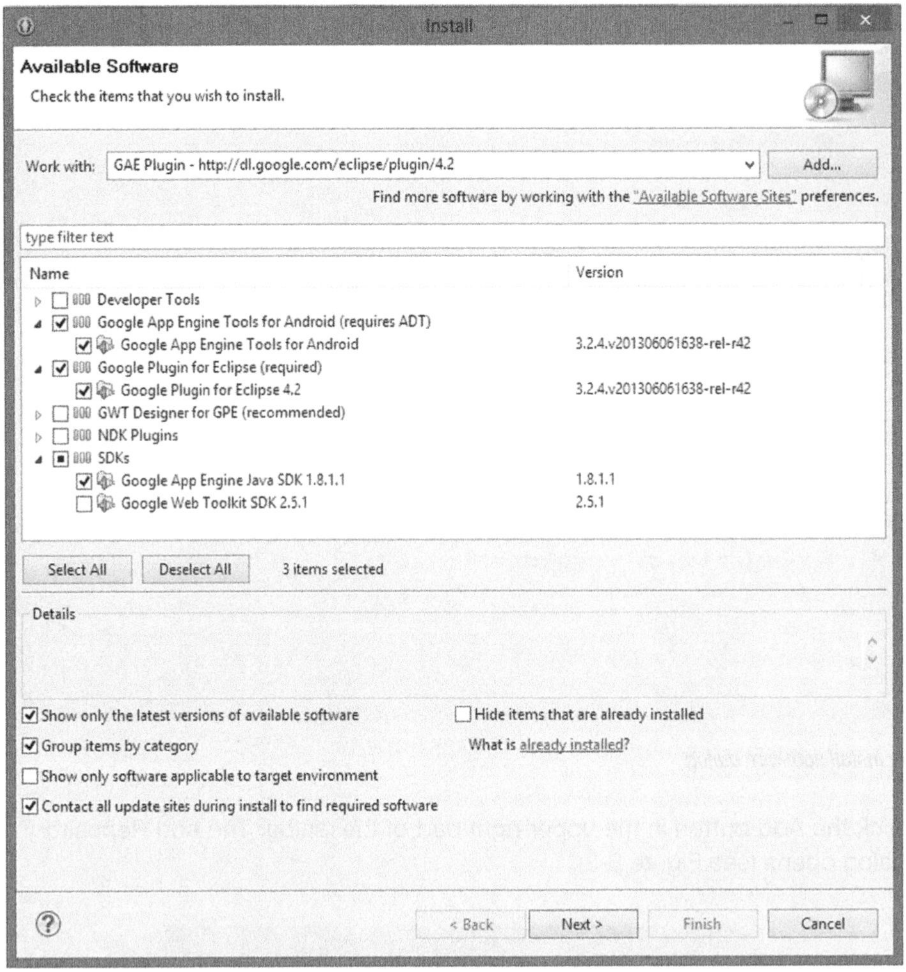

Figure 8-4. Choosing the plug-ins needed to support GAE

6. Expand the Google Plugin for Eclipse (required) item and select Google Plugin for Eclipse 4.2 (see Figure 8-4).

7. Expand the SDKs item, and choose Google App Engine Java SDK 1.8.1.1 (see Figure 8-4).

8. Click Next.

9. Click Next again on the Install Details dialog.

10. Review and accept the license agreements.

11. Click Finish and the software installs into ADT. You may be prompted to restart ADT.

We will also use the Jersey implementation of JAX-RS. For this example we will download and use the zip bundle of version 1.17.1 of Jersey from `https://jersey.java.net`. Decompress the archive into a location on your computer where you will get the JAR files needed for the project.

Create the Project

Now that you have the necessary components and SDKs downloaded, set up the project in Eclipse.

1. In Eclipse, in the GDT pull-down menu in the toolbar, choose New Web Application Project (see Figure 8-5).

Figure 8-5. Creating a new Web Application project

2. Enter a name for your project, such as AppEngineToDoService, and a Package name, such as com.example.todo (see Figure 8-6).

Figure 8-6. Setting up a new web application project for the ToDo service

3.   Uncheck the Use Google Web Toolkit option.

4.   Uncheck the Sample Code option.

5.   Click the Finish button. Eclipse creates the project structure.

Now that the project is created, we need to make a configuration change in the project to ensure compatibility between the GAE SDK and Jersey.

Configure the Project

The project requires some configuration changes in order to allow GAE to use the Jersey library. JDO/JPA version 2 conflicts with the version of Jersey in this example.

1.   Right-click the project in the Package Explorer, and choose Properties.

2.   Expand the Google item in the left pane, and then click App Engine
     (see Figure 8-7).

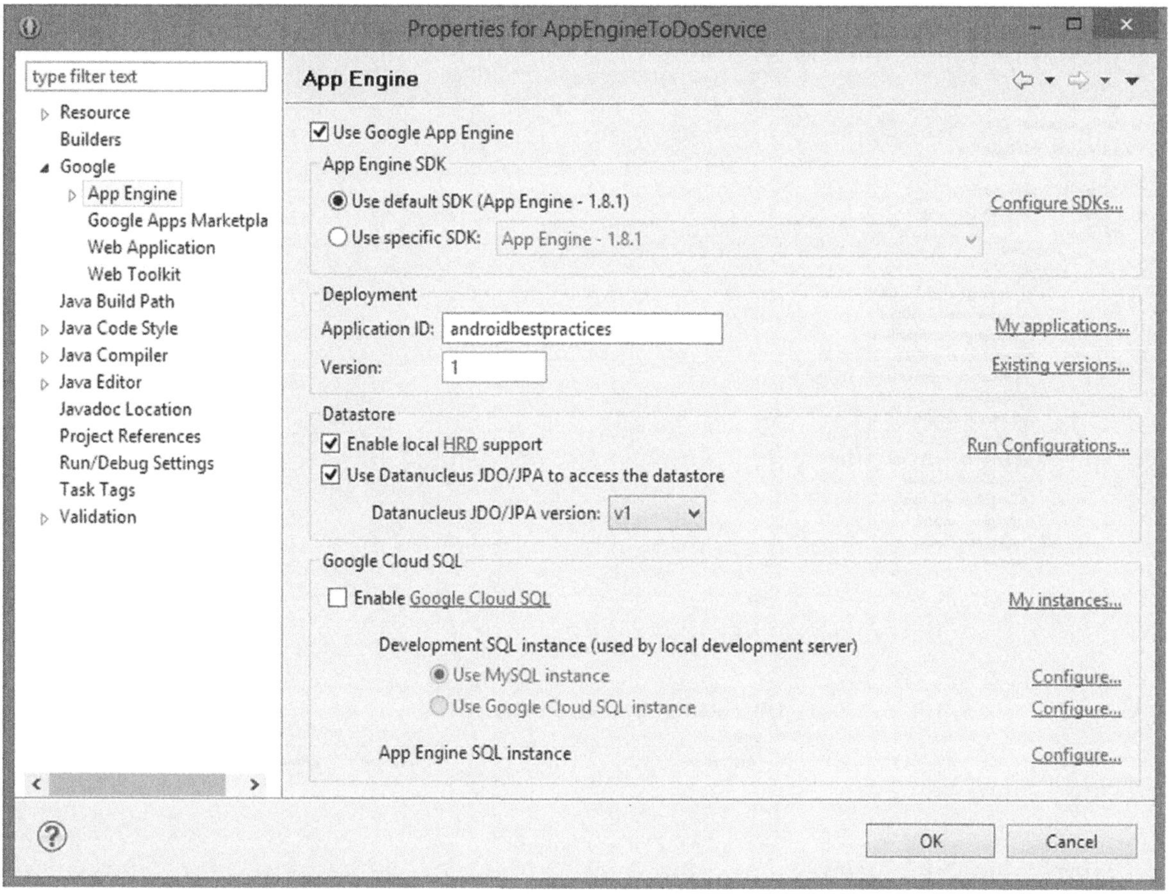

Figure 8-7. Changing the project configuration for GAE

3. Change the Datanucleus JDO/JPA version to v1 and click OK.

The project is now ready for us to import the Jersey JARs.

Add Jersey to the Project

Now that you saved the JDO/JPA version change in the project configuration, add the JARs that make up the Jersey library.

1. Expand the war, WEB-INF, and lib folders of your project in the Package Explorer (see Figure 8-8).

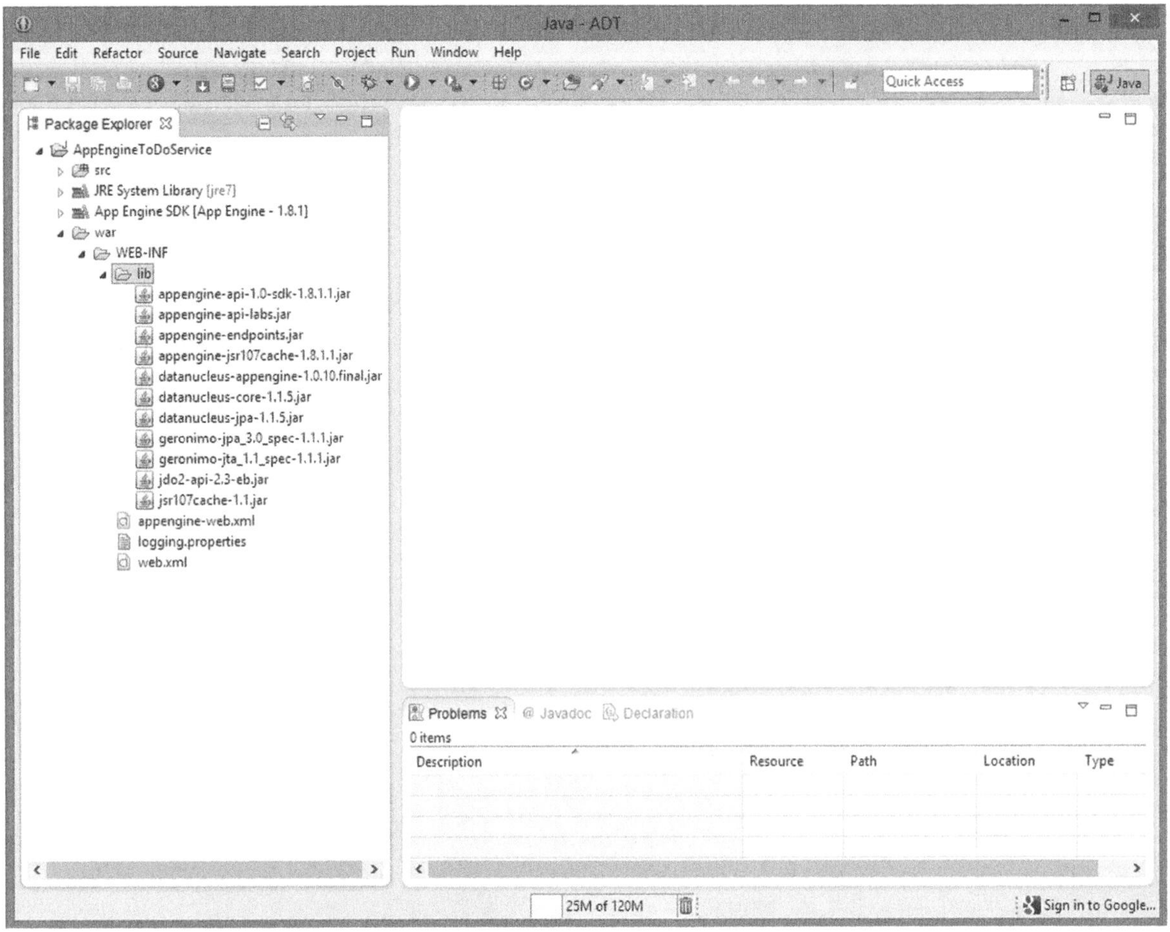

Figure 8-8. The project location for the Jersey JARs

2. Right-click the lib folder and choose Import.

3. Expand the General item.

4. Click the File System item under General (see Figure 8-9).

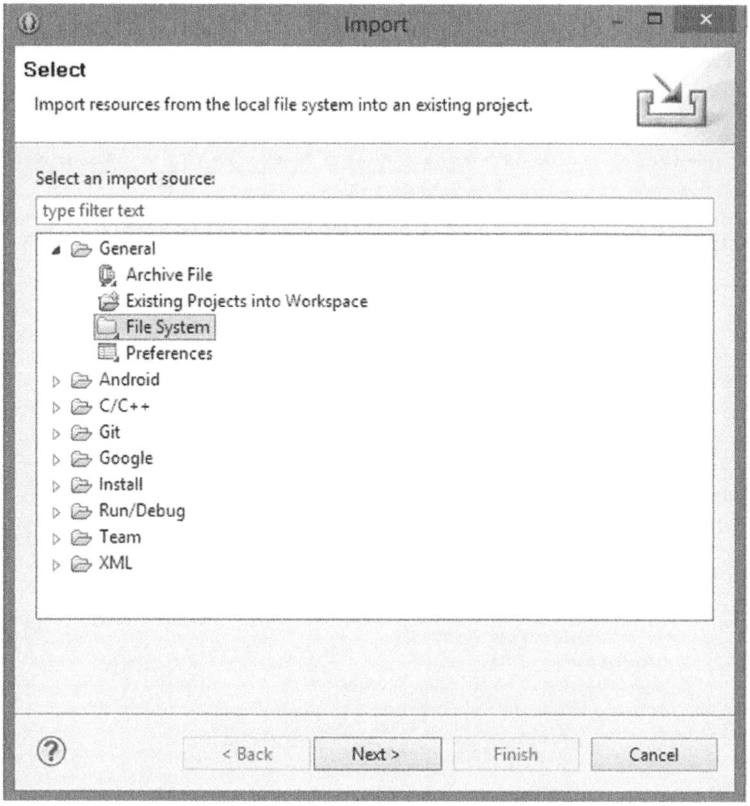

Figure 8-9. Importing from the file system

5. Click Next.

6. Browse to the location where you expanded the Jersey archive downloaded earlier and select the `lib` folder.

7. In the Import dialog, click the `lib` folder in the left pane, which selects all the jars in the right pane (see Figure 8-10).

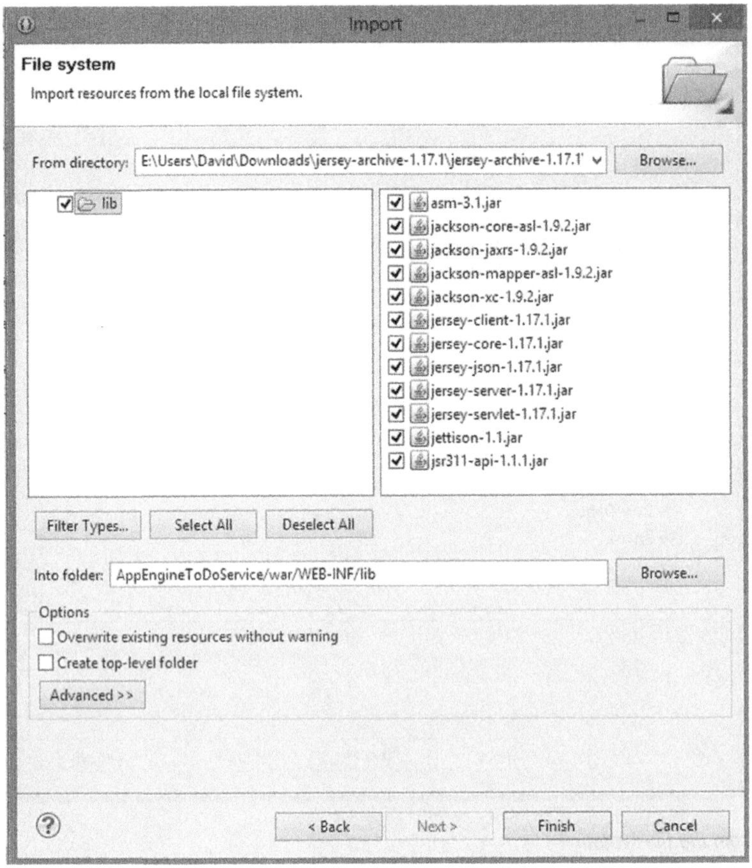

Figure 8-10. Importing the Jersey JARs

8. Click Finish.

Add Jersey to the Classpath

After adding the JARs to the project, you must add them to the Classpath in order for Eclipse to compile your project correctly.

1. Right click the project in the Package Explorer, and choose Build Path and then Configure Build Path (see Figure 8-11).

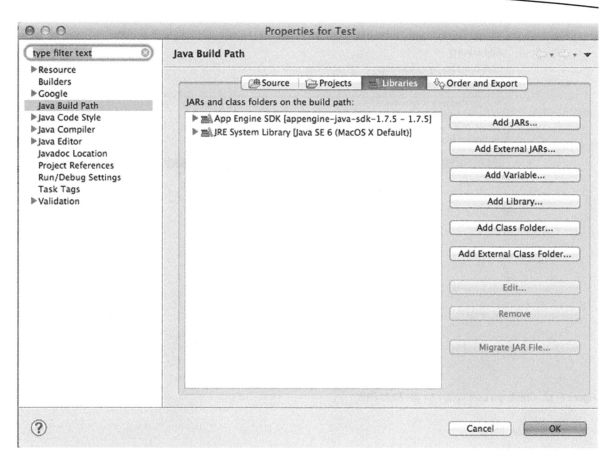

Figure 8-11. The Build Path dialog for adding Jersey as a library

2.   Click the Libraries tab.

3.   Click the Add Library button.

4.   Click User Library (see Figure 8-12).

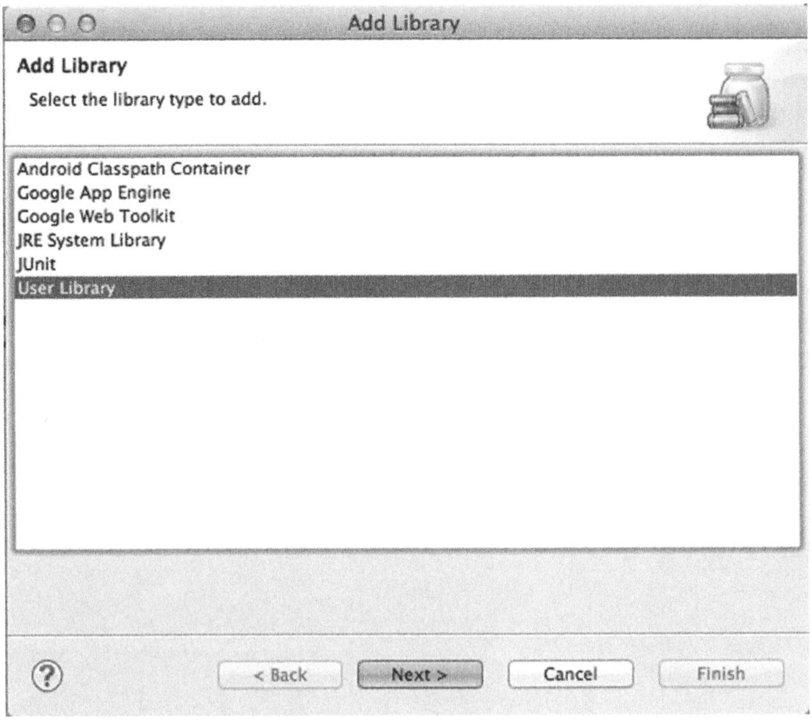

Figure 8-12. Creating a user library for the Build Path

5. Click Next.

6. Click the User Libraries button.

7. Click the New button on the right side of the Preferences dialog box.

8. Type Jersey for the library name.

9. Click the OK button.

10. Click the Add JARs button.

11. Select the JARs that belong to Jersey (see Figure 8-13).

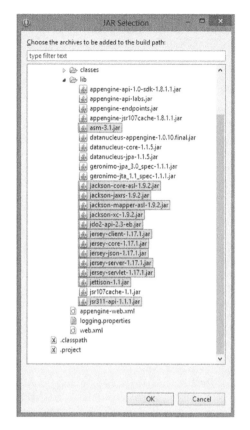

Figure 8-13. Choosing the JARs for inclusion in the User Library

12. Click OK.

13. Click the next OK button.

14. Click Finish.

15. Click the OK button. The Jersey Library should appear in the Package Explorer (see Figure 8-14).

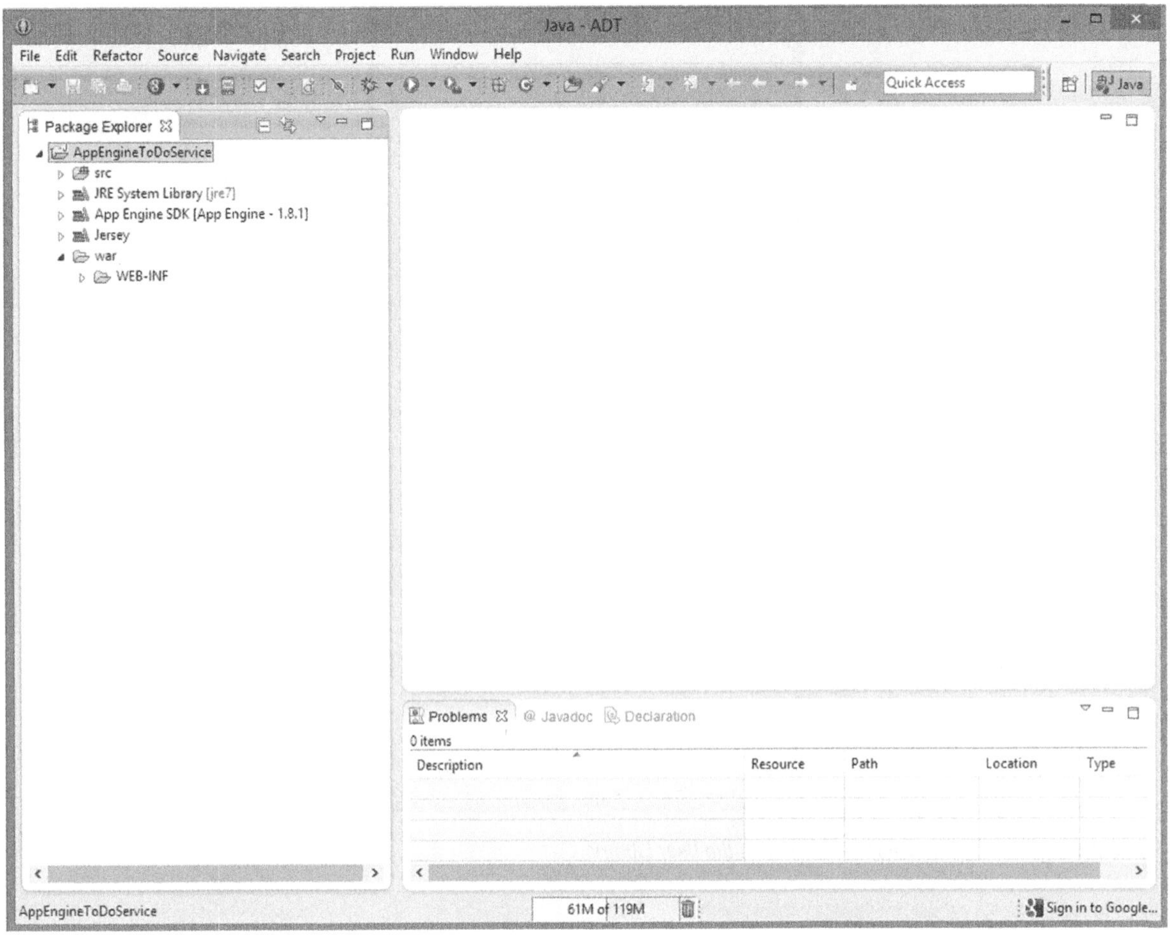

Figure 8-14. The result of adding the Jersey JARs as a User Library

Now that we have the libraries set up, we should configure the web.xml file for Jersey. The web.xml file is located in the WEB-INF folder of the project. Open web.xml, and you'll see a single XML tag, <web-app>. Take note that the version in this tag is 2.5, which is the servlet specification supported by Google App Engine currently.

Add the servlet tag within the <web-app> tag of web.xml as shown in Listing 8-16.

Listing 8-16. Servlet tag contents for the Jersey library

```
<servlet>
    <servlet-name>Jersey REST Service</servlet-name>
    <servlet-class>com.sun.jersey.spi.container.servlet.ServletContainer</servlet-class>
    <init-param>
        <param-name>com.sun.jersey.config.property.packages</param-name>
        <param-value>com.example.todo.service</param-value>
    </init-param>
    <init-param>
```

```
        <param-name>com.sun.jersey.api.json.POJOMappingFeature</param-name>
        <param-value>true</param-value>
    </init-param>
    <load-on-startup>1</load-on-startup>
</servlet>
```

Notice in Listing 8-16 that our package name is included in an `<init-param>` tag. This tells Jersey where to look for the classes that comprise our web service. The `POJOMappingFeature` is also important; it allows classes to automatically serialize to XML or JSON, saving us from writing code to map our classes to a format for the input and output of the web service.

Below the servlet tag we'll add a servlet mapping, but still inside the `<web-app>` tag as shown in Listing 8-17. The `<url-pattern>` tag in Listing 8-17 provides a way to map a base URI pattern for Jersey to listen for when receiving requests from clients. The mapping also allows web projects to host both web pages and services.

Listing 8-17. Mapping the base URI structure in web.xml

```
<servlet-mapping>
        <servlet-name>Jersey REST Service</servlet-name>
    <url-pattern>/api/*</url-pattern>
</servlet-mapping>
```

Create the Service

Now that the project is all set up, we can finally write some Java code for our service. We'll start with the data and work our way out of the service to the client.

The data will be stored using a NoSQL database built into GAE, known as the *datastore*. The datastore holds objects known as entities, which map to a Java classes in our service. Each entity contains properties, which map to the member variables of a Java class. Each entity we store must have a key unique among all stored instances of like entities. When an application deployed to GAE contains entity definitions, the datastore will be able to store those entities without any administrative work, such as creating a table or setting up a data schema. Additionally, the datastore can be manipulated from the Admin Console of the Google App Engine web site (see Figure 8-15).

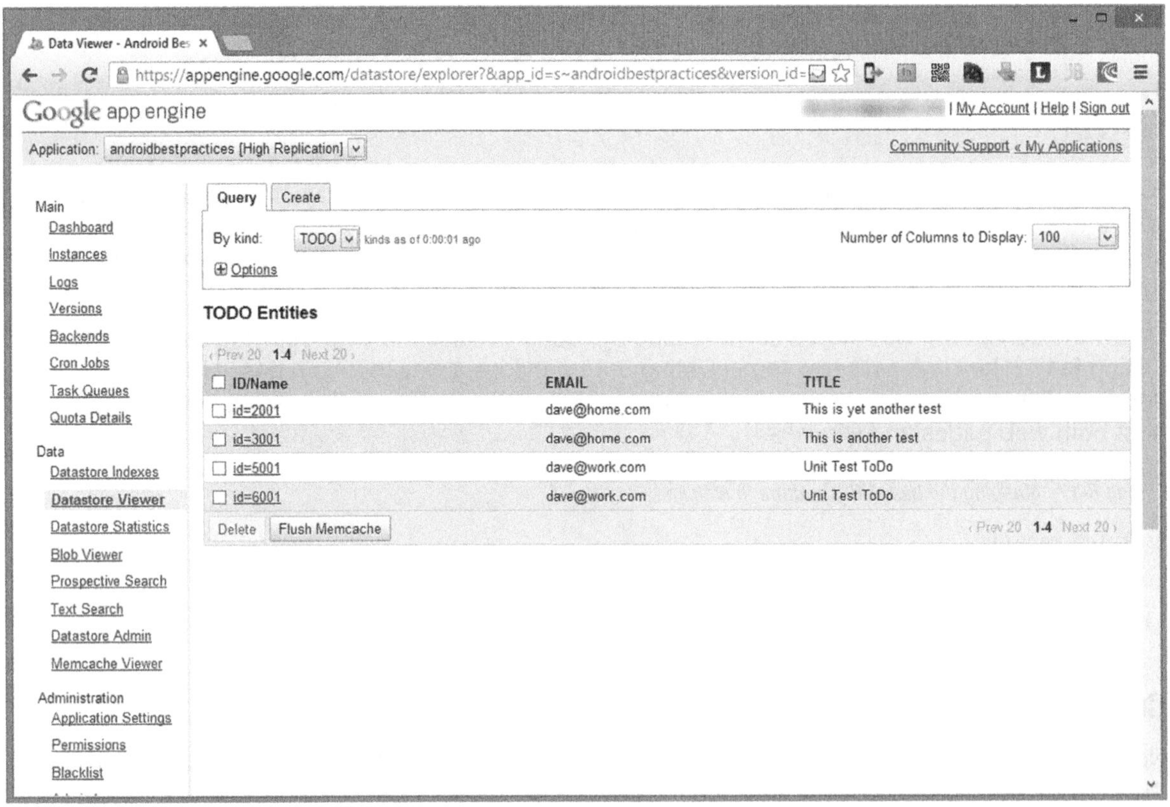

Figure 8-15. The GAE datastore management web page

Our service will utilize the JPA 1.0 implementation that ships with the Google App Engine SDK. This version is compatible with Jersey, which the JPA 2.0 version currently is not compatible with—even though it shares some libraries with Jersey; unfortunately, the Jersey and GAE JPA 2.0 use incompatible versions of these libraries.

Let's start with a ToDo class that is a slight variation on what we built earlier. The ToDo class will serve two purposes. The first is to act as the schema for the data we will persist on GAE. The second purpose is to provide a data structure that will become both input and output from our web service.

The class in Listing 8-18 is annotated with a number of JPA attributes, including @PersistenceCapable to tell JPA to persist this data structure, and @Persistent to mark the member variables that we want to save. Note that the primary key is a Long, which is a requirement for GAE, and that the primary key will be auto-generated when new records are created. We have also added an email address, so that we can store the records of many different users.

Listing 8-18. The ToDo data class annotated for JPA persistence

```
@PersistenceCapable
public class ToDo {

    @PrimaryKey
    @Persistent(valueStrategy = IdGeneratorStrategy.IDENTITY)
```

```
    private Long id;

    @Persistent
    private String title;

    @Persistent
    private String email;

    public Long getId() {
        return id;
    }

    public void setId(Long id) {
        this.id = id;
    }

    public String getTitle() {
        return title;
    }

    public void setTitle(String title) {
        this.title = title;
    }

    public String getEmail() {
        return email;
    }

    public void setEmail(String email) {
        this.email = email;
    }
}
```

Listing 8-19 defines different actions in a data layer to manipulate ToDo records in the GAE datastore:

- Create

- Delete

- List ToDos for a user

Listing 8-19. Data Layer Class for Manipulating ToDos in the Cloud

```
public class ToDoAppEngineData {
    //Ensure there is only one instance of the factory
    private static final PersistenceManagerFactory factory = JDOHelper
            .getPersistenceManagerFactory("transactions-optional");
    private PersistenceManager manager;

    public ToDoAppEngineData(){
        manager = factory.getPersistenceManager();
    }
```

```java
public Long createToDo(ToDo item) {
    ToDo newItem;
    Transaction trans = manager.currentTransaction();
    try {
        trans.begin();
        newItem = manager.makePersistent(item);
        trans.commit();
        return newItem.getId();
    } catch (Exception ex) {
        trans.rollback();
        return -1l;
    } finally {
        manager.close();
    }
}

public boolean deleteToDo(Long id) {
    ToDo item = getToDo(id);

    if(item == null)
        return false;
    Transaction trans = manager.currentTransaction();

    try {
        trans.begin();
        manager.deletePersistent(item);
        trans.commit();
        return true;
    } catch (Exception ex) {
        trans.rollback();
        return false;
    } finally {
        manager.close();
    }
}

public List<ToDo> getAll(String email) {

    if(email == null || email.isEmpty()) {
        return new ArrayList<ToDo>();
    }

    PersistenceManager manager = factory.getPersistenceManager();

    Query query = manager.newQuery(ToDo.class);
    query.setFilter("email == emailParam");
    query.declareParameters("String emailParam");
    List<ToDo> results;

    try {
        List<ToDo> temp = (List<ToDo>) query.execute(email);
        if (temp.isEmpty()) {
```

```
                return new ArrayList<ToDo>();
            }

            results = (List<ToDo>) manager.detachCopyAll(temp);
        } catch (Exception e){
            results = new ArrayList<ToDo>();
            e.printStackTrace();
        } finally {
            query.closeAll();
            manager.close();
        }
        return results;
    }
}
```

Most of the code in Listing 8-19 is fairly straightforward and somewhat repetitive. Each method retrieves an instance of a `PersistenceManager`, which takes the annotated ToDo class and performs CRUD operations wrapped in a `Transaction`.

The last function in Listing 8-19, `getAll()`, contains some interesting elements. This function creates a `Query` object and searches for the saved ToDo entities that match an email address specified in the input parameter. Also, the functions that read data call a function that detaches the objects from the `PersistenceManager`. The detachment action ensures that if consumers of our read functions modify any ToDo entities, those changes won't be accidentally persisted to the datastore.

Now that the ToDo entities are persistable, those CRUD operations can be exposed as web services by wrapping them in a class annotated with attributes from the Jersey library.

At the start of Listing 8-20, our class is annotated with the `@Path` attribute. This attribute provides Jersey with a piece of the URI that our class responds to. At this point, all the URIs mapped the function calls in our class will start with `http://localhost:8888/api/todo`. Remember that the `/api/` portion of the URI came from the Jersey configuration in `web.xml`. Each function may also have an `@Path` annotation that denotes additional elements of the URI needed for mapping incoming parameters.

Listing 8-20 A Jersey-Annotated Class Exposing ToDo Entities via REST Operations

```
@Path("/todo")
public class ToDoResource {

    private ToDoAppEngineData datastore;

    public ToDoResource(){
        datastore = new ToDoAppEngineData();
    }

    @GET
    @Path("list/{email}")
    @Produces(MediaType.APPLICATION_JSON)
    public List<ToDo> getToDoList(@PathParam("email") String email) {

        List<ToDo> result = datastore.getAll(email);
```

```
        return result;
    }

    @DELETE
    @Path("{id}")
    public void deleteToDo(@PathParam("id") long id) {

        if(!datastore.deleteToDo(id)) {
            throw new WebApplicationException(Response.Status.NOT_FOUND);
        }
    }

    @PUT
    @Consumes(MediaType.APPLICATION_JSON)
    @Produces(MediaType.APPLICATION_JSON)
    public ToDoId createToDo(ToDo item) {

        Long newId = datastore.createToDo(item);

        if(newId == -1){
            throw new WebApplicationException(Response.Status.INTERNAL_SERVER_ERROR);
        }

        ToDoId result = new ToDoId(newId);

        return result;
    }
}
```

Each function is annotated with the HTTP verb corresponding to the CRUD operation in the data layer class we created. There can be more than one operation per HTTP verb. For instance, our class could have more than one GET operation. The @Path annotation distinguishes these functions from one another in our REST URIs. Each function must be annotated with a unique combination of HTTP verb and @Path attributes.

The functions returning data are annotated with @Produces(MediaType.APPLICATION_JSON), which tells Jersey to serialize the output of the function into JSON. Additionally, the content type in the HTTP header of the response will be application/JSON, telling the consumers of our REST service to expect JSON in the response body. The functions that accept ToDo entities as input are annotated with @Consumes(MediaType.APPLICATION_JSON). This forces the client calling our REST function to add the content type application/JSON to the header of the incoming HTTP call. If this annotation is absent, the client could conceivably send XML or even plain text instead. Because mobile apps consume these services, JSON is our preferred format. If the content type were not set at the Android client, our service would throw an HTTP 400 error, indicating that the combined HTTP headers and body are not formatted properly.

Notice that none of the function calls contain any code converting the incoming messages from JSON or the outgoing results to JSON. In the web.xml file the POJOMappingFeature is enabled, which allows the Jackson library (included as part of the set of jars that make up Jersey) to perform the serialization of our ToDo objects to or from JSON automatically.

The createToDo() function returns a new type, the ToDoId class. This simple class simply returns the new id generated by the datastore when a new ToDo is inserted into the datastore.

By returning a class instead of a single number, clients to our API will get a JSON object and not just plain text in the body of the response which would happen if we simply returned a long. Notice the lack of annotations in Listing 8-21. We don't persist this class in the datastore; we simply use it as a data transfer object.

Listing 8-21. A Data Transfer Object for Returning Newly Generated ToDo IDs

```
public class ToDoId {

    public ToDoId(Long id){
        Id = id;
    }

    private Long Id;

    public Long getId() {
        return Id;
    }

    public void setId(Long id) {
        Id = id;
    }
}
```

For the version of Jersey that we are using, we need to create an application class that knows which specific Java classes we would like to expose as web services, as shown in Listing 8-22.

Listing 8-22. The Jersey Application object that registers the service class

```
public class ToDoApplication extends Application {

    public Set<Class<?>> getClasses() {
            Set<Class<?>> s = new HashSet<Class<?>>();
            s.add(ToDoResource.class);
            return s;
    }
}
```

Tools

Once we create a service, we want to be able to test our code. There are a few options for testing a service before we have built the Android client.

The first and most valuable tool for testing web services is to write unit tests. No matter which testing framework you choose, you can write Java code that calls the service. If you host the service remotely, tests can be a challenge, since the data is not local to the unit tests. The upside to unit tests is much greater than with manual testing because the unit tests can become part of a continuous integration (CI) cycle. The CI build provides regular feedback and may help development teams find and fix bugs in the service sooner than when the service is released for manual testing.

Another option to exercise a service is to use a pre-made REST client, such as Advanced REST Client for Google Chrome or RESTClient for Firefox (`https://addons.mozilla.org/en-us/firefox/ addon/restclient/`). These manual tools help you compose raw HTTP calls, including the HTTP method, headers and body. They also show the resulting HTTP response and headers.

We will test our service manually using Advanced REST Client for Google Chrome.

1. In ADT, run the web services project.

2. Open Google Chrome.

3. Follow this URL in Chrome (`https://chrome.google.com/webstore/detail/ advanced-rest-client/hgmloofddffdnphfgcellkdfbfbjeloo?hl=en-US`) and install the app.

4. Open a new tab in Chrome, and navigate to the installed apps. Click Advanced REST Client (see Figure 8-16).

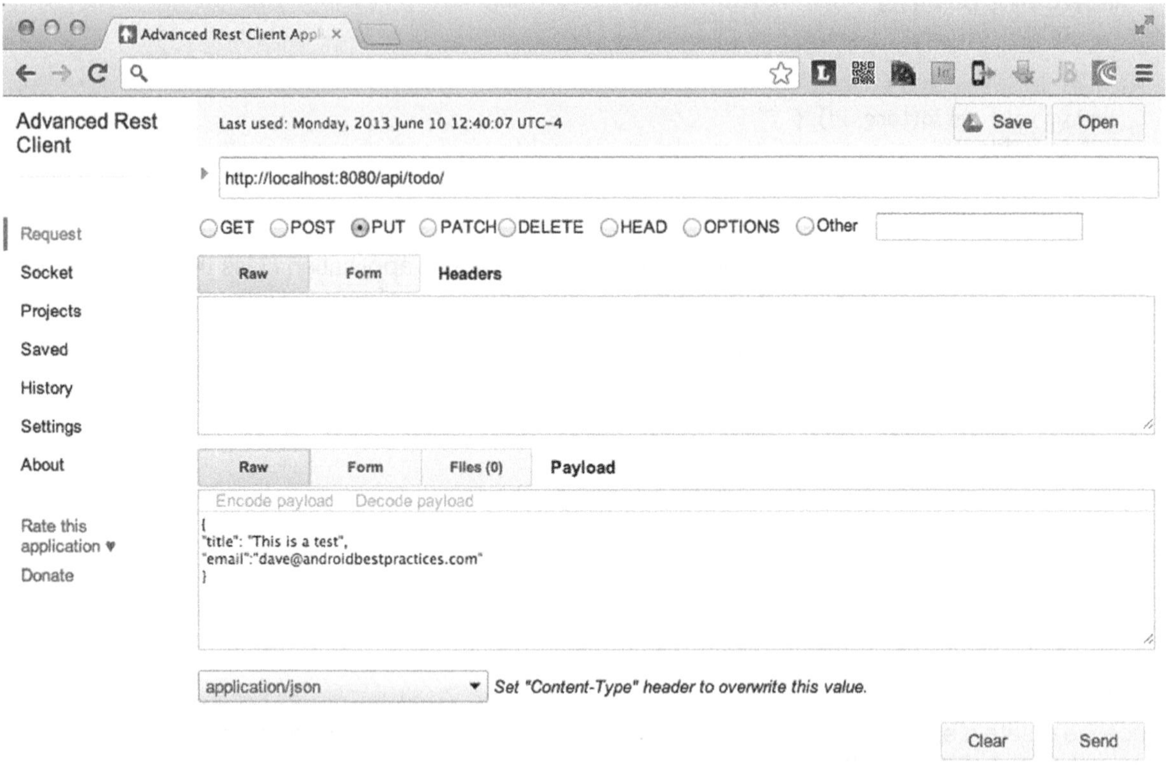

Figure 8-16. Advanced REST Client for testing the ToDo web service

5. In the URL box, enter `http://localhost:8080/api/todo/`.

6. Choose the PUT method.

7. In the Payload box enter:

```
{
"title": "This is a test",
"email":"dave@androidbestpractices.com"
}
```

8. In the drop-down list below the Payload box, choose `application/json`.

9. Click the Send button. The service should return a new ID for the record sent to the web service (see Figure 8-17).

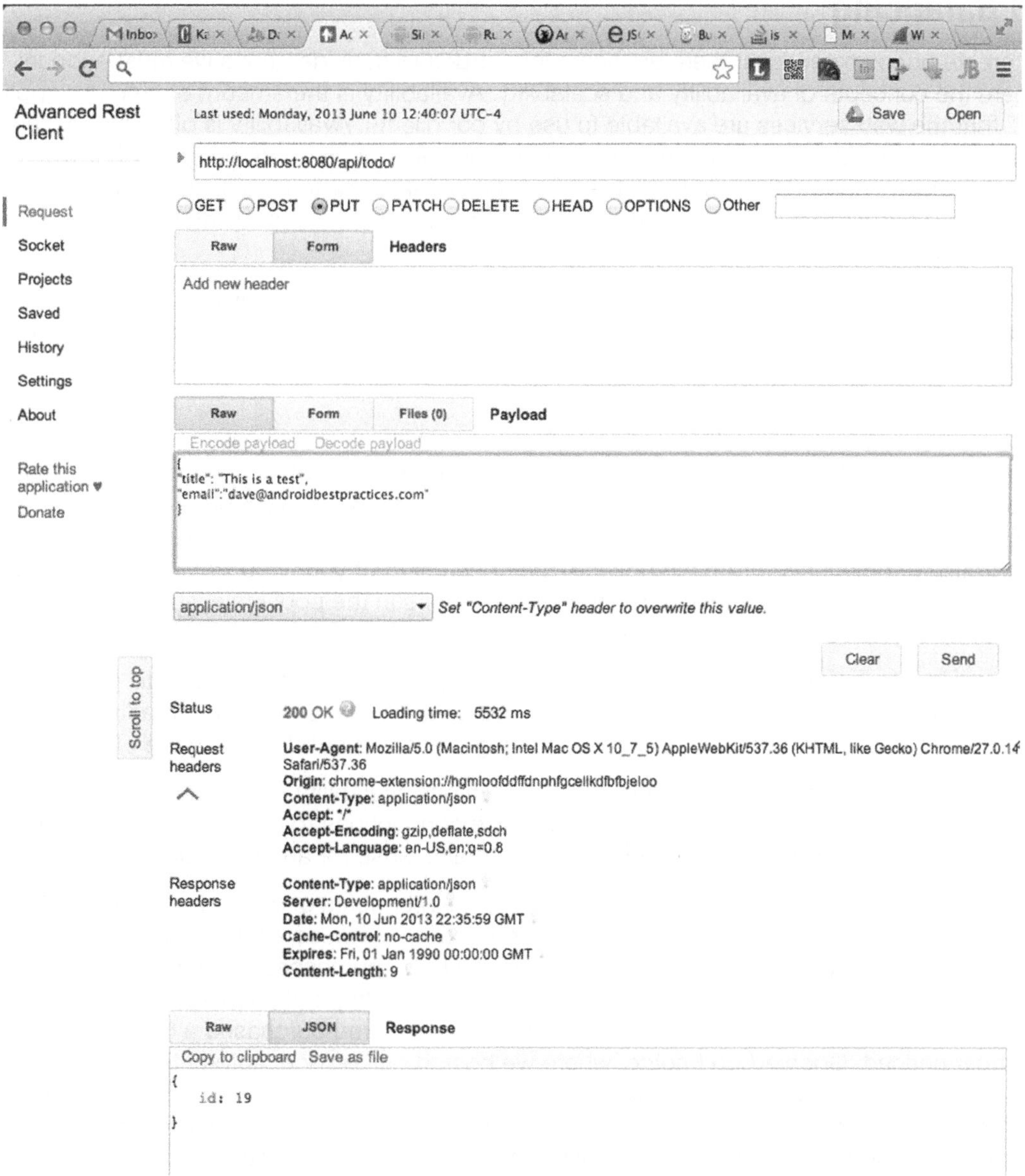

Figure 8-17. Inserting a new ToDo record using Advanced REST Client

Once you move from debugging the service to debugging an Android application, you may want to examine the raw HTTP message after the Android client generates it. An HTTP proxy set up between the Android emulator and the web server allows for capture and examination of the message and response. There are a number of HTTP proxy tools, including Charles Proxy (http://www.charlesproxy.com/), WireShark (http://www.wireshark.org/), and the PC-only Fiddler (http://fiddler2.com/). Device traffic can be captured if your computer is set up to share its wireless network connection and the Android device attaches to the computer instead of the normal wireless access point.

Load Balancing

As we create our own services, there are some infrastructure considerations we must account for. These are the concepts of availability and scalability. Availability is the amount of time our application is "up," that the web services are available to use by our clients. Availability is often expressed as a percentage, like 99.9%, or "three nines." That represents 8.76 hours/per year of down time, which translates to about 10 minutes of down time per week. A system gains availability by adding redundant servers, so that in the event that one server goes down, whether intentionally or not, another server is available to service requests.

Scalability, on the other hand, is the ability of your service to handle increasing numbers or spiking numbers of requests. If you build a successful mobile app using your own web services, you will eventually encounter scalability issues. You will need more servers to handle the increasing number of requests.

A load balancer is a network tool for managing both availability and scalability, provided by either software or dedicated hardware. A load balancer sits in front of a pool of servers hosting your web services. The load balancer distributes the requests among the available servers in the pool. Should the pool of servers increase or decrease, the load balancer automatically handles the situation, shifting traffic automatically. From the outside, the consumers of your web services see a single URL that is the load balancer, making the number of servers in the pool irrelevant to the consuming application.

Load balancing does not solve scalability problems completely, as an app could still generate more traffic than the pool of servers could handle. The load balancer does allow you to add or remove servers from the pool easily to adjust for the incoming traffic without disrupting the existing servers.

Additionally, your code can be written in a way that inhibits scalability. Your application code should be using memory and external resources properly, like connections to databases or the file system, in order to scale well. Poor design and coding is the main cause for an application to scale poorly.

If you host your web services in the cloud, one of the main benefits of a cloud platform is rapid scaling. Creating new server instances in quick and relatively easy, so an app scales up faster than with traditional hosting, where a hardware server needs to be purchased, configured, and deployed before your app can scale upward. Alternatively, if your traffic drops off, servers removed from the pool stop being a cost immediately, unlike the situation where you purchased a hardware server that is no longer needed. Google App Engine, where we hosted our service, automatically load balances and scales your application during its life cycle. GAE manages your application itself, automatically building the new servers and installing your application. Other cloud services, like Amazon's Elastic Beanstalk and Microsoft's Windows Azure, also offer automated scalability.

Summary

In this chapter we covered many aspects of web services as they relate to Android applications. We examined the types of web services, and saw that REST is the best fit for mobile applications. We also explored data formatting, noting that JSON is much smaller and better for data transfer over mobile networks.

We then looked at the many ways to access web services using Android, examining the design options, and how to transform JSON data into Java objects.

Finally, we built our own web services in the cloud, using Google App Engine and the Jersey REST library.

Index

Get the eBook for only $10!

Now you can take the weightless companion with you anywhere, anytime. Your purchase of this book entitles you to 3 electronic versions for only $10.

This Apress title will prove so indispensible that you'll want to carry it with you everywhere, which is why we are offering the eBook in 3 formats for only $10 if you have already purchased the print book.

Convenient and fully searchable, the PDF version enables you to easily find and copy code—or perform examples by quickly toggling between instructions and applications. The MOBI format is ideal for your Kindle, while the ePUB can be utilized on a variety of mobile devices.

Go to www.apress.com/promo/tendollars to purchase your companion eBook.

CPSIA information can be obtained at www.ICGtesting.com
Printed in the USA
LVOW03s1957040114

368094LV00012B/761/P